The Intuitive Arts on LOVE

The Intuitive Arts on LOVE

Arlene Tognetti and Lisa Lenard

A member of Penguin Group (USA) Inc.

Astrological charts in this book were generated using Astrolabe's Solar Fire software program.

International Standard Book Number: 1-59257-106-9
Library of Congress Catalog Card Number: 2003108343

05 04 03 8 7 6 5 4 3 2 1

Interpretation of the printing code: The rightmost number of the first series of numbers is the year of the book's printing; the rightmost number of the second series of numbers is the number of the book's printing. For example, a printing code of 03-1 shows that the first printing occurred in 2003.

Printed in the United States of America

Publisher: Marie Butler-Knight
Product Manager: Phil Kitchel
Senior Managing Editor: Jennifer Chisholm
Senior Acquisitions Editor: Randy Ladenheim-Gil
Book Producer: Lee Ann Chearney/Amaranth Illuminare
Development Editor: Lynn Northrup
Copy Editor: Keith Cline
Technical Editor: Reba Jean Cain
Cover Designer: Charis Santillie
Book Designer: Trina Wurst
Creative Director: Robin Lasek
Layout/Proofreading: Angela Calvert, John Etchison

Contents

Appendixes

Introduction

Claim your brightest destiny and fulfill your own essential nature.

More than ever, we are searching for an inner awareness that brings outer confidence, joy, and direction. The *Intuitive Arts* series—with volumes on Love, Family, Health, Money, and Work—gives readers looking for answers to questions of daily living tools from the esoteric arts that will help them look deeply, see, and make real changes affecting their futures. In each problem-solving volume, curious querents are presented exercises in the Intuitive Arts of Astrology, Tarot, and Psychic Intuition that examine, instruct, illuminate, and guide. In essence, you get three books for one—but also so much more!

An understanding of the interplay of the Intuitive Arts of Astrology, Tarot, and Psychic Intuition is something most people gain slowly over time, or with the aid of a professional Intuitive Arts practitioner who already has the knowledge to give in-depth readings that link the arts together.

In *The Intuitive Arts* series, expert author Arlene Tognetti shares her deep knowing of the arts of Astrology, Tarot, and Psychic Intuition to give you the best opportunity to work out solutions to life's problems and challenges with the benefit of the sophisticated relationships between the arts Arlene reveals chapter by chapter. By combining the Intuitive Arts together throughout each chapter's exercises, you'll gain insights that link the arts together—how, for example, the Tarot's Elements are present in your astrological Elemental Romance Signature, or what your ascendant, or rising sign, has to say about your openness to receiving psychic love messages.

Arlene Tognetti and New Age book producer Lee Ann Chearney at Amaranth Illuminare created this series for Alpha Books to respond to the public's growing fascination with all things spiritual. People (like you!) want to know how they can use the Intuitive Arts to solve everyday challenges, plan for the future, and live in the present, with hands-on advice and techniques that will make things better for them. We want to help you improve the issues surrounding your unique life situation by providing a multi-art approach that gives you multiple pathways to personal growth and answers your questions about family, health, love, money, and work.

Using Tarot's Major and Minor Arcana cards and spreads; Astrology's birth charts and aspect grids, sign, planets, and houses; and Psychic Intuition's meditations, affirmations, and inner knowing exercises—the innovative *Intuitive Arts* series provides a truly interactive, solution-oriented, positive message that enriches a personal synergy of mind, body, and spirit!

Read on to further your knowledge and understanding of how the Intuitive Arts work together to reveal deep insights. In this series volume, *The Intuitive Arts on Love,* learn how Astrology, the Tarot, and Psychic Intuition reveal your future romance!

Are *you* ready for love?

chapter 1

All You Need Is Love

Love meets the Intuitive Arts
Astrology: Love made in the heavens
The Tarot: Picture your love
Psychic Intuition: Follow your heart
What kind of love have you got?
A short history of love
The physiology of love
The psychology of love
Planetary cycles and love
The heart of love

No matter where you turn, love surrounds you. No one topic permeates our world quite so thoroughly or holds our interest quite so unwaveringly. Love doesn't just make the world go 'round, it's our soul and inspiration, our reason to believe, and, sometimes, our ball and chain. If you ask practitioners of the Intuitive Arts what people want to know about most, love tops the list. That's why, in this guide, we've married love and the Intuitive Arts—it's a marriage made in the stars, in the cards, and in your hearts. But before we show you how you can live the love life you've always wanted, we begin by introducing you to love through the lens of the Intuitive Arts of Astrology, Tarot, and Psychic Intuition.

Meet the Intuitive Arts

In this book, we focus on three of the Intuitive Arts: Astrology, the Tarot, and Psychic Intuition. Astrology requires some technical knowledge; the Tarot requires only a deck of Tarot cards; Psychic

Intuition you already have within, and it requires nothing more than some simple exercises to help you get in touch with it. We like to think of the Intuitive Arts as metaphors for the self and the lives we lead.

Astrologically, for example, a birth chart—a map of the heavens at the moment you were born—is a blueprint of your unique self. Studying the movements and patterns of the planets in the heavens and how they relate to you and your lover's birth charts can provide an extended metaphor for exploring your love relationship. For this reason, you'll want to have your birth chart on hand for the astrological love exercises we provide in this book.

To prepare your astrological birth chart, an astrologer needs to know the day, year, and time, as well as the place, of your birth. If you don't know your precise birth time, try to narrow it down to morning, afternoon, or evening. If you cannot determine anything more than the day and year of your birth, then use noon as your birth time. You can order a birth chart online or from your local metaphysical bookstore; there's more information on how to order a birth chart in Appendix A. We've also provided a sample birth chart with love connections highlighted in Appendix A.

But you don't have to turn to Appendix A to see what a birth chart looks like. You'll see chart examples throughout this book, and working with those charts will help you to interpret your own and your love partner's charts. Arlene used the computer software program Solar Fire 5 by Astrolabe, Inc. to generate the birth charts we've adapted as examples throughout this book. Charts are cast using the Geocentric view, Tropical Zodiac, Placidus house system, and True Node because these are the most common in modern Western Astrology. To get a birth chart you can use with this book, be sure to specify these parameters.

Even if you know nothing about what the symbols in a birth chart mean, take a moment to study the visual metaphor of a birth chart as a representation of a person—in this case, someone who's had a lot of experience in her own love life, actress Julia Roberts. Don't worry about what anything *means* in this image; simply look at it as a metaphor of Julia herself. Julia's circular birth chart appears here with her aspect grid, the triangular table at the lower left. Aspects reveal relationships between heavenly bodies in a birth chart.

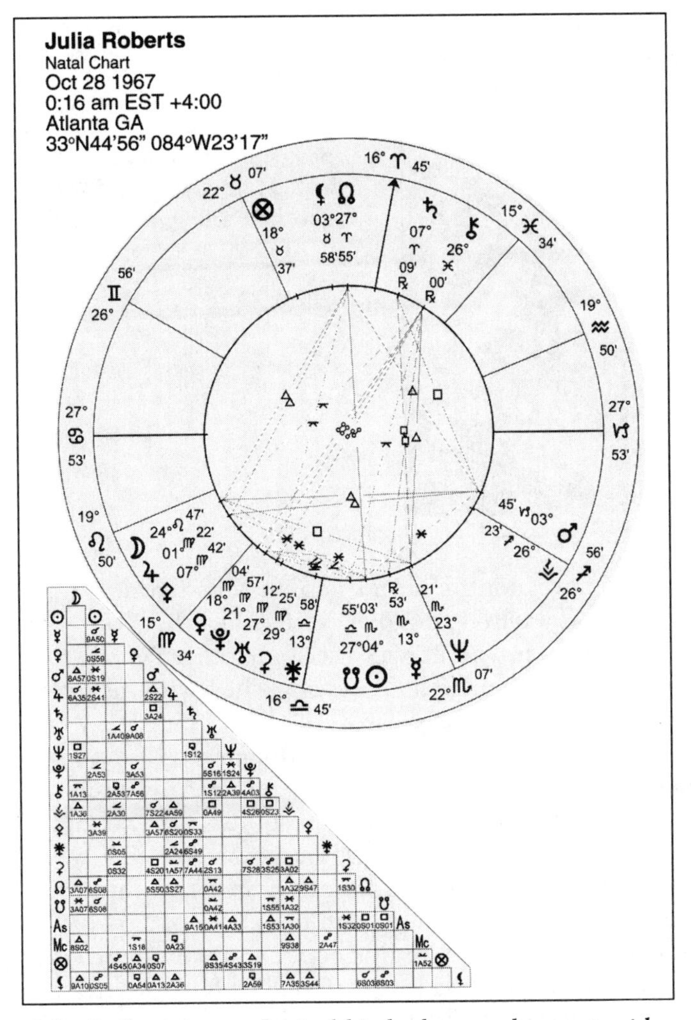

Julia Roberts's astrological birth chart and aspect grid.

Like your birth chart, and Julia Roberts's—the 78 cards of the Tarot can also be thought of as a metaphor. Astrology and Tarot present visual representations as a way of seeing both within yourself to your unconscious and beyond yourself to the bigger picture of your place in the universe. In Appendix B, you'll find a picture of each of the cards in the Universal Waite Tarot deck we'll be using to illustrate this book, along with several love keywords for each card. But, as we'll stress throughout, we think that the best way to learn to intuit the Tarot's imagery is to not rely on these keywords, but instead to let the cards' imagery communicate to you directly. To help you understand how Tarot imagery works, we're going to begin with one card, the Fool, the card that leads off Tarot's Major Arcana.

The Fool is the first card in Tarot's Major Arcana. Would you follow this guy down the path of new, or re"new"ed, love?

Your first impression of Tarot's Fool may be that it is likely this guy's about to walk off a cliff—and love can feel like that! Upon further observation, however, you may notice some other details, too: the pattern on his shirt, the bundle he's carrying, the joy of his little dog, to name but three. Like all Tarot cards, the Fool's message when it comes to love will vary depending on the question asked of him, but you can be sure when the Tarot's Fool shows up a new love adventure awaits you!

If Astrology and Tarot are visual metaphors for you and your place in the world, then Psychic Intuition, the sixth sense that we all possess within us, is the catalyst that leads you to their true interpretation and full self-awareness. As you work with the Intuitive Arts of Astrology, Tarot, and Psychic Intuition in this book, you will discover more about yourself and about how you love—as well as how to attract and keep the love you've always desired. As we will for Astrology and the Tarot, we'll be providing you with a variety of exercises that make tuning in to your own Psychic Intuition as easy as, well, falling in love!

We suggest you begin a new notebook dedicated to the exercises in this book (a binder into which you can insert loose pages can work quite well), but you can of course use any type of paper you want and just keep all your notes in one place. You can even save your exercises in a word processing program if you'd like!

So are you ready for love?

A Love Made in Heaven: Love and Astrology

What's your sign? Even if you know nothing else about Astrology, chances are you know what your Sun ☉ sign is. Just in case you don't, however, we've provided a Zodiac wheel where you can discover your Sun sign simply by finding your birthday.

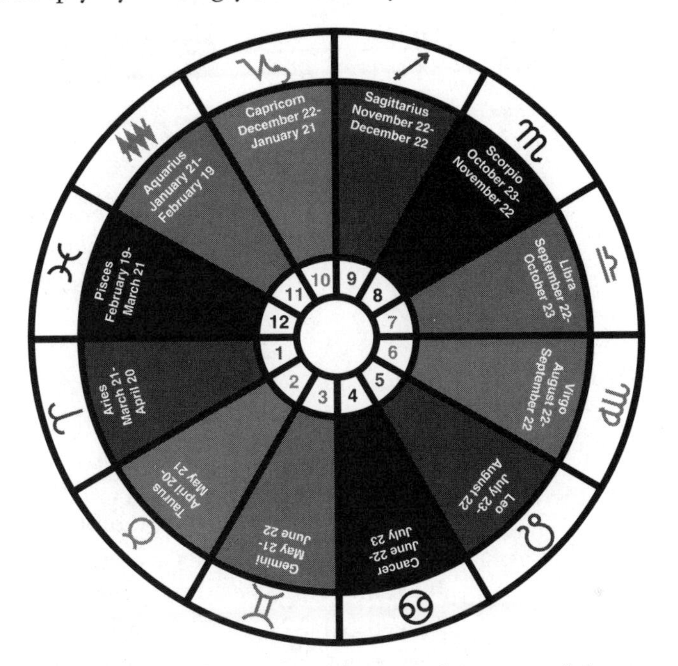

To find your Sun ☉ sign, simply note the name of the astrological sign that correlates to your birth date.

According to Astrology, each of the 12 signs of the Zodiac represents certain characteristics. What makes you unique is that you are far more than your Sun sign: At the moment you were born, each of nine planets (in basic Astrology, the Moon is included and the Earth is not) was in a particular sign and house (the 12 segments in the Zodiac wheel). Because each of the planets is constantly moving around the Sun ☉, even someone born seconds before or after you will have a different astrological birth chart.

Astrological Keywords

Relationship Astrology, or synastry, involves matching up your birth chart with someone else's—whether a current lover or a potential one—to find out how compatible you may or may not be. For now, though, all that's necessary is to familiarize yourself with the basic astrological symbols and their keywords. The more you learn about Astrology, the more this shorthand will become second nature to you. Let's begin with the symbols and keywords for each sign.

Astro Sign	**Symbol**	**Dates**	**Keywords**
Aries	♈	March 21 to April 20	Energetic, take-charge, pioneering
Taurus	♉	April 20 to May 21	Sensual, grounded, down-to-earth
Gemini	♊	May 21 to June 22	Resourceful, quick-witted, mercurial
Cancer	♋	June 22 to July 23	Empathetic, nurturing, emotional
Leo	♌	July 23 to August 22	Charismatic, fun-loving, confident
Virgo	♍	August 22 to September 22	Resourceful, practical, analyzing
Libra	♎	September 22 to October 23	Principled, balanced, harmonious
Scorpio	♏	October 23 to November 22	Passionate, powerful, profound
Sagittarius	♐	November 22 to December 22	Adventurous, fun-loving, enthusiastic
Capricorn	♑	December 22 to January 21	Serious, hard-working, responsible
Aquarius	♒	January 21 to February 19	Idealistic, humanitarian, persistent
Pisces	♓	February 19 to March 21	Spiritual, compassionate, dreamy

Note that if your—or your sweetie's—birthday falls on a date that appears in two signs, you were born on what is called a "cusp," and you'll want to read the keywords for each sign carefully to determine which sign is most likely your Sun sign.

In a birth chart, Astrology involves exploring which of the astrological signs each of the planets appears in. Like the signs, each planet has a symbol and a keyword to help you remember its character. Here's a list of those.

Planet	Symbol	Keyword
Sun	☉	Explores
Moon	☽	Senses
Mercury	☿	Communicates
Venus	♀	Enjoys
Mars	♂	Engages
Jupiter	♃	Benefits
Saturn	♄	Cooperates
Uranus	♅	Innovates
Neptune	♆	Dreams
Pluto	♇	Transforms

The last part of basic astrological lingo you'll want to learn is houses. The 12 houses of Astrology are those pie slices you probably noticed in Julia Roberts's chart. The following figure shows you the keyword for each house within the house itself.

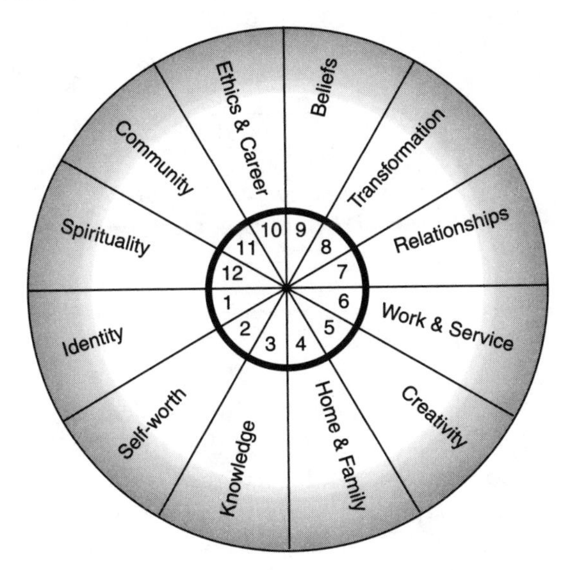

Each of your birth chart's 12 houses represents an area of your life.

Exploring the Zodiac

To help you begin to memorize the symbols and meanings for Astrology's signs, planets, and houses, take another look at Julia Roberts's birth chart. To make it easy, here it is again.

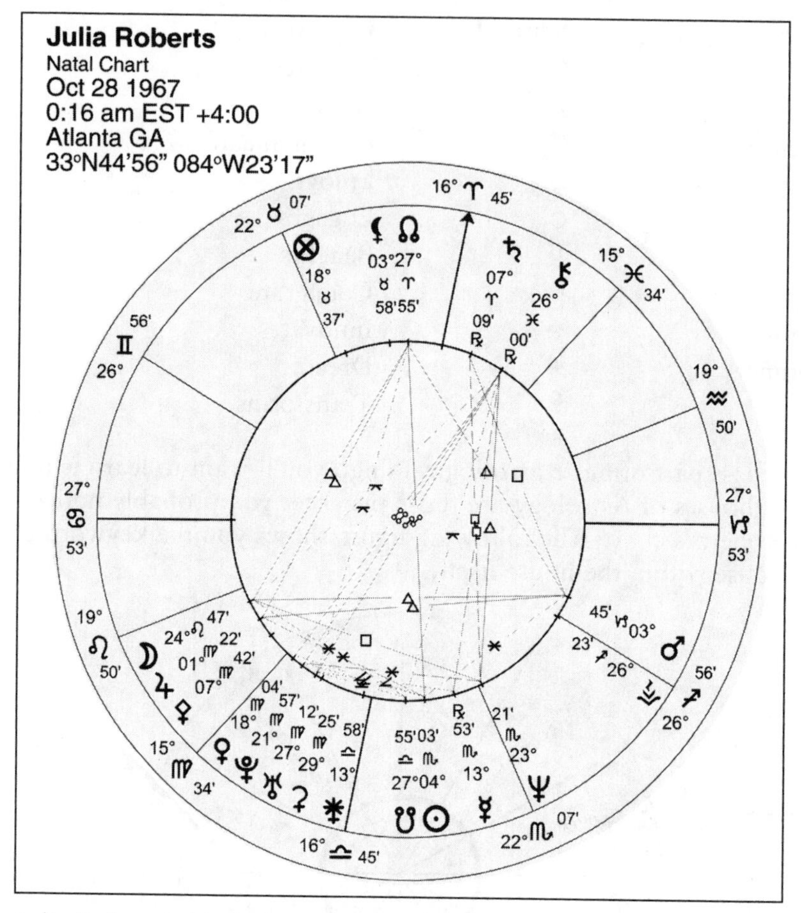

Julia Roberts's birth chart.

One at a time, look in the houses of Julia's birth chart to find the symbol for each of the planets in the list that follows. When you've found it, you'll also see a symbol for a sign. This means that in Julia's birth chart, that planet appears in that sign in that house. Her Sun ☉, for example, is in Scorpio ♏ in her 4th house of home and family. As you discover the astrological sign and house for each planet, note them and their keywords in the following table. By the time you've finished, you will have taken a big first step toward learning these important symbols and keywords. When you have your own birth chart on hand, do this exercise for your own planets in their signs and houses (and your sweetie's, too!), and keep this information in a special place in your Intuitive Arts notebook so you can refer to it as you need to.

Julia Roberts's Planets in Their Signs and Houses

Planet	Planet Keyword	Astro Sign and Symbol	Astro Sign Keyword	House	House Keyword(s)
Sun ☉	Explores	Scorpio ♏	Passionate	4th house	Home and family
Moon ☽					
Mercury #					
Venus ♀					
Mars ♂					
Jupiter ♃					
Saturn ♄					
Uranus ♅					
Neptune ♆					
Pluto ♇					

Picture Your Love: Love and the Tarot

The Tarot deck is tailor-made for looking at love. While at first glance these cards may seem overwhelming, the more time you spend with them, the more you begin to see how their images mirror what's going on inside of you and in the situations surrounding you.

There are literally hundreds of Tarot decks to choose from, but in this book we use the traditional images offered by the Universal Waite Tarot deck, published by U.S. Games Systems, Inc. Basically, a Tarot deck is divided into 22 Major Arcana cards, which represent a metaphorical karmic journey through life, from the Fool to the World; and 56 Minor Arcana cards, which are divided into 4 suits of 14 cards each, and reveal our everyday free-will decisions. Tarot's Wands are the suit of enterprise and growth, Cups represent creativity and emotion, Swords are the cards of action, and Pentacles are the cards of abundance. To begin our exploration of love and the Tarot, we've selected 5 cards, one to represent the 22 cards of the Major Arcana, and one for each of the 4 suits of the Minor Arcana.

The Lovers, the 2 of Cups, the Ace of Wands, the 3 of Swords, and the 10 of Pentacles.

Meet the Tarot

One of the most important things to understand about interpreting Tarot cards is that there are no hard-and-fast meanings. Even though many books—including this one—will give you suggested meanings for each card, ultimately a particular card's image and position in a reading will suggest different things depending on both the question asked and how you feel about the image relative to the question. If the

Tarot card for the Lovers appears in a position representing the person asking the question, the querent, for instance, it may well represent the traditional divinatory meaning of a love-related choice. At other times, however, this same card may stand for blessings from above, marriage, or even indecision (especially if it's reversed, or upside down). So depending on where you and your love partner are now, different Tarot cards will have different meanings.

Take a few minutes to individually study each of the cards in the image above, thinking about where you and your partner are now when it comes to love. If you already have a Tarot deck, remove these cards and study them individually. Consider these questions:

- What do you want to learn about love?
- What do you feel you already know about love?

Don't rush your reactions to the cards. Let the individual images "speak" to you. When you're ready to record your impressions, use the spaces provided here to record your thoughts on each card, or you may choose to record these impressions, and all of your exercises for this book, in your Intuitive Arts notebook.

The Lovers ____

____

____

2 of Cups ____

____

____

Ace of Wands ____

____

____

3 of Swords ____

____

____

10 of Pentacles ____

____

____

After you've taken the time to ponder these cards yourself, take a look at some of the following possible meanings. Remember, though, each card's love meaning is connected to the larger question; it's never something written in blood (or ink).

- *The Lovers.* Upright meanings: choices, romance, inspiration; reversed meanings: indecision, delays, learning to make choices
- *2 of Cups.* Upright meanings: new relationship, cooperation, a thoughtful partner; reversed meanings: misunderstanding, stubbornness, possessiveness
- *Ace of Wands.* Upright meanings: new energy, self-esteem, creative upsurge; reversed meanings: delay in start, time to regroup, something missing
- *3 of Swords.* Upright meanings: heartbreak, separation, argument; reversed meanings: apology, difficulties ending, healing of a broken heart
- *10 of Pentacles.* Upright meanings: lifetime rewards, a stable foundation across generations, family security; reversed meanings: dispute over inheritance, financial loss, instability

Before you move to the Tarot exercises throughout the rest of this book, take some time to familiarize yourself with the rest of the cards in a Tarot deck (either by purchasing a deck of your own or meditating on the pictures we've provided in Appendix B).

Follow Your Heart: Love and Psychic Intuition

As one of the catch phrases for listening to your Psychic Intuition is "follow your heart," it should be no surprise that there's much to be learned about love from this most fundamental of the Intuitive Arts. Psychic Intuition is really nothing more than paying attention to your inner voice, a way of learning things without consciously thinking about them. If you've ever had a hunch or flash of insight, a dream that turned out to be precognizant, or strong feelings about someone you've just met, you've already encountered your own Psychic Intuition.

The best way to fine-tune your intuition is by developing a meditation practice. Meditation helps still both the body and the mind, thus allowing a quiet space into which those intuitive nudges can more easily flow. Ways of meditating are as individual and unique as, well, your birth chart, and you may need to try out a few before you settle on a meditation method that works for you. If you've never meditated before, the simple meditation that follows can provide a starting point.

Chances are, you picked up this book because you want to learn more about love, and especially your own love life. Meditations are simple ways of getting in touch with your inner self to discover what you're really thinking. For this first meditation, we've provided a question for you to ponder as you meditate. The more you meditate, the more you'll come to discover what works best for you.

Here's the question: *What kind of love have you got?*

1. Find a place where you can sit or lie down, uninterrupted by sounds or people around you. This may be a room you can dedicate to your meditation practice, or it may be in your bathtub. The important thing is that you not be interrupted during your meditation. The machine will answer the phone, the doorbell (if no one else is home) will go unanswered, and your dryer will not buzz to let you know it's time to unload. Meditation time is your quiet time. Place this book, your Intuitive Arts notebook, and a pen or pencil nearby.
2. Think about your love life as it is right now. What kind of love have you got? Is there a special someone in your life, or are you recovering from a broken heart? Maybe you're ready to try love again, or maybe you're trying love for the first time.
3. If you could ask one question of your Psychic Intuition about your love life, what would it be? Write that question here, or in your notebook.

 ____

4. Now, make yourself comfortable. Close your eyes. Focus on relaxing each part of your body, one part at a time. Begin with your toes or begin with the hairs on your head, concentrate on what you feel, and then consciously relax them. Work from top to bottom or bottom to top until you have relaxed your entire body.

5. When you're fully relaxed, take another look at the question you wrote down earlier. Repeating the question aloud, simply let your mind wander, paying attention to each thought as it comes and goes but not allowing yourself to be dragged in by details. Meditation should not be like those nights you can't sleep because you're obsessively reviewing the details of the day before and planning the day to come. Watch your thoughts enter your mind, and then watch them leave again.
6. If something comes to you that you want to remember because it relates to your question, open your eyes and write it down. Just as we think we'll remember those middle-of-the-night inspirations and dreams but then don't, the insights that come to us in meditation can be lost if we don't write them down. This is why, when you began this meditation, we had you place your notebook and pen nearby. When you're done writing, close your eyes and resume your meditation.
7. When you're ready, open your eyes and slowly take in the room around you. Note the temperature, the colors, the sounds, smells, and feel of things. Allow the things you take for granted to take on the immanence of the extraordinary, and nothing about love will ever be ordinary for you again. You will come out of your meditation renewed, refreshed, and reinvigorated. Plus, you'll have a new understanding of what you want when it comes to love!

What's Love Got to Do with It?

So what is it about love, anyway? Sure, we can look in our *Webster's* and find it defined as "a deep and tender feeling of affection for or attachment or devotion to a person or persons." But that's just the first of the 15 definitions in the dictionary. Others include "sexual passion" and "to feel delight in." Part of our continuing passion for love may be that, at least in English, we depend on one little word to mean oh, so much!

A Short History of Love

According to Diane Ackerman, author of *A Natural History of Love* (Vintage, 1995), the concept of romantic love is a relatively recent invention. Until the Crusades in the eleventh and twelfth centuries, the idea of romance probably never crossed anyone's mind; quite simply, women were property, and marriages were for producing children.

Until 1,000 years ago, love didn't have a whole lot to do with it.

Ackerman credits the wandering troubadours whose appearance roughly coincided with the Crusades with popularizing the idea of romantic love. These strolling minstrels' tales of ill-fated lovers like Abelard and Heloise and Romeo and Juliet set many a heart a-flutter with the notion of similar passions. The rise of chivalry also played a role in idealizing what had been a businesslike relationship; as part of their code of honor, knights paid homage to damsels who in return pledged their devotion.

Knights in shining armor were among the first to pay homage to the idea of romantic love.

The invention of the printing press helped spread the notion of romantic love still more, and many far more recent inventions also fueled the fire: Witness the telegram, the phonograph, and our own contemporary, e-mail. Love is uniquely suited to be communicated in modes other than face to face, it seems, which may be why books, songs, and films embrace the notion again and again.

Lovers soon realized that communication is the alchemy of creating a lasting love relationship.

The Physiology of Love

When we talk about love, the language we use reveals a great deal about both the physiology of love and our blissful ignorance about that physiology. We say we "fall in love" or are "blindsided by love." We refer to the heart as, well, the heart of love. But what really happens when we "fall in love"? Where does love "happen" in the human body? And why does love matter so much to us?

Studies indicate that our ability to give and receive love is learned in infancy. At its most basic, love is shown by stroking, cuddling, and close body contact. Researchers believe that if we receive love at this earliest, most needful stage, we will learn its lessons—both giving and receiving—and carry them throughout our lives.

Love is hardwired into us—body, mind, and soul—from birth. Let love blossom and lead you to contentment and joy.

One of the hormones that plays a role in love has been called "the infatuation chemical." Phenylethylamine (let's call it PEA—that's what biologists do) has been likened to amphetamine ("speed"). When we're attracted to someone, PEA leaps in to rush the news throughout the body. If that newly fallen-in-love feeling feels like an addictive "high," that's because, in short, it is. Because of PEA, love makes us happy—euphoric, even. It makes us feel young, even if we no longer are. When we're in love, we feel good about ourselves and giddy about our lover. No wonder PEA can be addictive: Once you've had a romantic "high," you may crave that same elation over and over.

There's nothing quite like the excitement of a romantic "high."

But just as PEA can make you feel high, the day-to-day love that follows can send you into despair. Coming down from a PEA high means returning to normal speed, which seems not just slow but positively drudgelike in contrast. Everyday love can seem dull when compared to new, PEA-fired love, and for some, it's just not enough. No wonder fairy tales end at "happily ever after": Their authors may not have understood or even been aware of the biology, but they knew that once the PEA sheen had faded, the excitement that fueled the love story would be gone as well.

PEA flares up any time you take a risk where the result is uncertain. Some lovers can't get enough of danger, and others prefer love in the slow lane. How much PEA an individual produces helps explain this difference among us.

A romantic "low" can send lovers straight to the chains of perdition.

Do We Need Love?

On the scale of human needs developed by Abraham Maslow in 1954, love holds center stage. Among the many aspects of human motivation it maps, Maslow's Hierarchy of Needs shows that once fundamental needs—food, shelter, security—are met, people seek fulfillment in more and more enlightened ways. Take a moment to study this simplified version of Maslow's model.

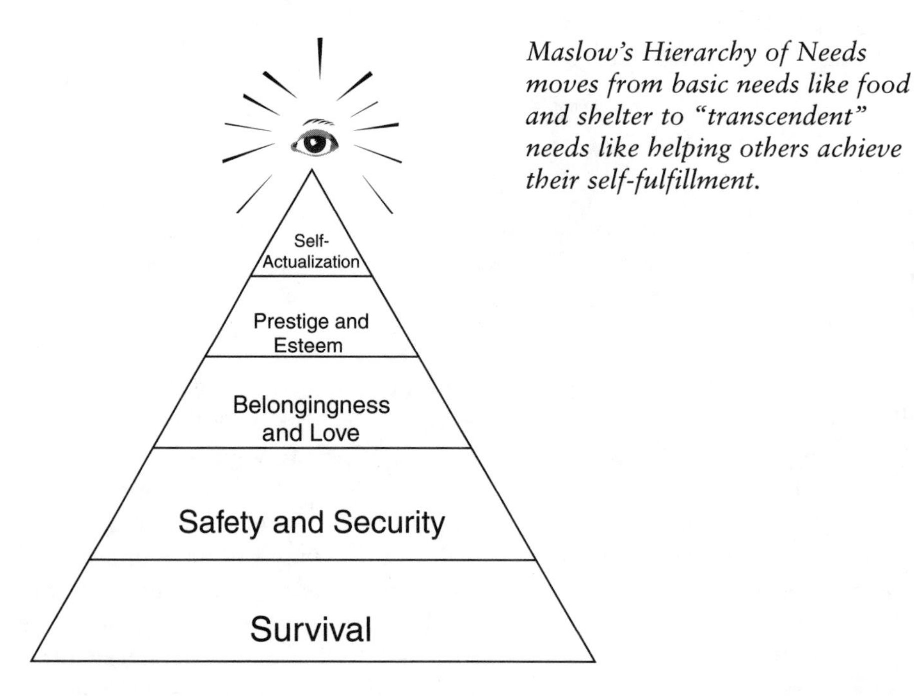

Maslow's Hierarchy of Needs moves from basic needs like food and shelter to "transcendent" needs like helping others achieve their self-fulfillment.

As you can see, Maslow divided needs into two groupings: deficiency needs and growth needs, which are in turn divided into four groupings each. The following table lists which needs fall into each of these categories.

Deficiency Needs

Physiological	**Safety/Security**	**Belonging/Love**	**Esteem**
Hunger	Out of danger	Affiliation with others	Achievement
Thirst		Acceptance	Approval
Bodily comfort		Recognition	

Growth Needs

Cognitive	Aesthetic	Self-Actualization	Transcendence
To know	Symmetry	Self-fulfillment	Help others find self-fulfillment and realize their potential
To understand	Order	Realizing one's potential	
To explore	Beauty		

Deficiency needs—those of physiology, safety, love, and esteem—must be met before growth needs can be considered. So we must feel warm, safe, loved, and competent before we can begin to reach beyond ourselves. This isn't, however, a ladder you climb up once and then never descend again. There are times when each of us feels as if one or more of our deficiency needs isn't being met. At our most basic, sometimes we're hungry, thirsty, or hot or cold. Sometimes we're frightened; sometimes we feel unloved, unaccepted, or misunderstood. But the more we focus on growth needs—learning, reaching out, creating and appreciating things of beauty, following our bliss, and helping others—the less time we spend worrying about our deficiency needs. In other words, a person who is self-fulfilled is also someone who's attractive to others.

Are you busy juggling your needs like the 2 of Pentacles, or are you secure and grounded like the 9 of Pentacles?

Up and Down and All Around

No matter how self-confident you are, you already know that, like life, love has its ups and downs. What you may not know is that there are certain ups and downs astrologers can predict because they are connected to regular astrological cycles. Throughout this book, we look at planetary cycles both large and small. In this chapter, we start with two very basic cycles: retrogrades ℞ and eclipses.

Retrograde ℞ is the astrological term for the time when a planet appears to move backward from our perspective here on earth. When a planet is retrograde, we perceive its usual, or direct, energy in a different way. When Mercury ☿, the planet of communication and technology, is retrograde—this happens three times a year for three weeks—love letters get lost, assignations are missed, and plans go awry. The following table lists the major planetary retrogrades and what you can expect when they occur. Consulting an astrological calendar so that you are aware of when planetary retrogrades occur could save your relationship when you realize that your miscommunication with your honey could be due to a retrograde planet rather than a sudden change of heart!

Planet	Direct Keyword	Retrograde Keyword(s)
Mercury ☿	Communicates	Stalls
Venus ♀	Enjoys	Reconsiders
Mars ♂	Engages	Rethinks
Jupiter ♃	Benefits	Exceeds limits
Saturn ♄	Cooperates	Restructures
Uranus ♅	Innovates	Reforms
Neptune ♆	Dreams	Reexamines
Pluto ♇	Transforms	Reviews

Like retrogrades, solar and lunar eclipses similarly cause unexpected glitches. Because they are far shorter in duration than retrogrades (minutes as opposed to weeks and months), eclipses, by their very nature, often cause dramatic change. Although we may not be able to physically "see" eclipses from our vantage point here on earth, we nonetheless feel the effect of one planet momentarily "blocking" the energy of another as dramatic upheaval. Depending on the planets involved, an eclipse can be the cause of dramatic global change, or of transformation on a more personal level.

Like Astrology, the Tarot has its own version of "retrogrades." In a reading, when a Tarot card appears reversed, or upside down, it reveals the polar energy of the card when it is upright. Reversed cards are denoted with an "R" after the name of the card (for instance, the Tower R). Just as astrological retrogrades ask you to reconsider, Tarot's reversed card images ask you to reexamine a card's energy in a new way. Astrological retrogrades and reversed Tarot cards may indicate delays, rethinking, or they can show decisions made in a new direction. Avoid the temptation to interpret these messages as "bad" or "negative." Every message presents a positive opportunity to move toward the love you seek!

Eclipses can feel a lot like the Tower card of the Tarot, like an unexpected jolt of lightning. Upright, the Tower signifies sudden shift or change; reversed, the Tower R may mean you are avoiding an issue or change you need to make.

The Tarot can also help you be more aware of when events in your love readings are likely to occur. That's because when you do a Tarot spread to answer a question, certain cards address the timing surrounding the question directly.

Tarot Cards	Tarot Timing
Ace through 10	1 to 10 days, weeks, or months (depending on the card, of course)
Page	11 days, weeks, or months
Knight	12 days, weeks, or months
Queen and King	Unknown time—it's up to you!

Tarot Suits	Tarot Suit Timing
Wands	Days to weeks
Cups	Weeks to months
Swords	Days, fast!
Pentacles	Months to years

In addition, Tarot cards are numbered. The Major Arcana, or karma cards, are numbered from 0 for the Fool to 22 for the World. Tarot's Minor Arcana suits, after the royalty cards, go from the Ace as number 1 to number 10. (The number 10 returns to the energy of the number 1.) These numbers can shed further light on timing. Or the cards can resonate simply to the energy each number holds. When doing your Tarot love readings, pay attention to the number resonance for each card in your spread.

Number	Keywords
1	Drive and determination
2	Balance and union
3	Creative enthusiasm
4	Practical planning
5	Impulsive spontaneity
6	Nurturing concern
7	Serene contemplation
8	Powerful achievement
9	Spiritual completion

The Heart of the Matter

Now you're ready to take the next step: using the Intuitive Arts to help you make your love relationships all they can be, and to determine with whom you should—and shouldn't—be having those relationships. So grab your astrological birth chart, Tarot deck, Psychic Intuition, and Intuitive Arts notebook, and join us as we show you how you can find the romance you desire.

While you don't *have* to change your love life as you explore Astrology, the Tarot, and Psychic Intuition, you'll likely find that the additional knowing provided by the Intuitive Arts will encourage you to evolve and grow your experience of love, to blossom in new and wonderful ways!

chapter 2

The Yin and Yang of Love

Do opposites attract?
Yin and *yang* keywords
Yin and *yang* meet Astrology's inner planets
Yin and *yang* meet the Tarot's Major Arcana
Finding the Chariot's balance
Yin and *yang* meet Psychic Intuition
"Put Yourself in My Shoes"
Rediscovering equilibrium

Yin *and* yang. *While you've likely encountered this ancient Chinese symbol for the duality that is one, you may not have given much thought to what it really represents. The concept of* yin *and* yang *is intrinsic to the Intuitive Arts, and, more important to our discussion here, to the ways of love and lovers. According to Chinese mythology, everything is comprised of these two opposing forces, which exist in a mutually dependent but complementary delicate balance. Some of the dichotomies represented by* yin *and* yang *are negative and positive, dark and light, indirect and direct, cold and warm, Earth and Heaven, and internal and external. And of course, there's that most basic dichotomy of all: feminine and masculine. We'll show you what this really means when it comes to love, and how finding the right* yin *and* yang *balance can help you create and maintain equilibrium in your love life.*

Do Opposites Attract?

At its most basic, everything has one polarity or another, and so is either *yin* or *yang*. The symbol for this ancient Chinese concept illustrates the interdependence of these two polarities, showing how they feed into each other, complete each other, and complement each other, over and over and over again.

Yin *and* yang *represent the mutually interdependent opposing forces that underlie the essence of all things.*

Before you read further in this chapter, we hope you take a few moments to study this image. Note how each half of the equation both feeds and supports the other, creating the perfect circle that is wholeness endlessly and without end. In the next section, we list some of the keywords for *yin* and *yang* so that you can begin to forge your own understanding of just what this dichotomy represents. But first, let's take a look at the origin of this concept.

According to ancient Chinese myth, *yin* and *yang* first existed in a giant egg, pushing against each other until the egg broke open to reveal Pan Ku, creator of the world. As Pan Ku emerged from the egg, Heaven and Earth separated, and Pan Ku kept them apart. It took this god 18,000 years to create the world. His tools were a hammer and chisel, and his assistants a dragon, a phoenix, a unicorn, a tiger, and a tortoise.

Although the concept of *yin* and *yang* may have originated in myth, at its heart is the scientifically supported knowledge that opposites attract. If Pan Ku had not succeeded, Earth and Heaven and *yin* and *yang* would soon have reunited. Whether magnets, electrical polarities, or potential lovers, the concept of opposites attracting that is *yin* and *yang* is intrinsic to what makes the world go 'round.

Yin and Yang Keywords

The following table lists some of the most common keywords for *yin* and *yang*. Note that although the first pairing listed is feminine/masculine, this isn't meant in the classic female/male sense. Rather, "feminine" suggests inward, quiet energy, whereas "masculine" represents outward, more active energy.

Nor is "negative" meant in its "negative" sense: To begin to understand them, it may help to think of the pull of *yin* and *yang* as the halves of an electrical polarity or the push/pull of magnetic forces.

Yin	Yang
Feminine	Masculine
Negative	Positive
Indirect	Direct
Cold	Warm
Receptive	Active
Earth	Heaven
Internal	External
________________	________________
________________	________________
________________	________________
________________	________________

What other oppositions that complete each other can you think of, to fit into the *yin/yang* equation? You can use the extra spaces provided in the table to complete your own *yin/yang* equation. Coming to your own understanding about the push/pull of *yin/yang* can help you understand a great deal about your own love relationships—as you'll soon find out.

Yin and Yang Meet Astrology

Each of the 12 astrological signs is either *yin* or *yang*, and this energy, when coupled with its element (as discussed in Chapter 3), helps create a distinctive picture of that particular sign. The following table lists the energy for each sign.

Yin	**Yang**
Taurus ♉	Aries ♈
Cancer ♋	Gemini ♊
Virgo ♍	Leo ♌
Scorpio ♏	Libra ♎
Capricorn ♑	Sagittarius ♐
Pisces ♓	Aquarius ♒

Now, this doesn't mean that a relationship between a Taurus and a Cancer or an Aries and a Gemini is bound to fail because the energy is predominantly *yin* or *yang*. Your birth chart includes all of the signs, and it's the combinations and their particular complementarity that create the push/pull of a perfect mix.

Looking at two astrological birth charts together, we can begin to see a more complete picture of how *yin* and *yang* work in astrological relationships. Let's look at several examples—three couples who've been together for years and a couple who've now gone their separate ways—to see how *yin* and *yang* work in love relationships.

Love Matches Made in Heaven

On the following pages you'll find the astrological charts for three couples whose marriages have more than passed the test of time. Even if you know little about Astrology, take a few minutes to study these paired charts to see what you notice about them. And notice that we've been determinedly apolitical in our choices!

When we look at birth charts for the *yin* and *yang* of relationships, one of the things we look for is balance. Is there a complementarity between the charts that bodes well for the long term? In the case of these three couples, the answer is a resounding "yes."

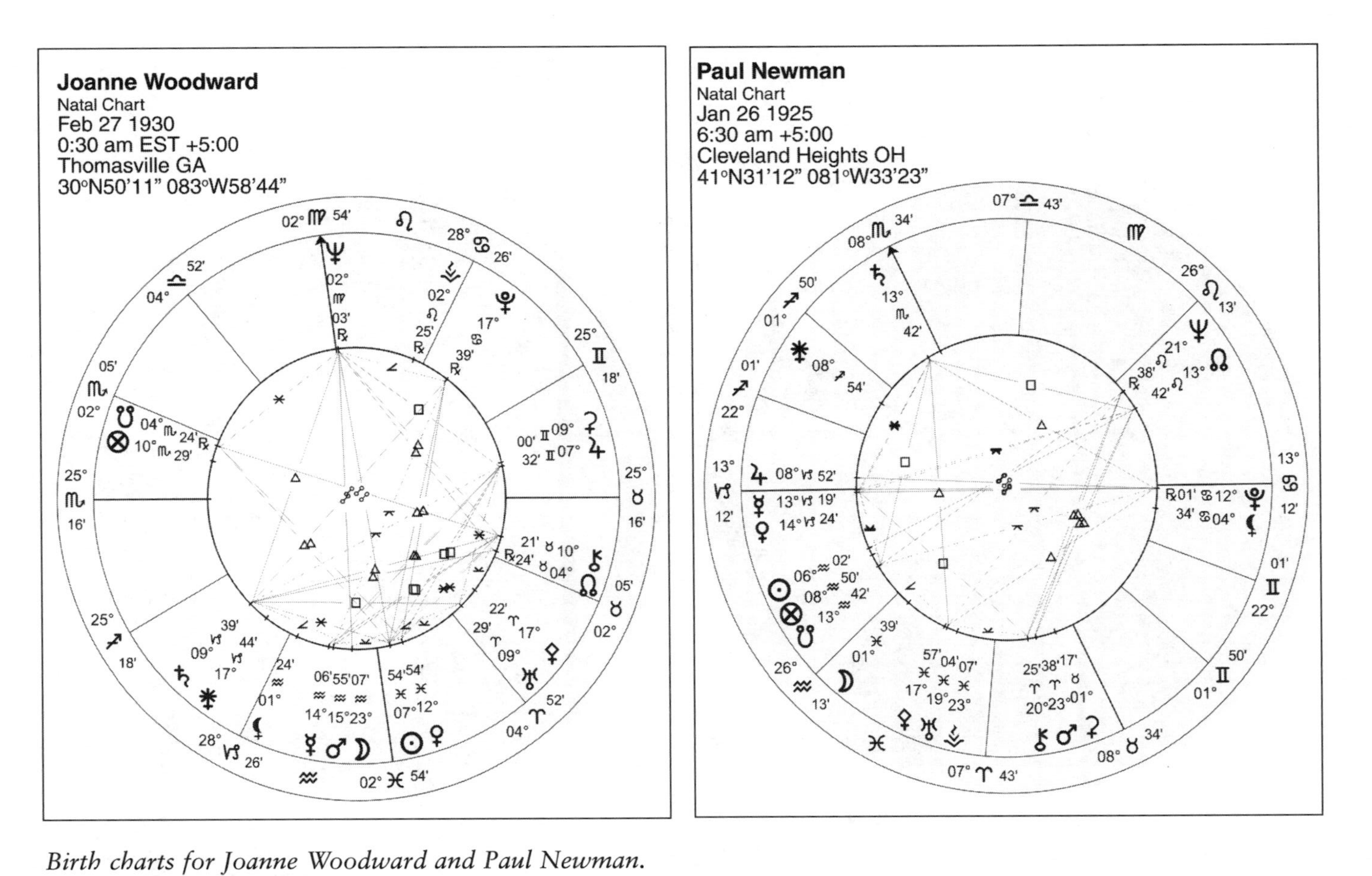

Birth charts for Joanne Woodward and Paul Newman.

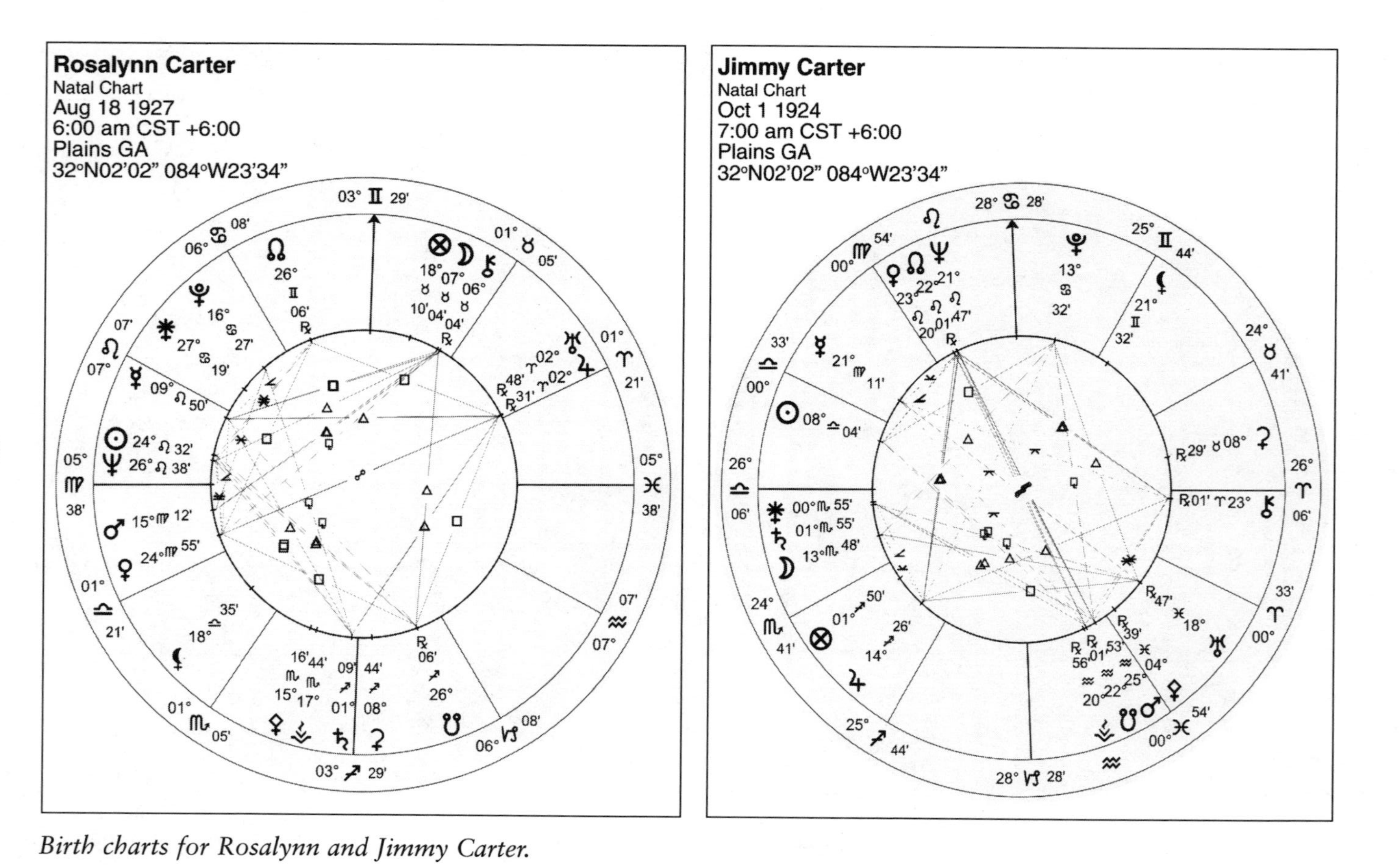

Birth charts for Rosalynn and Jimmy Carter.

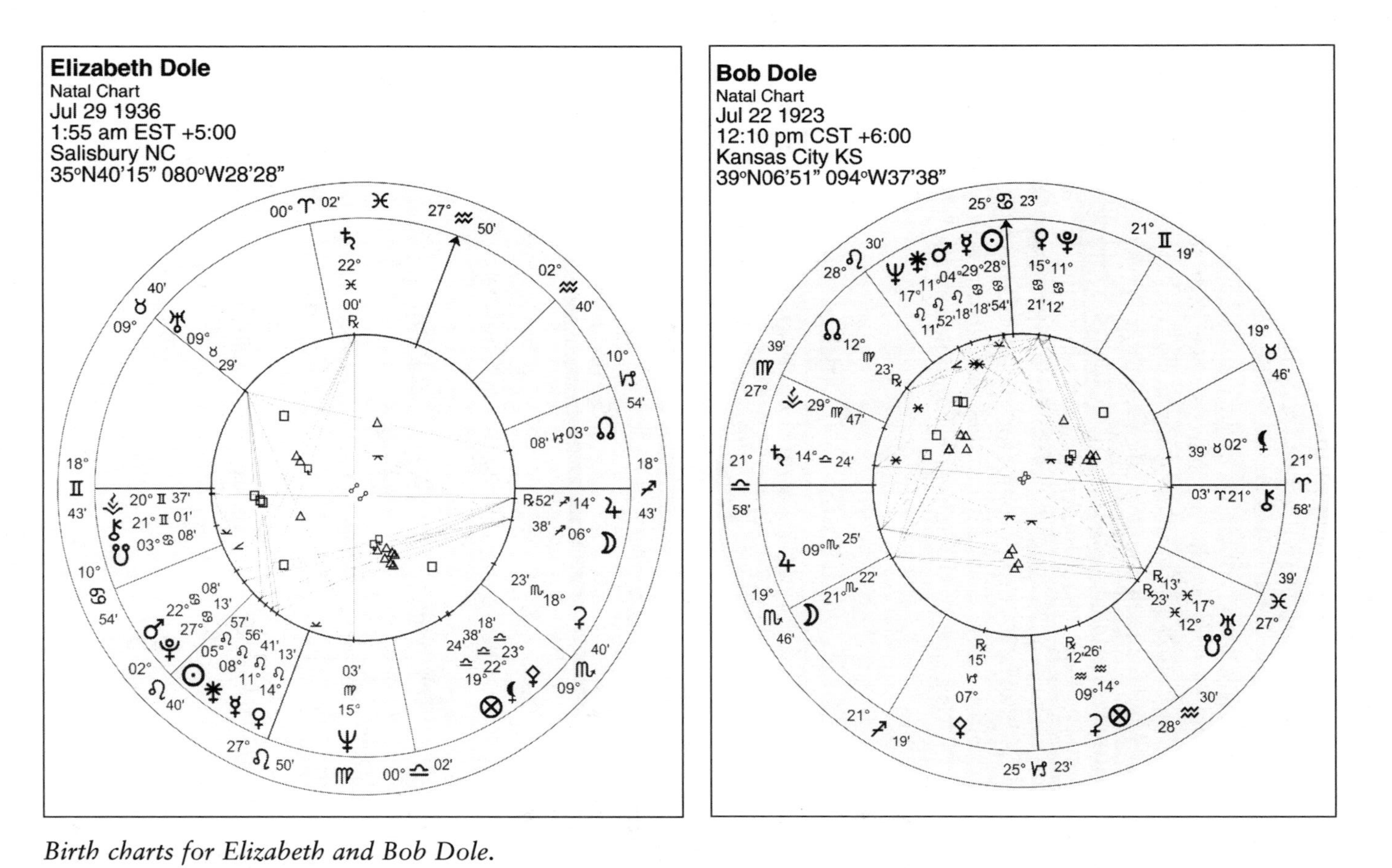

Birth charts for Elizabeth and Bob Dole.

To help you begin to examine birth charts on your own, we've devised a table to look at the signs of the inner planets of each of these couples. We don't look at the outer planets in the same way because they move much more slowly, often remaining in the same sign for many years. If you look at the Pluto ♇ on the six charts shown here, for example, you'll find that it's in Cancer ♋ for all six people. For this reason, we look at the *yin* and *yang* for each couple's Sun ☉, Moon ☽, Mercury ☿, Venus ♀, Mars ♂, Jupiter ♃, and ascendant. (Also called the "rising sign," this is the astrological sign that appears on the cusp of the 1st house.)

Next, we note which signs are *yin* and which are *yang*. We like to use the letter "X" (as in X chromosome) for *yin* and the letter "Y" (as in Y chromosome) for *yang*. Not only are these designations easy to remember, the letter "X" is a universal symbol for feminine and the letter "Y" for masculine!

Inner Planets Reveal Love's Yin and Yang

Inner Planets	**Joanne Woodward**	**X/Y *Yin/Yang***	**Paul Newman**	**X/Y *Yin/Yang***
Sun ☉	Pisces ♓	X	Aquarius ♒	Y
Moon ☽	Aquarius ♒	Y	Pisces ♓	X
Mercury ☿	Aquarius ♒	Y	Capricorn ♑	X
Venus ♀	Pisces ♓	X	Capricorn ♑	X
Mars ♂	Aquarius ♒	Y	Aries ♈	Y
Jupiter ♃	Gemini ♊	Y	Capricorn ♑	X
Ascendant	Scorpio ♏	X	Capricorn ♑	X

Inner Planets	**Rosalynn Carter**	**X/Y *Yin/Yang***	**Jimmy Carter**	**X/Y *Yin/Yang***
Sun ☉	Leo ♌	Y	Libra ♎	Y
Moon ☽	Taurus ♉	X	Scorpio ♏	X
Mercury ☿	Leo ♌	Y	Virgo ♍	X
Venus ♀	Virgo ♍	X	Leo ♌	Y
Mars ♂	Virgo ♍	X	Aquarius ♒	Y
Jupiter ♃	Aries ♈	Y	Sagittarius ♐	Y
Ascendant	Virgo ♍	X	Libra ♎	Y

Inner Planets	Elizabeth Dole	X/Y *Yin/Yang*	Bob Dole	X/Y *Yin/Yang*
Sun ☉	Leo ♌	Y	Cancer ♋	X
Moon ☽	Sagittarius ♐	Y	Scorpio ♏	X
Mercury ☿	Leo ♌	Y	Cancer ♋	X
Venus ♀	Leo ♌	Y	Cancer ♋	X
Mars ♂	Cancer ♋	X	Leo ♌	Y
Jupiter ♃	Sagittarius ♐	Y	Scorpio ♏	X
Ascendant	Gemini ♊	Y	Libra ♎	Y

You'll likely notice the balance between each couple's *yin* and *yang* as you study this table. But something else caught our eyes—the complementarity that occurs in each of these charts. Look, for example, at Joanne Woodward and Paul Newman's Sun and Moon: Her Sun is in Pisces and his in Aquarius, while her Moon is in Aquarius and his in Pisces. A perfect *yin/yang* complementarity!

When we look at the Woodward and Newman birth charts together, we immediately see the energy flow between them. Because the *yin* and *yang* are balanced, the flow of energy generates respect for each other's egos, understanding of each other's emotional natures, and acknowledgment of the other's public identity. In addition, the Air sign Aquarius, a fixed (*yang*) sign that ensures longevity, appears in both charts, revealing both their humanitarian and independent sides. At the same time, because of their *yin/yang* complementarity, these two know how to cooperate well. Finally, the Water sign Pisces (*yin*) and Earth sign Capricorn (*yin*) are also here, and this combination provides emotional and sexual support to the relationship.

As we all know, this couple has certainly given great support to each other over the years; at the same time, they are well known for their common goals concerning community and humanitarian causes. This is truly a classic example of how love, independent thinking, peaceful coexistence, and genuine concern for others can be the makings of a great marriage.

Let's try the same thing for Rosalynn and Jimmy Carter. Here the *yin/yang* complementarity occurs in their Mercury (communication) and Venus (love) signs. Her Mercury is in Leo, his in Virgo; her Venus is in Virgo, his in Leo. Good communication and mutual understanding of goals are indicated with this complementarity. With their unique balance of intelligence and emotional complementarity, these two can overcome great obstacles not only through their devotion and loyalty to each other, but their devotion and loyalty to the focus of their intelligence and emotion. This pair is particularly focused by a willingness to allow the other to speak his or her own truth, even when they disagree. "I agree to disagree" can be the focal point of a great marriage, as it indicates a diplomatic willingness to keep the doors of communication open. Rosalynn and Jimmy Carter have clearly learned this lesson well.

The most striking *yin/yang* complementarity occurs in the charts of Elizabeth and Bob Dole. See if you can find it yourself. (Hint: Look for the Cancers and Leos.)

What did you discover? The Doles' complementarity occurs between their Sun (exploration), Mercury (communication), Venus (enjoyment) signs, hers in Leo and his in Cancer; and her Mars (engagement) in Cancer and his in Leo. All this translates to a couple who not only enjoys communicating, but, because the Leo and Cancer signs "flip," so to speak, share a complementarity between how they communicate and how they interact. There's a further *yin/yang* balance in their Moon (sensual) and Jupiter (beneficent) signs, too, with hers in Sagittarius and his in Scorpio.

Quite simply, complementarity is *yin/yang* at work. When the balance is there, the match truly does seem made in heaven.

We return to these couples' birth charts throughout this book. After all, it takes more than *yin/yang* complementarity to make a perfect marriage. But as you can see, *yin/yang* complementarity is a great start.

Two for the Seesaw

As you may recall from those magnets in physics class, the flip side of *yin/yang* complementarity is friction. Although there may be initial attraction, ultimately, when there is too much similarity, the result is a pushing away rather than the natural attraction found with a *yin/yang* balance.

Here, for example, are the birth charts of actors Demi Moore and Bruce Willis. Take a moment to study these charts before moving on to the table that shows their inner planets' *yin* and *yang*.

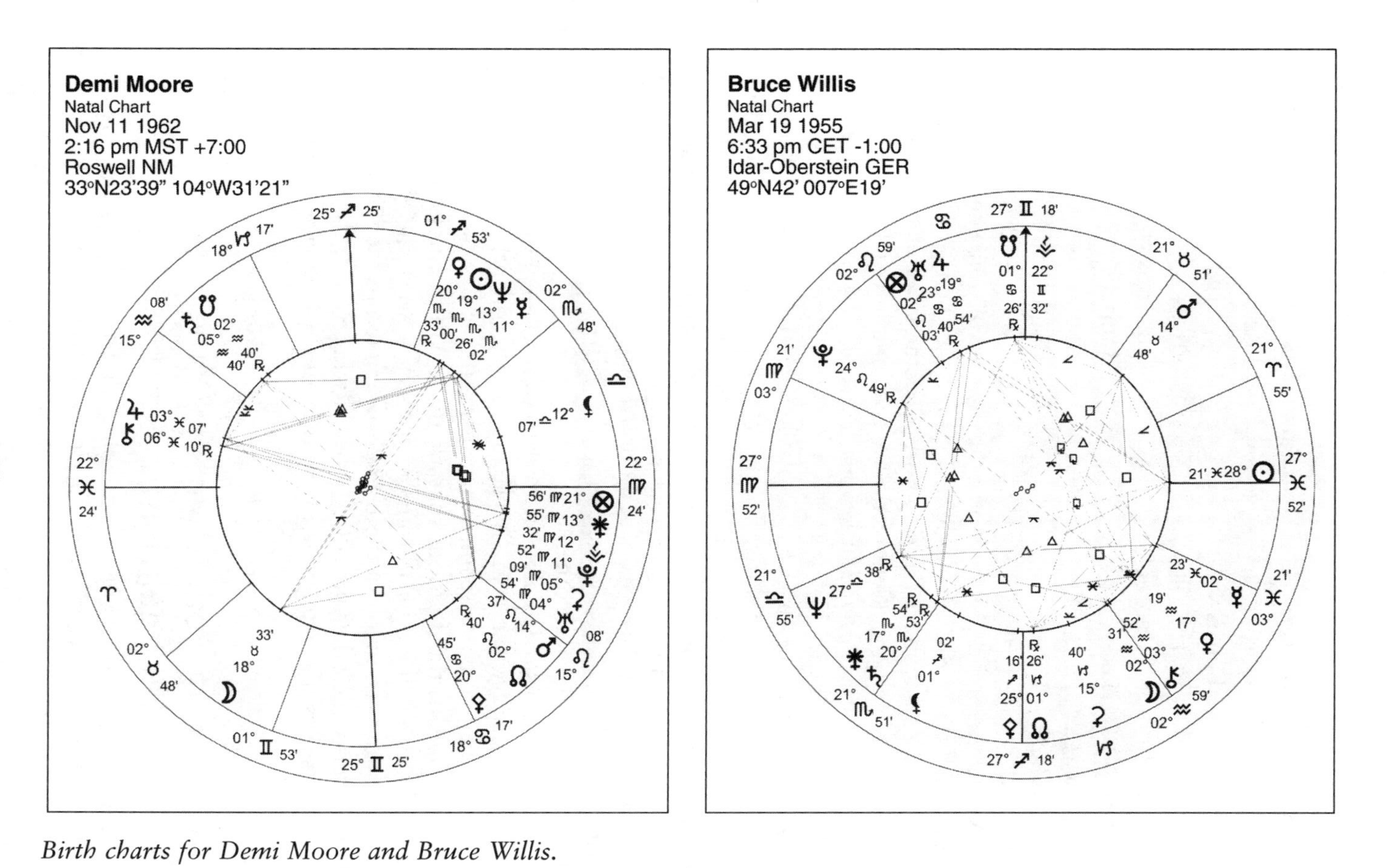

Birth charts for Demi Moore and Bruce Willis.

Inner Planets	Demi Moore	X/Y Yin/Yang	Bruce Willis	X/Y Yin/Yang
Sun ☉	Scorpio ♏	X	Pisces ♓	X
Moon ☽	Taurus ♉	X	Aquarius ♒	Y
Mercury ☿	Scorpio ♏	X	Pisces ♓	X
Venus ♀	Scorpio ♏	X	Aquarius ♒	Y
Mars ♂	Leo ♌	Y	Taurus ♉	X
Jupiter ♃	Pisces ♓	X	Cancer ♋	X
Ascendant	Pisces ♓	X	Virgo ♍	X

What's the first thing you notice about the *yin/yang* energies for this couple? All those X's! That's right: This is a pairing that is so predominantly *yin,* it's a wonder there was any directness in this relationship! *Yin* energy, remember, is indirect, receptive, and internal, and when a couple has a lot of *yin* and little *yang* between them, no one may be willing to take the lead.

Yin energy can be emotional, volatile, secretive, and subject to sudden and illogical mood shifts. For this reason, too much *yin* energy can lead to those weepy moments where neither one is listening to the other because both are upset. At the same time, even though there may be no basis in reality, jealousy or envious feelings can surface. While such feelings often arise because of past emotional baggage rather than anything that's occurring right now, the couple won't likely realize this, and so will instead blame each other.

Finally, because *yin* energy is receptive rather than direct, a couple with too much *yin* can actually be emotionally codependent with no leader or logic to guide them. When this is the case, either no decisions will be made, or the decisions that are made will be emotionally rooted, which in turn will only lead to more conflict between the two.

The initial attraction in the Demi/Bruce union to the mirror image of *yin* energy the other provided, especially in terms of their emotional makeup, seems ultimately one of the reasons the marriage couldn't continue.

Discovering Your Own Yin/Yang Astrological Equation

Discovering your own *yin/yang* astrological equation is as close as your birth chart—and your sweetie's. Begin by setting up a table like the ones we've done for the previous couples. You can use the following table if you'd like, or you can copy it into your own notebook.

Inner Planets	Name 1: ___________	X/Y Yin/Yang	Name 2: ___________	X/Y Yin/Yang
Sun ☉	___________	________	___________	________
Moon ☽	___________	________	___________	________
Mercury ☿	___________	________	___________	________
Venus ♀	___________	________	___________	________
Mars ♂	___________	________	___________	________
Jupiter ♃	___________	________	___________	________
Ascendant	___________	________	___________	________

Now, looking first at your own birth chart, find the sign for each of the planets listed. Here are handy lists of the symbols for each of the planets and signs to help you begin to memorize them, if you haven't already.

Astro Sign	Astro Symbol	Planet	Astro Symbol
Aries	♈	Sun	☉
Taurus	♉	Moon	☽
Gemini	♊	Mercury	☿
Cancer	♋	Venus	♀
Leo	♌	Mars	♂
Virgo	♍	Jupiter	♃
Libra	♎	Saturn	♄
Scorpio	♏	Uranus	♅
Sagittarius	♐	Neptune	♆
Capricorn	♑	Pluto	♇
Aquarius	♒		
Pisces	♓		

After you've found the sign for each of the planets in each of your charts and noted them in the table, you can use the following chart to determine whether each of those signs is *yin* (X) or *yang* (Y). We've provided a place for you to do so in the earlier blank table as well.

Yin (X)	**Yang (Y)**
Taurus ♉	Aries ♈
Cancer ♋	Gemini ♊
Virgo ♍	Leo ♌
Scorpio ♏	Libra ♎
Capricorn ♑	Sagittarius ♐
Pisces ♓	Aquarius ♒

When you've finished filling in your form, you'll first want to look for any *yin/yang* complementarities that may exist, such as those we noted when we compared the charts of Joanne Woodward and Paul Newman, Rosalynn and Jimmy Carter, and Elizabeth and Bob Dole. Does your Sun match his or her Moon while his or her Sun matches your Moon? If so, you've got the makings of a strong and long-lived relationship. Other complementarities offer strong potential as well, so take your time as your compare all of the planet's signs.

The next thing you'll want to look at is the *yin/yang* balance. If both of your charts are predominantly *yin* or *yang,* you may have already noted an imbalance in your relationship, even if you haven't been able to pinpoint it until now. Still, *yin/yang* imbalance can be offset by any number of factors; so don't assume that, just because you don't have a *yin/yang* balance, your relationship is doomed to fail. Toward the end of this chapter, we show you how you can work to achieve a *yin/yang* balance in your relationship even if it's not readily apparent in your birth charts.

Once again, take your time looking at your charts and beginning to compare them. As you learn in future chapters, *yin* and *yang* are only the beginning of relationships that seem heaven on Earth.

Yin and Yang Meet the Tarot

Although the Tarot doesn't assign specific *yin/yang* labels to the cards, you can nonetheless see how this energy is reflected in the cards yourself. To try this, take out your Tarot deck and follow these steps:

1. Separate the Major Arcana from the Minor Arcana.
2. Set the Minor Arcana cards aside.
3. Lay out all 22 Major Arcana cards in order, beginning with the Fool and ending with the World.

4. Now, one at a time, look at each of these Major Arcana cards. Does it feel *yin* to you or *yang*? If necessary, you can refer to the table of *yin* and *yang* keywords at the beginning of this chapter. Create two new rows of cards, one for *yin* and one for *yang*.
5. As you move each card to your *yin* row or *yang* row, go with your first impulse, as always. When you're finished, you'll have 2 new rows of cards which will likely contain 11 cards each: a row of *yin* energy cards, and a row of *yang* energy cards.

Here are the cards that we came up with when we did this exercise:

Our Yin Major Arcana cards are the Magician, the High Priestess, the Empress, the Lovers, Strength, Justice, the Hanged Man, Temperance, the Star, the Moon, and the World.

Our Yang Major Arcana cards are the Fool, the Emperor, the Hierophant, the Chariot, the Hermit, the Wheel of Fortune, Death, the Devil, the Tower, the Sun, and Judgement.

Were your choices similar to ours? We're betting they were, as these cards seem to naturally divide into indirect and direct energies. If your cards sorted differently from ours, however, that's fine. In the next part of this exercise, we show you why we picked the cards we did, and you have the opportunity to explain why you selected the cards you did.

Discovering Your Own Yin/Yang Tarot Equation

Don't put your cards away yet! Instead, get out your notebook so you can record the next part of this exercise. When you're ready, pick up the first card in your *yin* row. As you look at your first *yin* card, think about what made you decide it represented *yin* energies. Here, for example, is our list of why we picked the Magician:

The Magician = *yin*

Intuitive
Receptive
Flowers
Cup (emotion)
Infinite
Gold and white
Flowing
Fecund

One at a time, go through each of the cards in your *yin* row and make a similar list. Each card's list will have similarities and differences. To show you what we mean, here's our list for another of our *yin* cards, the Moon.

The Moon = *yin*

Moon
Water
Intuitive
Animals
Fecund
Receptive
Darkness

As you can see, some words, such as *receptive* and *intuitive,* appear in both lists, but most do not. Your determinations of masculine and feminine qualities will likewise be your own. *There are no right or wrong answers.* This exercise is designed simply to help you learn to work with the imagery of the Tarot on your own terms.

When you've completed your row of *yin* cards, repeat the exercise with your *yang* selections. Here, for example, are our lists for the Emperor and the Sun.

The Emperor = *yang*
Man
Armor
Red bearded
Strong
Aggressive
King

The Sun = *yang*
Boy
Positive
Victorious
Blonde
Light
Forward motion
Solid foundation

After you've made a list of words for each of your cards, review the words you've chosen to represent *yin* energy and *yang* energy. From these words, select the five that to you seem most representative of that particular polarity. We've listed ours here.

Yin	**Yang**
Intuitive	Active
Receptive	Strong
Infinite	Positive
Flowing	Aggressive
Dark	Light

Here's a table for you to fill in your own *yin* and *yang* keywords.

Yin	Yang
______________	______________
______________	______________
______________	______________
______________	______________
______________	______________
______________	______________
______________	______________

Whether a card in a particular Tarot reading represents *yin* or *yang* energy ultimately depends on the question you are asking and the cards' relationships within the reading itself. However, armed with your *yin/yang* keyword list, you'll be far better equipped to consider a Tarot reading's *yin/yang* love equation.

A Sample Tarot Spread: What Do You Desire in a Relationship?

Before we set you loose to try your own Tarot spread about what you desire in a relationship, we thought we would show you someone else's Seven-Card Spread asking the same question. A Seven-Card Spread is particularly effective when your question requires more than just a yes or no answer, but some divine wisdom as well. As the number of wisdom and higher knowledge, 7 is uniquely suited to help you discover what may not be readily apparent on the surface, as well as determine your feelings about the question itself. The Major Arcana card that bears the number 7 is the Chariot—a card that considers the two sides of the issue, balancing opposing forces, light and dark. Sounds pretty *yin/yang* to us!

Study the Chariot and look for the yin/yang symbolism its images contain.

Tarot's Seven-Card Spread is laid out very simply, with the cards in a row as shown here.

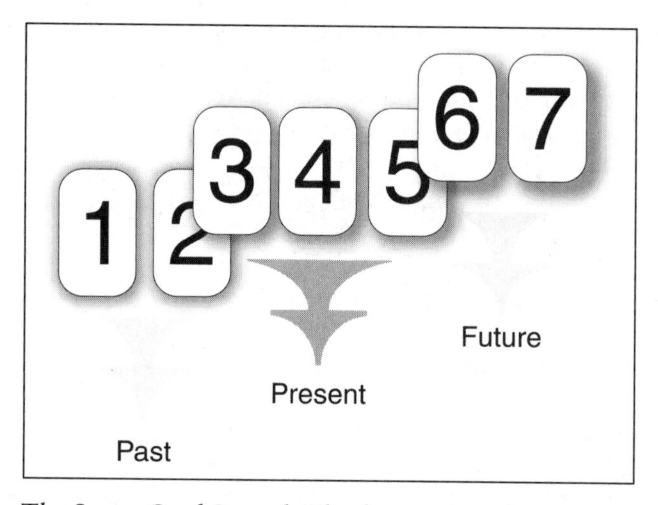

The Seven-Card Spread. The first two cards represent the past, the next three cards represent the present, and the last two cards represent the future.

Suzanne has spent the several years following her divorce fantasizing about her "knight in shining armor," but not doing anything to find this elusive partner. For this reason, Suzanne's question is "What do I desire in a relationship?"

Arlene begins by having Suzanne shuffle the cards until she feels they are ready, and then has her cut the deck. Arlene then deals the spread for Suzanne. Here is her Seven-Card Spread:

Suzanne's Seven-Card Spread: "What do I desire in a relationship?"

The Past. Right away, we can see that in Suzanne's past, she had decisions, 2 of Swords, to make about home life and marriage, the Empress. In fact, Suzanne was divorced after what was at first a good relationship slowly grew apart. Suzanne said she wasn't afraid of relationships because she felt her marriage had been basically good, and that no major traumas remained with her. Read on to see if you agree with her assessment.

The Present. At present, Suzanne is reevaluating. She's contemplating love or romance again, 4 of Cups, but cautiously. Because Suzanne is not entirely sure how she should approach a new relationship, Knight of Cups, she has spent several years focused on *wanting* a relationship rather than *pursuing* one. As the 8 of Swords indicates, Suzanne has some strong fears that hold her back from making a decision, but the fears are self-imposed, and she can change them by examining her own attitudes—if she wants.

The Future. The 7 of Cups indicates that in the immediate future Suzanne will contemplate the fantasy of a great relationship and romanticize for a while longer. At the same time, these two cards show

Suzanne moving back and forth between the emotional fantasy of the 7 of Cups and the logical thinking of the Queen of Swords. Suzanne will continue to bounce between emotion and logic until she decides not only what her desires are, but how she will go about them. The Knight of Cups in the middle of the spread is waiting for her—if and when she decides!

What's especially interesting about this spread is that the question of Suzanne's desire in a relationship is hidden among the cards rather than spelled out directly. This is because Suzanne is hiding the answer from herself, moving between emotional fantasy and logical thinking. At least for now, in Suzanne's case, the push and pull of *yin* and *yang* is all internal!

Your Own Seven-Card Tarot Love Spread

Now that you've read Suzanne's Seven-Card Spread, you're probably ready to try one of your own. Your question doesn't have to be worded the same way as Suzanne's question: You may want to ask about a specific person, or you may want to ask about a relationship you're already in. Keep in mind the *yin/yang* balance you seek.

Begin by writing your question here:

____

Shuffle the cards in your Tarot deck until you feel they are ready to answer your question. You can cut the cards if you want as well. Now, lay out the seven cards. Remember: *The first two cards represent the past, the next three cards represent the present, and the last two cards represent the future.*

Without looking at the Tarot card love keyword meanings provided in Appendix B, contemplate the images on the Tarot cards in the spread you've dealt. It may help you to think of the spread as a story about your question, with the figures in the cards representing you and the other person (or people) you asked about.

Very often, you will immediately identify a particular image in a particular spread as something that connects directly to your question. The blindfolded woman in the 2 of Swords and 8 of Swords, for example, seems to sum up Suzanne's feelings about her question very well—as well as represent the *yin* passivity that's at the heart of her current response. The imagery of the Tarot cards often illustrates what you've felt has been going on in a relationship in a way you may not have previously thought about, but that makes perfect sense when you see it represented in the cards' pictures.

Note both the Tarot cards in your spread and your initial thoughts about them on the following spread form. Only then should you look in Appendix B for the love card interpretations—and only if you feel you need that additional input.

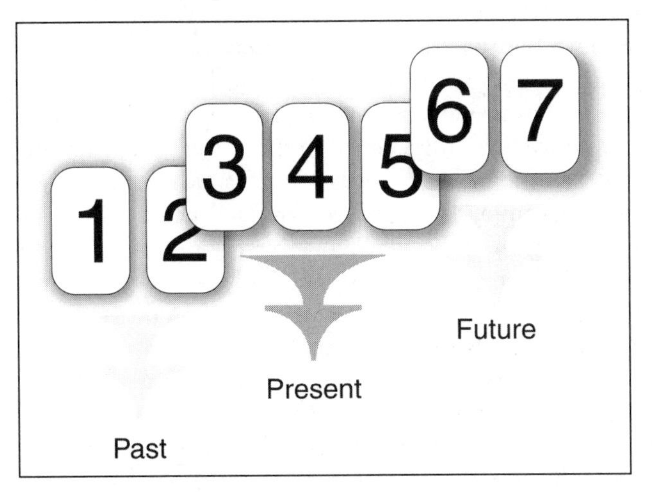

Yin and Yang Meet Psychic Intuition

Intuitive consultant Lynn Robinson, M.Ed. notes that her female clients ask predominantly about love and her male clients predominantly about work. Is this yet another "men are from Mars, women are from Venus" equation? We would suggest that not only does this idea connect with *yin* and *yang,* there could be compelling reasons for these differences.

Women produce far higher levels of the hormone oxytocin than men. As the hormone responsible for nurturing and cuddling, oxytocin may well be the reason women naturally focus more on relationships than men. At the same time, if you think about our cave-dwelling ancestors, CavePapa was likely out killing supper while CaveMama kept the home fires burning. According to Darwinian natural selection, those most successful at fulfilling these chores would also have been most likely to succeed—and reproduce.

So while men may not exactly be from Mars, their predisposition to behave in the ways symbolized by the planet Mars ♂—directly, forcefully, and actively—do give them a *yang* focus. Similarly, women are often more Venus ♀ and *yin*like: intuitive, empathetic, and receptive. To put it in *yin/yang* terms, we say, "*Vive la difference!*"

You can use your Psychic Intuition to explore this difference and see for yourself that *yin/yang* differences are cause not for argument but celebration. Here's an exercise to help you do just that.

"Put Yourself in My Shoes"

"Put Yourself in My Shoes," croons a recent country-western song. We bring this up because this is a good way of using Psychic Intuition to investigate the *yin* and *yang* of your love life. To begin, think of a recent moment shared between you and your partner. This can be a nice moment or a more difficult one, something that occurs regularly, or something out of the ordinary. It could be a conversation you had over breakfast, for example, or a look that passed between you while someone else was doing the talking. Whatever the moment, envision it in your mind. If you are currently without a love partner, return to the last important love relationship in your life; use a memory from that relationship to help you gain insights into your current situation.

Go over the situation or memory in detail. Where were you? Who said what? How did you feel about the moment, both while it was going on and afterward? You may want to make some notes at this point, before you go on to the next part of the exercise.

Now, for the next part of the exercise, you're going to figuratively climb into your partner's head. This means that whatever *you* think about the moment no longer applies. Your memory of the moment is no longer there. Immerse yourself in your partner's point of view. See yourself from there. Try to imagine what your partner is thinking as this moment occurs. Do not allow your point of view to intrude. Simply envision the moment through his or her eyes. Write down what you see.

If you truly allow your Psychic Intuition to work through this exercise, you will have put yourself in your partner's shoes and seen this moment from a whole new perspective that is not your own. Were you surprised by what you thought, saw, and heard? How did it feel to be on the other side of your love *yin/yang* balance? Did the things you said sound different when you heard them through another set of ears?

Putting yourself in your partner's shoes can be particularly helpful at those moments when you simply can't see eye to eye, and allowing yourself to "see" through his or her eyes can help reestablish the *yin/yang* balance between you. At their best, *yin* and *yang* shouldn't represent a seesaw, but the equilibrium of a balanced and secure relationship.

chapter 3

True Love Is Elemental

Elemental keywords
Every astrological sign has an Element—find yours
Every Tarot suit has an Element
Your Elemental Romance Profile
Discover your astrological Elemental Romance Signature
A Tarot spread for your daily Elemental romantic outlook
Exploring the intuitive Fire, Earth, Air, and Water within
Experimenting with Elemental reactions—
from nurturing stability to courting explosives!

Fire, Earth, Air, Water. The Elements are elemental to everything—and everyone. Astrologically, you may already know if your birth sign's Element is Fire, Earth, Air, or Water. But did you know that you've got an Elemental Romance Signature beyond the Element of your birth sign? Or that, by comparing your Elemental Romance Signature to that of the one you love (or hope to love), you can find out what unique alchemy you and your loved one might create? Each of the Tarot's four suits—Cups, Wands, Swords, and Pentacles—represents an Element as well, so we use the imagery of the Tarot as our stepping-stone toward connecting the Elements to your love life; along the way, we show you how much you intuitively know about the Elements already. Whether you're in love, falling in love, falling out of love, or looking for love, the Elements can help you discover what love's got to do with it.

It's Elemental

What is an Element, anyway? Simply put, each of the four Elements is shorthand for certain personality characteristics. Along with *yin* and *yang,* discussed in Chapter 2, the Elements are a simple way of understanding some of the differences among people—including those we love. Whether we're talking Astrology, Tarot, Psychic Intuition, or any other Intuitive Art, we instantly know a number of things about someone when we use this shorthand—and so can you.

Let's begin by establishing some keywords for each of the Elements.

Fire	**Earth**	**Air**	**Water**
Enthusiastic	Productive	Inventive	Sensitive
Visionary	Practical	Mindful	Emotional
Courageous	Hardworking	Thoughtful	Empathetic
Forceful	Complacent	Social	Romantic
Passionate	Physical	Mental	Intuitive

Next, let's find out which astrological sign is associated with which Element.

Fire	**Earth**	**Air**	**Water**
Aries ♈	Taurus ♉	Gemini ♊	Cancer ♋
Leo ♌	Virgo ♍	Libra ♎	Scorpio ♏
Sagittarius ♐	Capricorn ♑	Aquarius ♒	Pisces ♓

Now, let's look at which Tarot suit is associated with which Element.

As you look at these relationships between Tarot, Astrology, and the Elements, you'll see surface connections. Intuitive as they may seem, however, it is important to remember that first impressions are not always enduring ones. Fire and Water might appear on first look to not make a good match: After all, forceful Fire is ready to roar in a burst of creative exploration, while intuitive Water wants to flow and feel its way to discovery. At the same time, however, there's nothing like Fire's passion to ignite Water's romance, so this might be a match worth kindling. Whether it is Fire and Water, Earth and Air, or any other Elemental combination, deeper meditation on the Elements at play and the individuals who possess them is needed to understand how these raw forces work in love.

Wands are Fire; Pentacles are Earth; Swords are Air; and Cups are Water.

To begin our deeper exploration, let's use your Psychic Intuition to discover what you already know about love and the Elements.

Love Is a Rock

Okay—love's not really a rock. But for this exercise, a rock may be one of the objects you'll be using. That's because, for the first part of this exercise, you'll be finding something in your immediate surroundings (no, you may not go to Crate & Barrel as part of this assignment) that represents each Element to you. Inside, outside, or both, it's up to you—the point is to find four simple objects, one to represent each Element.

Even if you can't venture far, and are pressed for time, you can still look for things that represent each Element to you. Maybe you're sitting at your desk. We're sitting at ours, and so—quick as we can—we're going to find a representation for each Element.

Element	Arlene	Lisa
Fire	Lamp	Light on answering machine
Earth	Amethyst crystal	Small wooden bowl of ocean rocks
Air	"Hal," her computer	Open books
Water	Rain outside the window	Water in water bottle

Get the idea? Good. Gather your four Elements and meet us back here. Got 'em? Okay. Write them down in the following table under Object.

Element	Object	Words and Ideas
Fire	________________	____________________________
Earth	________________	____________________________
Air	________________	____________________________
Water	________________	____________________________

You probably noticed there's a blank Words and Ideas column. That's there because, for the second part of this exercise, you're going to meditate on each object and then write down the words and ideas that come to mind as you do. You can even draw pictures, if you're a more visually oriented person. Start by selecting one object. Pick it up (if you can—otherwise, touch it). Hold it in your hand and feel it. Smell it. Taste it (if you can). Shake, rattle, and roll it. Then, still holding it in your hand, close your eyes and sense the object in your mind's eye. What words come to mind? What feelings? Are there pictures, scents, or sounds in addition to those you saw with your eyes open?

When you're ready, open your eyes and, in the previous chart, record what you've discovered about this object. Then do the same for each of your other objects. Take your time. By the time you've completed this exercise, these objects will have become your own personal symbols for each of the Elements, so that every time you hear "air" from now on, you'll think of your object first, and then everything that you associated with it in this exercise. In other words, you'll have made the Elements your own.

For the third part of this exercise, you're going to look at these objects from a slightly different angle—what you want in someone you love. If you want a love that's "like a rock," for example, the rock you selected as your Earth Element would be an easy representation—and someone with an Earth emphasis in his or her chart might be an excellent match.

To discover what Elements you seek (or already have found) in a lover, answer the following questions:

- Which of my objects most clearly represents what I desire in a lover? Why?
- Which Element does this object represent?
- Do I particularly like any characteristics of this Element?
- What are they?

- Which of my objects most clearly represents what I *don't* want in a lover? Why?
- Which Element does this object represent?
- Do I particularly dislike any characteristics of this Element?
- What are they?

After answering these questions for two Elements, go back and answer them for the other two Elements as well. In this way, you'll have painted a portrait of the one you love—or hope to.

Your Elemental Romance Signature

To find your astrological Elemental Romance Signature, you need to take a look at your birth chart. If you've got a sweetie or potential sweetie's birth chart, after you've discovered your own Elemental Romance Signature, you can make a note of his or hers as well.

To help you see how this works, we begin with an example. Following is the birth chart of Russell Crowe, the heartthrob actor with a temper, who is a gladiator with a beautiful mind!

To begin, let's note Crowe's sign for the Sun ☉, Moon ☽, Mercury ☿, Venus ♀, and Mars ♂, as well as his ascendant or "rising sign." These five personal planets, along with the rising sign, are what we like to call the Elemental Romantic Signature. Note that Crowe's is a noon chart. His Moon and ascendant signs could be different, depending on how many hours from noon his precise birth time is.

Planet	Crowe's Astro Sign	Element
Ascendant	Gemini ♊	Air
Sun ☉	Aries ♈	Fire
Moon ☽	Aquarius ♒	Air
Mercury ☿	Taurus ♉	Earth
Venus ♀	Gemini ♊	Air
Mars ♂	Aries ♈	Fire

Next, we wrote down the Element for each of these signs and then used the following table to total up how many of each Crowe has in each Element.

Element	Number of Astro Signs
Fire	2
Earth	1
Air	3
Water	0

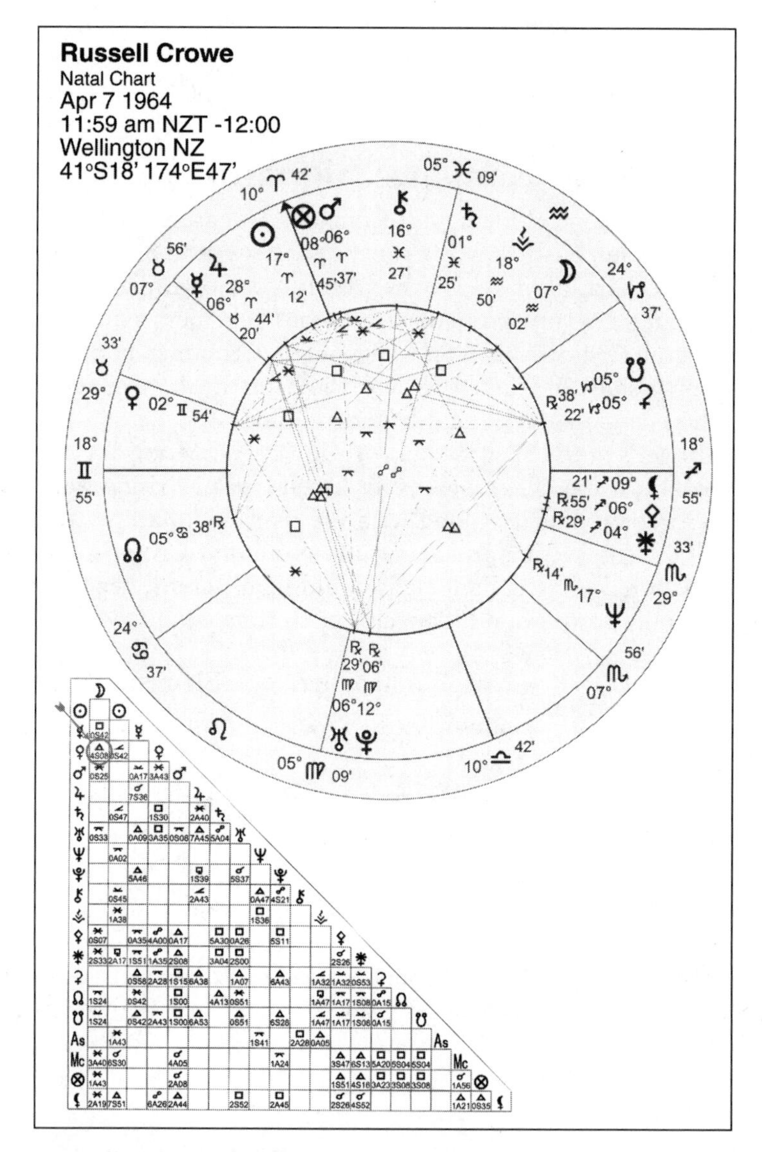

Russell Crowe's birth chart and aspect grid.

From this, we can see that Russell Crowe's Elemental Romantic Signature is an intriguing combination: three Air signs and two Fire signs, grounded by an earthy Mercury in Taurus. This suggests that, when it comes to romance, Crowe's pioneering and innovating spirit, represented by his fiery Sun and Mars, harmonizes with his intellectual and imaginative Air signs of Gemini (both his rising sign and Venus) and his Aquarian Moon. Crowe can use the energy of his Fire signs—symbolizing personal charisma, power, and zest for life—and direct it to the mental, verbal signs of Air. Plus, with three Air signs, he can verbalize exactly how he feels.

Crowe's Sun and Mars in fiery Aries suggest that he will be very intense about whomever he's attracted to. Crowe thinks about things as well as acts upon them; so, while his romantic energy in Air and Fire won't be overly emotional, he will nonetheless be very enthusiastic about getting to know the person he's with, including getting into her head, thoughts, and ideas. Beauty is important, too, with his Venus/Moon trine, so Crowe's romantic ideal is someone with both charisma and intelligence. Because of his passion, he can't have one without the other. In Astrology, a trine △ is a harmonic planetary relationship; you can see the Venus ♀/Moon ☽ trine △ highlighted in Russell Crowe's triangular aspect grid in the illustration. Most important, Crowe needs someone who can communicate at his level—on the airy intellectual plane of his Elemental Romantic Signature. Love is in the Air for Russell Crowe and we wish him the best in creating a beautiful home and family with the woman he loves!

Now try the same thing with your own birth chart. Identify and record the sign for each of the planets noted, as well as your ascendant. You can use the following chart to do so.

Planet	Your Astro Sign	Element
Ascendant	____________________	____________________
Sun ☉	____________________	____________________
Moon ☽	____________________	____________________
Mercury ☿	____________________	____________________
Venus ♀	____________________	____________________
Mars ♂	____________________	____________________

Refer to the table at the beginning of this chapter if you need to and write down the Element for each of those signs. Then use the following table to total up how many signs you've got in each Element.

Element	Number of Your Astro Signs
Fire	______________________
Earth	______________________
Air	______________________
Water	______________________

Which Element appears most in the first five planets of your chart, along with your ascendant or rising sign? That's your Elemental Romance Signature. Of course, it's colored by the other Elements in which you have signs—that's part of what makes you unique. But as we did for Russell Crowe, you can study your own particular Elemental combination to discover just what it is you want from your lover—and what you're willing to do for her or him.

By the way, if you already knew this was your Element Romance Signature when you first read each Element's keywords at the beginning of the chapter, your intuitive "hunch" system is working very well!

An Elemental Romance Tarot Spread

Every day carries an Elemental Romance Signature of its own, and you can find out your daily Elemental Romance Signature with a simple Tarot spread. For this exercise, you use the Minor Arcana cards only, so go through your Tarot deck now and set the 22 Major Arcana aside.

As you shuffle the remaining 56 cards, meditate on finding out the day's Elemental Romance Signature. When you feel ready, cut the deck into four separate stacks (they don't have to be even), and then turn each of the stacks over. The cards on the bottom of each stack represent the day's Elemental Romance Signature.

Odds are that two cards will be from one suit and the others from one suit each. If that's the case, the two-carded suit represents the strongest Elemental Romance Signature of the day, while the others add their own touch of spice.

This isn't the only possible outcome, of course. One card may come from each suit, in which case it will be a day whose romantic flavor is evenly distributed among the Elements. Or three cards may come from one suit—meaning a particular Element's characteristics will predominate. There will even be the rare spread when all four cards come from the same suit. On a day like that, you'll be glad you prepared in advance!

With a daily Elemental Romance Signature like this one, you can expect a day where romantic energy is evenly spread among the Elements.

In addition to noting the suits of your four cards, study the imagery of your Elemental Romance Spread. The "story" we see here, for example, to us indicates a tendency to daydream, a Knight (in shining armor!), a need for self-protection, and a desire for escape. From this we might conclude that on this day, the love of our dreams might arrive—but we might not be ready to let down our own guard.

You may want to do this reading on a daily basis—it's not only simple, it's simply revealing.

Exploring the Fire, Earth, Air, and Water Within

Especially when it comes to love, every Element has more than one side. Just as a single drop or a roaring cascade can represent Water, how the Element Water behaves in your love life can vary widely. So to better understand how the Elements interact, let's first take an in-depth look at each Element individually.

Fire: From Slow Burn to Conflagration

It's springtime in north central New Mexico, and yesterday, like her neighbors, Lisa was out in her orchard, gathering and burning the past winter's tumbleweeds. Just as she lit her first stack, the wind picked up, and, not only did her tumbleweeds burn, but the still winter-brown grass around her fire soon lit as well. Poor little Lisa quickly shoveled dirt over the little grass fires, but the lesson about fire was clear: All it takes is a little wind (read: Air) to turn a slow burn into a conflagration.

If you look up the word *fire* in a thesaurus, you'll quickly see just how many kinds of fire there really are. We've taken some of those words and sorted them by type to discover more about this Element.

I	II	III	IV
Spark	Flame	Blaze	Intensity
Combustion	Burn	Inferno	Animation
Kindle	Heat	Conflagration	Energy
Light	Candle	Firestorm	Power

Let's start with the words in the first column: spark, combustion, kindle, and light. These words describe the beginning of fire. When it comes to romance, this is the stuff that songs are written about: "Some Enchanted Evening," "Strangers in the Night." Quite simply, this type of fire energy takes two, and represents love at its inception.

In the second column are the words flame, burn, heat, and candle. These words represent the second stage of a fiery love, after the fire has been ignited. This kind of fire is warm and intoxicating—as you already know if you've ever been mesmerized by a campfire or fireplace fire. No fire is as romantic, which is why we love candlelit dinners, moonlit walks, a whirlpool tub surrounded by scented candles, or a glass of wine next to that fireplace or campfire.

The words in the third column—blaze, inferno, conflagration, and firestorm—represent fire at its most intense (and most dangerous, as we Westerners know all too well). Out-of-control fire can destroy everything—and everyone—in its path. It's important to be aware of this destructive side of fire—because it's also one thing that makes fire so very attractive in the first place.

In the fourth column, we find intensity, animation, energy, and power. In this incarnation, firepower is a positive force. Without burning out of control, as it does in the third column of words, fire here has been harnessed. This slow-burning fire represents long-lasting love, enduring romance, marriages where the spark never goes out, and relationships whose energy stands the test of time.

The Major Arcana Tarot card, The Magician, represents all of the Fire Element's romantic incarnations. Take this card from your Tarot deck now, if you have a deck, or study the following black-and-white representation.

The Magician represents all of Fire's incarnations in love.

If romance is about making magic, Tarot's Magician card is romance incarnate. Nothing is beyond the Magician's fiery power, whether it's igniting the fire, or keeping it burning. While he holds the Wand that represents Fire high over his head to wield his magic, the Magician also has the romantic equivalents of the other Elements on his table. Surrounded by his magical tools, the Magician is ready to fire the romantic imagination—and romance itself. Tarot's Magician resonates to the number 1, the number of achievement and driving determination. Sound like Fire?

Earth: Building from a Solid Foundation

Just as Fire has many aspects, there's more to Earth than initially meets the eye. Far more than the solid foundation on which we walk, Earth also represents a warm and nurturing place for growth, the rewards of hard work, an appreciation of the sensual, and the enjoyment of earthly delights—sometimes, a bit too much enjoyment.

Let's look at one of Earth's astrological signs, Taurus ♉, to explore the various facets of this Element from a romantic standpoint. Think about what you already know about Taurus. It's represented by the bull—down-to-earth, with all four feet planted firmly on the ground. Taurus's ruler is Venus ♀, the planet of sensuality and financial security, and not only does Taurus represent possessions, it represents possessiveness as well.

When it comes to love, Earth is in it for the long haul. Security and stability are the hallmarks here, and earthly romance is a love that lasts. With an Earth lover, there will be an emphasis on the physical and the sensual—the feel of silk, the taste of chocolate, the sound of rustling leaves, the sight of lush green hills, the scent of a rare perfume. Earth is the Element of fertility and fecundity, too—as represented by its most famous incarnation, Mother Nature.

Tarot's Major Arcana card the Empress gives us a Tarot-eye view of Mother Nature. Relaxed and comfortable on her pillowed throne, the Empress is surrounded by the beauty of living things—from the green forest behind her, to the pomegranates that decorate her dress, to the field of wheat at her feet. This is a well-rounded Empress who clearly enjoys all of life's sensual pleasures, and she's perfectly happy to lie back on her throne and let love come to her, because she knows it will. Although shown here in black and white, the actual colors of this card are warm and earthy, too—the gold of the wheat and the sky, the green of the forest, and the warm reds of the Empress's throne—all combine to symbolize the pleasures of earthly romance. Tarot's Empress resonates to the number 3, the number of creative enthusiasm.

Tarot's Empress represents all of Earth's romantic incarnations.

Take a few moments to meditate on this card. Use your intuition to connect with this card's symbols and ideas, as well as its connection to the Element Earth in all of its romantic incarnations.

Air: The Stuff of Dreams—and Flights of Fancy

Air is the Element of ideas, and from this lofty plane, the idea of romance is as important as the romance itself. To explore this Element's varied romantic sides, it's time to think about some questions. Write down your answers in the space provided. Then read on to learn what your answers reveal about this thoughtful Element.

How do you think about love?

____

____

____

____

What do you think about love?

____

____

____

____

Perhaps most important, *who* do you think about when you think about love?

____

____

____

____

No Element is more thoughtful than Air, as evidenced by its astrological signs of Gemini ♊, Libra ♎, and Aquarius ♒. When it comes to love, Air's mental capabilities can make for inventiveness and creativity, although the romance may sometimes seem almost abstract to more concrete sorts. True to its name, Air makes for lighthearted love. At the same time, something about Air seems to attract the love and admiration of others; maybe it's the air of unattainability that comes from its abstractedness, or its seeming flightiness—this Element flourishes above the Earth, remember.

Tarot's Major Arcana card the Lovers represents Air's finest possibilities. Take this card from your Tarot deck, or meditate on the black-and-white image shown here.

Tarot's Lovers represent all of Air's love possibilities.

The angel Raphael, the angel of air, gives this romantic pair his own special blessing in this card. We also see representations of the Tree of Knowledge (behind the woman) and the 12 signs of the Zodiac (behind the man). That's because this is a card that represents the idea of love as much as it represents love itself. With this kind of divine inspiration, love exists on a lofty, more spiritual plane. Whether it's a match made in Heaven or the idea of a match made in Heaven, airy love is about both creativity and harmony. Tarot's Lovers card resonates to the number 6, the number of nurturing concern.

Water: True Romance—and Tears

Water is the most intuitive Element, so for this reason we're going to ask you to explore it intuitively. Select the Major Arcana card the Moon from your Tarot deck, or use the following black-and-white image. Gaze at this card for a few moments, noting its imagery without judging or drawing any conclusions. When you're ready, write down your impressions in the space provided.

Tarot's Moon represents all of Water's emotional and spiritual love possibilities.

Your impressions of this card: ______________________________

____

____

____

When we meditate on this lovely Tarot card, the Moon, we see all the facets of romantic Water: the flow of Water itself and the life that Water generates; as well as the emotion (the raindrops) and confusion (the Moon and howling dogs) that love often brings with it. This is love at its most intuitive, where the heart leads the head. Nighttime, rule by the Moon, is the domain of Water romance, so there's often more here than can be seen in the light of day. Tarot's Moon resonates to the number 9 (key 18 reduced to 1 + 8), the number of spiritual completion.

Of course, Water can be too sensitive, too emotional, or too romantic. Water, like the astrological signs its Element represents—Cancer ♋, Scorpio ♏, and Pisces ♓—"goes with the flow," and so can get caught up in the emotional aspect of romance at the expense of the vision of Fire, the practicality of Earth, or the thoughtfulness of Air. At its best, however, the Element Water represents true romance and the immortal love embodied by mythic lovers from Romeo and Juliet to Jack and Rose at sea in the film *Titanic*.

Elemental Reactions

Now that you've made the shorthand of the Elements your own, it's time to have some romantic fun, and mix and match them. It is important to note that there are no perfect Elemental matches, just as there are none that should absolutely be avoided. Every Elemental coupling creates its own unique chemistry, and even if, like for us, science wasn't your strong suit, you may recall that some combinations could create either success or disaster, depending on how they were mixed.

Fire and Fire

Because every picture tells a story, we are going to use some Tarot imagery to help you see the various Elemental interplays. Let's start with Fire and Fire. For this combination, we've selected the Queen and King of Wands.

The King and Queen of Wands inspire passion!

This is a pair that fires passion! The colors of their robes (the King's a pumpkin orange, the Queen's a golden yellow) combine just as you would expect if you were to pair Fire with Fire—bright bursts of flame, coupled with energy, enthusiasm, and vision. Remember, too, that the best way to fight Fire is with Fire. That's because there's no stopping this forceful Element once it's begun to burn.

The problem with Fire and Fire is that there's nothing to feed or sustain it. Sure, they are two strong, courageous, and visionary individuals, but what happens when they get where they're going? Matching Fire with Fire tells the story leading up to "happily ever after": Once these two have arrived, the fuel may have been burned and the passion passed. Still, if kept to a nice, slow ember, fire can burn a long, long time.

Fire and Earth

Next up is Fire and Earth. Our Tarot cards for this match are the Knight of Wands and the 9 of Pentacles.

The fiery Knight of Wands and the earthy lady 9 of Pentacles.

The fiery Knight of Wands can hardly hold back his anxious steed, while the lovely woman in the 9 of Pentacles is too content in her garden to worry much about where he's off to this time, or when he'll be back. Fire and Earth romance is a lot like this couple—one can't wait to try something new and exciting, while the other is content to keep the home fires burning.

This can be a good, long-lasting match: Steadfast Earth slows down quick-to-jump Fire, while Fire's passion appeals to Earth's sensuality. The story here is at first glance of one who's off to fight another battle while the other stays behind, but the untold story is of equal interest: The one who stays behind is perfectly content there! And don't assume it's always the woman who brings Earth's rootedness to this relationship—many's the fiery woman who's excited the practical man.

Fire and Air

Now look at Fire and Air, and their Tarot representatives, the Page of Wands and the Page of Swords.

The Page of Wands cloaked in Fire and the Page of Swords fed by Air's inventiveness.

These two bring out the best in each other—you can see that by the way they look beyond themselves. The Page of Wands is cloaked in Fire, and yet knows that more is needed to bring out the best, a best fed by Air's inventiveness. Remember that Air feeds Fire, and that, at the same time, Fire's milieu is Air. Enthusiasm and vision begin all ventures, but it is ideas that keep them going strong.

If this combination has a downside, it's a lack of grounding or emotional foundation, but that is not to say that this is a bad thing. Some of the best relationships (and marriages) are built on intellectual stimulation rather than sensual connections, and when it comes to combining Fire and Air, you may well discover a passion fueled by ideas.

Fire and Water

The last of our Fire pairings is Fire and Water, represented by the Ace of Wands and the 2 of Cups.

The Ace of Wands is the torch of Fire's enthusiasm coupled with Water's empathic understanding in the 2 of Cups.

When we touch the emotional energy of the 2 of Cups with the magic Ace of Wands, it can herald the beginning of steam heat—a romance whose passion continues in a slow burn. Water's emotional nature can be fed by Fire's enthusiasm, and, in turn, Fire's need for excitement can be met by Water's intuitive understanding.

When Fire and Water first meet, an instant attraction often occurs, but Fire's quickness may send sensitive Water into hiding, which will in turn appeal to Fire's desire for conquest. Because Fire won't take "no" for an answer, Water will find Fire's fervent desire romantic, and, once these two finally do get together, Fire will find Water's empathy feeds Fire's passion. Yes, Water can drown out Fire, but, carefully tended, this is a romance that can last and last and last.

Earth and Earth

Now look at Earth and Earth. We selected the King and Queen of Pentacles to represent this combination.

Slow and steady wins the race. Of course, romance isn't a race, but to an Earth and Earth match, especially as shown by the King and Queen of Pentacles, racing isn't where the interest lies in the first place. To this pair, it's all about setting down roots, working hard, making sure everything is tended to and growing well, and enjoying the good things in life. When we look at the people in these two cards, they look as if they've put down some roots themselves!

The King and Queen of Pentacles set down earthy roots!

Earth plus Earth won't create any fireworks, but fireworks aren't what they're about. Chances are, you already know a couple like this—everyone seems to gravitate toward their house on Sunday afternoons, and there's always enough food and drink to go around, as well as comfortable chairs to sit on, good conversation, and time to enjoy the finer things in life. An Earth/Earth combination isn't in the fast lane—but it's a warm and comfortable relationship to be in—till death do you part.

Earth and Air

Earth and Air are the next Elemental couple to examine. Their Tarot combination for our purposes is the 4 of Pentacles and the 2 of Swords.

The earthy 4 of Pentacles and airy 2 of Swords hold on to what they've got!

Both the man in the 4 of Pentacles and the woman in the 2 of Swords are holding tightly to what they've got, and that's a good indication of a relationship between Earth and Air—caution and thoughtfulness, every step of the way, on both sides. Earth, remember, is the most practical and grounded of the Elements, whereas Air is committed to ideas and harmony. Imagine one without the other, however, and you begin to see just what such a match might offer.

At the horizon where Earth and Air meet is the realm of possibility, and with this match, anything is possible. Mind over matter? Matter over mind? How about mind plus matter: That's what Air plus Earth equals—the best of both worlds. Passion isn't the lodestar here, nor is romance. Instead, what you'll find is a meeting of thought and practicality, a relationship where, again, anything is possible—and may well last a long time.

Earth and Water

Next look at Earth and Water, as shown by the 7 of Pentacles and the Ace of Cups.

The earthy 7 of Pentacles plants while the Ace of Cups nurtures and waters.

The man in the 7 of Pentacles knows the fields he has planted need Water, and the Ace of Cups is just his match. The mixing of Earth and Water is optimum for growth. Sensitive Water needs the stability of Earth to contain its flow, while steadfast Earth finds flowing Water feeds its sensuality. In addition, empathetic Water will happily see that complacent Earth has a home that truly is a castle to both of them.

You won't see this pair in the headlines, however, and you won't find them out inventing—or re-inventing the wheel. To an Earth and Water romance, home is not only where the heart is, it's where the hearth is, and that hearth will be the center of this relationship that will create its own special synergy, a match made not in Heaven, but right here on Earth, fed by Earth's most bountiful Element, Water.

Air and Air

Air and Air is the next couple up, represented by the King and Queen of Swords.

The King and Queen of Swords have their heads in the clouds!

Here's a pair with their heads in the clouds—quite literally. Air is the realm of the King and Queen of Swords, and with so much going on up here, the breeze might just turn into a windstorm! This is a serious pair, because each has got a lot on his or her mind. Air plus Air combinations bring to mind scientific couples like the Curies or political couples like Franklin and Eleanor Roosevelt. Where these two meet is in the realm of ideas. Air and Air is an intellectual pairing. They may forget to eat—they may even forget to buy groceries—but they'll be so caught up in their intellectual pursuits, neither one will notice.

The problem with an Air/Air pairing, as you may have gathered, is a distinct lack of any grounding—but this is not necessarily a negative. If you recall, some of the most romantic scenes in the film *Crouching Tiger, Hidden Dragon* had couples literally walking on air. It can be heady up there—just be careful you don't fly away.

Air and Water

Then there's Air and Water, and their Tarot cards, the Knight of Swords and the 3 of Cups.

The Knight of Swords flies through the air; his love lifts a cup in celebration!

Here's another Knight flying off through the air, while his lady love, left behind, happily dances with her friends. She's celebrating her happy romance, yes, but she's not celebrating it with her romantic object—he's got his head in the clouds! All kidding aside, Air and Water make a rather nice match. Think: cologne. Think: champagne. Think: light, misting rain. Nothing heavy is produced when Air and Water are mixed; instead, Air's thoughtfulness remembers Water's sensitivity, while Water's empathy fuels Air's ideas.

However, no one may be keeping this couple's feet on the ground. Air/Water pairings might do well to have independent incomes, as practicality is not the strong suit for either Element. Still, chances are, they'll be too happy dancing and dashing to notice—and between Air's social skills and Water's intuition, everyone around them will be dancing, too.

Water and Water

The last Elemental couple to look at is Water and Water. For this pairing, we selected the King and Queen of Cups.

Water, water, everywhere ... Put together Water and Water and you could be in for a deluge—or simply true romance. Both the King and Queen of Cups have their hearts firmly pinned to their sleeves, and the King's throne literally floats on the water, while the Queen's throne rests comfortably at water's edge.

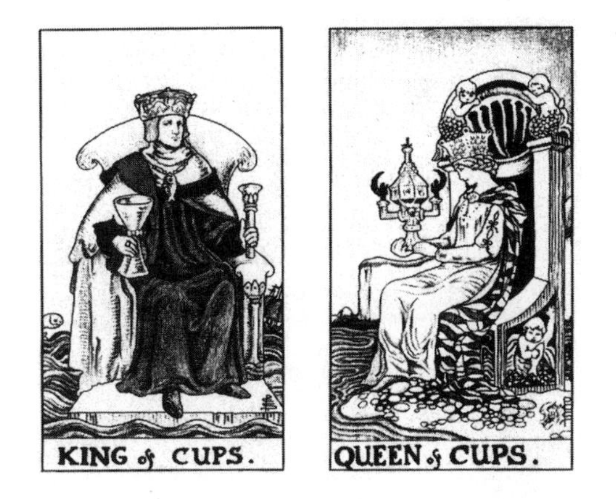

The King and Queen of Cups go with the flow!

This is a sensitive, intuitive couple—so sensitive that it can be all emotion, all the time. What can save this pair from a soap opera life is that both are also empathetic and intuitive, and so will sense the other's needs as if they were their own. A Water/Water match is not for everyone, but it is for anyone who has an Elemental Romantic Signature of Water. The only problem here may be that this couple is so awash in emotion they may forget that not everything has an emotional side. But with Water plus Water, neither one will care, either.

Elemental Love

Whether it's enthusiastic Fire, productive Earth, inventive Air, or sensitive Water, an understanding of how the Elements' energies behave and interact can add a whole new dimension to how you approach love and romance. Now that you've read this chapter, you can add your new understanding of the Elements to your intuitive sense of these four aspects of love—and generate a romantic Elemental synergy that's uniquely your own.

chapter 4

Attracting the Love You Want

Always dating duds?
The romance patterns of our love lives
Learning to separate fantasy from reality
Astrological houses and aspects: Within you, without you
Tarot's Star Spread: What qualities do you want in a lover?
Uncover your dream lover
Attracting the love you want

Does it seem as if your love life is a series of leaps from the frying pan into the fire? Does every promising prince or princess turn out to be a frog or frogette? It could be that it's not the people you're choosing but your own unconscious romance patterns that keep you from the love you want. In this chapter, we show you how to take a closer look at yourself to see how you approach love and potential lovers. We show you how you can learn to spot your unconscious love patterns by using your birth chart to explore the astrological houses where your personal planets reside and what your planets' aspects, or relationships to each other, reveal. We provide a Tarot reading that you can use to learn more about your dream lover, and then a dream meditation to help you uncover how to attract that love.

Always Dating Duds?

If you're a fan of the hit HBO series *Sex and the City,* you can probably identify with Carrie's, Miranda's, Charlotte's, and Samantha's ongoing quests to attract the "perfectly-right-for-me" lover. Or, you tune in to late-night reruns of *Seinfeld* and see Jerry, Elaine, Kramer, and George complaining nonstop about their ex or soon-to-be ex who (fill in the blank): cries too much, laughs too much, high-talks, low-talks, has "man hands," wants to be called only "maestro," and so on and so on. Sometimes looking for the right love partner is like playing that classic girl's board game (sorry, we know there are sexist overtones, here!), *Mystery Date,* where you open the plastic door in the middle of the game board and the door handle catches on … well, hopefully not the dud.

So how *do* you find the "perfectly-right-for-*you*" lover? Does a perfect someone for you even exist? And, if so, can the Intuitive Arts help you find that special someone's phone number (or e-mail address)?

Although we can't provide that phone number or e-mail address, we *can* tell you the first thing to realize is that, good or bad, the familiar is what's usually the most comfortable. This means that, whether they make us happy or not, we will fall into the same romance patterns—and people's arms—over and over again. By the same token, this also means that we may be unconsciously rejecting people who don't fit into that pattern, when one of these untried suitors may be the great love of our lives. So how do you begin to break out of *your* love pattern? By first discovering just what that pattern is.

The Romance Patterns of Our Love Lives

In the world of *Sex and the City,* "modelizer" is a term for someone who only dates models. Chances are, your scope is a little bit wider than that, but you may still be choosing your lovers by a surprisingly narrow and predictable method. We've designed a quiz to help you determine what your own particular romance pattern is. As always, there are no right or wrong answers. How you respond will help you understand your own expectations in a relationship, which will in turn help you see what kind of person you're drawn to—and whether that's a true love match for someone like you.

For each hypothetical situation here, check the response that most closely resembles how you believe you would react.

1. At the opening of a friend's first group gallery show, you feel someone looking at you across the room, and when you look back, you feel an instant attraction. You:

 ____ a. Make eye contact and wait for the person to come to you.

 ____ b. Make your way across the room and introduce yourself.

____ c. Find your friend and ask who the person is, then decide if you want to meet him or her.

____ d. Do nothing.

2. You are standing in the checkout line at the local supermarket on a Saturday night, buying a quart of Ben & Jerry's ice cream and renting the DVD of *Sleepless in Seattle,* when a sexy voice behind you asks you what flavor Ben & Jerry's that is. You:

   ____ a. Ignore the voice.

   ____ b. Answer that it's Cherry Garcia.

   ____ c. Ask what flavor your admirer would like.

   ____ d. Offer to share it.

3. You decide to redo your lover's apartment as a surprise. When you get an angry, ungrateful reaction, you:

   ____ a. Would never redo your lover's apartment as a surprise.

   ____ b. Accuse your lover of being a control freak.

   ____ c. Realize you may have overstepped your bounds and apologize.

   ____ d. Act surprised.

4. You and J. have been going out nearly every Saturday night for the past four months. Now, Thanksgiving is approaching. You usually go to your parents' house, but you're hoping to spend it with J. You:

   ____ a. Tell your mother you have other plans, then hope J. asks you.

   ____ b. Ask your mother if J. can join you, then invite J. to your parents' house.

   ____ c. Ask J. what his or her plans are and then ask to be included.

   ____ d. Pray J. will take the lead and do nothing.

5. You've been dating W. for a month when his or her birthday arrives. You:

   ____ a. Ask W. what he or she would like.

   ____ b. Ask his or her secretary what W. would like.

   ____ c. Reserve that corner table where you had your first romantic dinner a month ago.

   ____ d. Say "happy birthday" when W. mentions it.

6. You've been planning for a special event for months. But an hour before the big event, C. calls to tell you he or she won't be able to make it. You:
   ____ a. Break up with C. on the spot.
   ____ b. Tell C. it is okay, but by the end of the evening you burst into tears.
   ____ c. Wonder why things like this always happen to you.
   ____ d. Understand and have a great time without C.
7. You come home after a hard day and are looking forward to a spontaneous date night with your unsuspecting loved one. You:
   ____ a. Find your lover's favorite chair and plop into it without a word.
   ____ b. Holler that you need attention, too, and start a fight.
   ____ c. Call your love at lunchtime and plan your evening's romantic encounter.
   ____ d. Announce to your lover that a foot massage, or more, is on the evening agenda.
8. M. has been looking for a new job for months. On a whim, he or she decides to quit that boring, thankless job to devote full-time effort to getting the perfect new job. You:
   ____ a. Tell M. that once he or she finds that job it is *your* turn to indulge a dream.
   ____ b. Are furious that M. did this without consulting you.
   ____ c. Counter M.'s decision by doing 10 small things you know he or she finds irritating.
   ____ d. Give M. the silent treatment.
9. You give L. jewelry for Christmas; he or she gives you a card. You:
   ____ a. Ask for your gift back.
   ____ b. Peek in the envelope then ask where the gift is.
   ____ c. Praise L. as a thoughtful person and then tell L. where he or she is taking you to dinner.
   ____ d. Register disapproval in your eyes, but say not a word.
10. It seemed as if you really hit it off on your first date, but now it's been a week and your phone calls and e-mails are going unanswered. You:

____ a. Tell yourself he or she is out of town on business.
____ b. Wait and wonder why this always happens to you.
____ c. Park across from his or her apartment and watch his or her comings and goings.
____ d. Write him or her off as a jerk.

Here's how to determine your score. For each question, circle the number in the following answer grid that appears next to the letter you checked off in the quiz.

1.	2.	3.	4.	5.	6.	7.	8.	9.	10.
(a) 3	(a) 2	(a) 2	(a) 4	(a) 3	(a) 1	(a) 2	(a) 3	(a) 1	(a) 2
(b) 1	(b) 3	(b) 1	(b) 3	(b) 4	(b) 4	(b) 4	(b) 1	(b) 3	(b) 1
(c) 4	(c) 4	(c) 3	(c) 1	(c) 1	(c) 2	(c) 3	(c) 4	(c) 4	(c) 4
(d) 2	(d) 1	(d) 4	(d) 2	(d) 2	(d) 3	(d) 1	(d) 2	(d) 2	(d) 3

Next, tally up how many 1s, 2s, 3s, and 4s you have. Whichever you have the most of represents your approach to love. Read that section below to find out the pros and cons to that pattern of loving. Get your partner to take the quiz and see how your love styles mesh—or clash!

The extrovert can be impulsive, cantankerous, quick to choose, and hasty, but also generous with ready love and affection.

Mostly 1s: The Extrovert. Why sit around and wonder when the answer's just one question away? With a direct approach to love, you're not afraid to take the lead, and you're happiest when you're in control. Chances are, you've got a good sense of humor and an overall healthy approach to love, but at times you can be just a little too controlling for your lover's comfort. Sometimes you're so certain you're right, you never stop to think whether your lover feels the same way, and you wonder sometimes why your actions spark so much controversy. Although honesty's a good thing, sometimes a little tact can go a long way toward creating or maintaining harmony—and at times, you might learn something by slowing down and looking, at least a little, before you leap. You may find a similarly outgoing lover feels more like a competitor than a partner, or you may love setting off together on a lifetime of adventures!

At heart, the introvert is a truth seeker, waiting, watching, and contemplating, but rooted in a cozy, comforting garden of love.

Mostly 2s: The Introvert. What? Me say something? If your answers are mostly 2s, chances are you prefer a good book to a good party, Mozart to Eminem, and not knowing to having to ask—let alone confrontation. If you haven't yet met Mr. or Ms. Right, you may not even be certain you care: After all, a partner could intrude on your solitude. But we suspect you may want a partner after all to snuggle into your homey nest with. It may surprise you to learn that you could do quite well with a more gregarious love partner; after all, a night on the town every now and then can be exciting. Of course, there's a great deal to be said for a pair of 2s keeping the home fires burning, too—you just have to find each other!

Logic takes precedence over romance when you're a practical sort who protects, ponders, and examines, but is eager to build love on a solid foundation.

Mostly 3s: The Logician. You're so practical when it comes to love, your lover won't have any trouble figuring out where you stand. You make your positions clear. At the same time, you won't abide any nonsense, and if you feel someone's playing you for the fool (or the hermit or the Devil, for that matter), you'll walk away without a further moment's thought. Sometimes, however, you're so practical your lover may occasionally long for a bit of romance. You examine everything and act with precision and purpose. And when you build, you build for strength and durability—where's the logic in love built on a shaky foundation? You can do quite well with both outgoing and more subdued love partners—and it's possible even a passive/aggressive type will have met his or her love match with logical you at the helm!

Strong emotions come to the surface when passive/aggressive lovers bear the burden, feel the pain, and sneak their desires. But their love can be charmed when balance and care nurture the partnership!

Mostly 4s: The Passive/Aggressive. Chances are there have been times you kept things in for so long, you finally exploded, surprising the heck out of your lover—and maybe yourself. Passive/aggressive lovers may seem to take the path of least resistance, but in actuality you are storing up emotions in your body, mind, and soul until you can't hold them in anymore. You can show unbelievable charm, overarching compassion, unusual empathy—no one's as good as the good side of your love. But watch out for the straw that breaks your back and starts the flood of emotions flowing to the surface. Your mercurial turns may keep your love partner guessing at your true feelings. You may find yourself more assertive with a quiet partner, or more submissive with a more outgoing partner. Instead of resorting to subtle or not-so-subtle manipulations and tactics, nurture the abundant love you have within for your partner by expressing your needs with honest, open balance.

Within You, Without You

When we look at an astrological birth chart to determine how you approach love relationships, we look first, as we did with Russell Crowe in Chapter 3, at your Elemental Romantic Signature, the five personal planets plus the ascendant, or rising sign. When astrologers examine the unconscious patterns that affect your love life, they add the influence of the astrological houses to this signature.

It may help your understanding if you think of astrological houses as actual places, because they are indeed where the action of your planets in their signs takes place. Although each house "houses" a number of areas of your life, we've provided just one key term for each house to make it easier for you to remember each house's area of specialty.

House	Key Term
1st	Identity
2nd	Self-worth
3rd	Knowledge
4th	Home and family
5th	Creativity
6th	Work and service
7th	Relationships
8th	Transformation
9th	Beliefs
10th	Ethics and career
11th	Community
12th	Spirituality

Let's look at Julia Roberts's birth chart to see how adding the influence of the houses works.

Planet	Julia's Astro Sign	Element	House
Ascendant	Cancer ♋	Water	1st
Sun ☉	Scorpio ♏	Water	4th
Moon ☽	Leo ♌	Fire	2nd
Mercury ☿	Scorpio ♏	Water	4th
Venus ♀	Virgo ♍	Earth	3rd
Mars ♂	Capricorn ♑	Earth	6th

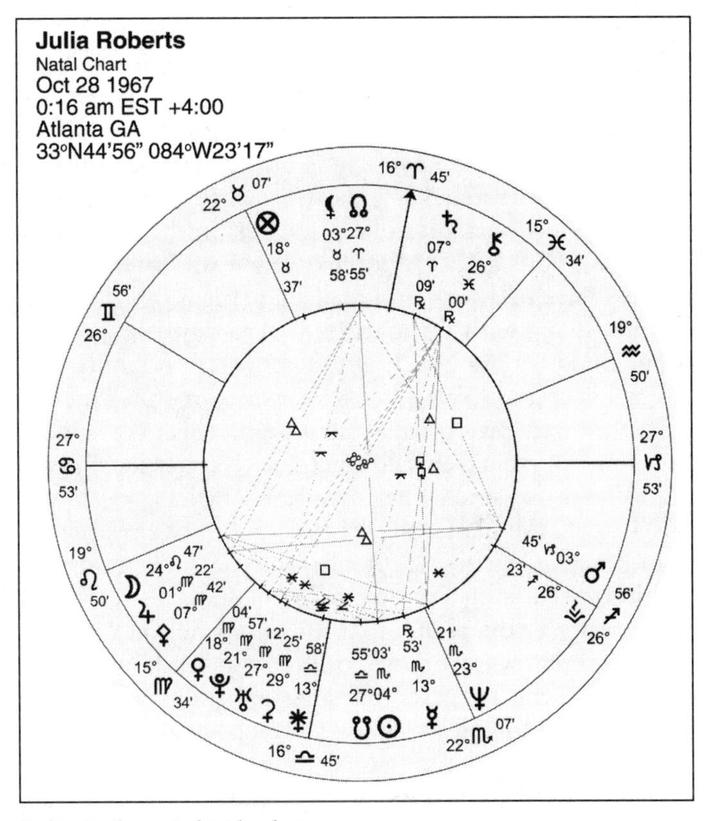

Julia Roberts's birth chart.

As you can see, Julia's Elemental Romantic Signature is predominantly Water. This suggests that, when it comes to romance, Julia will be ruled by emotion first. Let's take a closer look, however, because the role each of these planets and the house it falls in play in one's romantic approach is what reveals our particular pattern, which in turn makes each of us romantically unique.

The first planet we look at for Julia is Venus ♀, the planet of love. Julia's Venus is in Virgo ♍ in her 3rd house, the house of knowledge and physical environment, whose natural ruler is Mercury ☿. Now, earthy Virgo does not approach relationships the same way a Romantic Signature of Water would. Earth signs prefer a more, well, down-to-earth approach. This means that right away, a potential conflict exists between Julia's desire for romance (all that Water) and her more practical earthbound Venus in Virgo. Because this is in the 3rd house, Julia will most likely seek love through knowledge.

Next, we look at the Moon ☽. Julia's Moon is in Leo ♌ in the 2nd house of self-worth and possessions. A fiery Leo Moon indicates a person who feels primarily with her heart (after all, this is the sign of the lion) and who's openly affectionate, but at the same time a Leo Moon will feel neglected any time he or she is not the center of his or her lover's universe. Leo Moons have a strong sense of pride, and because a Leo Moon will feel hurt any time pride gets in the way, marriage is unlikely to turn out as a Leo Moon expects it to. Often, a Leo Moon first becomes infatuated with an idealized perception of the beloved, and then, once living with this partner day to day, begins to wonder just who this person is! A Leo Moon will be devoted to family and career, so great financial success is likely, but love, which requires matching ideals and reality, is a dicier proposition. Because all this takes place in Julia's 2nd house, she will regard this conflict between her ideal love and day-to-day reality as a measure of her own self-worth.

Julia's Mars ♂, the planet that reveals her outward approach to things, is in practical earthy Capricorn ♑ in her 6th house of work and service (which goes a long way toward explaining her career choice), while her Mercury ☿, the planet that illustrates her method of communication, is in secretive watery Scorpio ♏ in the 4th house of home and family. Essentially, this suggests that although Julia may appear to be direct, there may be things she doesn't reveal—even to herself—and that she will often feel a conflict. For Julia, this conflict will likely seem like a literal polarization between work and family. If her ego and emotions aren't kept in balance, jealousy may be a factor as well, whether her partner's jealousy or her own. Julia's chart path suggests that she needs to learn about conflicts between becoming too self-sufficient versus too self-sacrificing. It's a hard seesaw to play out, as we've witnessed in her love life so far. In the 6th house, Julia's Mars will find its greatest satisfaction in work and service, while in the 4th house her Mercury will seek its strongest connections through home and family. This classic push/pull between work and family may well have something to do with Julia's love life as well.

Finally, with a Scorpio ♏ Sun ☉ in the 4th house and Cancer ♋ rising, for Julia the song may well be "Falling in Love with Love." Arlene predicts at least four marriages for Julia—and that doesn't include all the relationships in between! Julia's 4th house Sun in addition to her 4th house Mercury emphasizes her strong identification with home and family, and in this case is reinforced by her Cancer ascendant, as Cancer itself is the sign of home and hearth.

Looked at in this way, Julia's pattern when it comes to love is surprisingly straightforward: While she finds her identity in home and family, she seeks her fulfillment in work and service. The conflicts inherent in romance patterns like Julia's patterns can be easier to deal with once we're consciously aware of them.

Discover Your Own Romantic Pattern

Now it's time for you to explore your own birth chart to discover your patterns and conflicts when it comes to romance. First, using the following table, list the signs, elements, and houses for each of your inner planets and ascendant.

Planet	Your Astro Sign	Element	House
Ascendant	________	________	________
Sun ☉ *Explores*	________	________	________
Moon ☽ *Senses*	________	________	________
Mercury ☿ *Communicates*	________	________	________
Venus ♀ *Enjoys*	________	________	________
Mars ♂ *Engages*	________	________	________

One planet at a time, consider what the sign and house reveal about your approach to love relationships. We like to begin with Venus ♀, as we did for Julia Roberts. Then we look at the Moon ☽, Mercury ☿ and Mars ♂, and finally, the Sun ☉ and ascendant, or rising sign. Write what you see in your birth chart in the following spaces.

Venus ♀: ____

Moon ☽: ____

Mercury ☿ and Mars ♂: ________________________________

Sun ☉ and Ascendant: __________________________________

One of the things to consider especially carefully is potential areas of conflict within your own chart. As we discovered with Julia Roberts's chart, patterns like these are often key to relationship difficulties, because we often are unaware of our own conflicts, and instead "project" them onto those with whom we're involved. For example, if you have an Aquarius ♒ Moon ☽ while your Venus ♀ is in Cancer ♋, it would likely result in a relationship conflict within yourself between a desire for distance and closeness.

Looking at Every Aspect

Another place astrologers look in your birth chart to determine the type of love you're seeking is your planetary aspects. Aspects show the relationships of planets, or, more precisely, their angle to each other, within a person's birth chart. Depending on their angles, aspects can be favorable or challenging—or both. Here is a list of the astrological aspects, along with their symbols and keywords, to help you understand each aspect's significance.

Astro Aspect	Symbol	Keyword(s)
Conjunction	☌	Focus, shared energy
Sextile	⚹	Favorable
Square	□	Challenging—pushes for change
Trine	△	Ease, extremely favorable
Opposition	☍	Difficulty, extremely challenging
Quincunx	⚻	No shared energy, nothing in common

When it comes to relationships, astrologers look at the aspects between your planets to uncover hidden patterns. No one's chart is without these patterns—they're what make each of us unique. At the same time, they are key to the type of person to whom we'll be attracted, and the type of person who will best complement our particular desires and needs.

To show you some of the patterns that aspects reveal, we provide Whoopi Goldberg's birth chart and triangular aspect grid here. The grid reveals how the planets in Whoopi's birth chart aspect each other.

You likely noticed right away that Whoopi has a lot of planets sitting at the top of her birth chart in her 8th, 9th, and 10th houses. Planets that are grouped in this way are considered a focal point on the chart, so astrologers know right away that Whoopi's Sagittarius ♐ midheaven (on the cusp of her 10th house), with her 10th house Venus ♀, 9th house Sun ☉ and Moon ☽, and 8th house Mercury ☿, reveals a major emphasis on areas of ethics and career, beliefs, and transformation. After several marriages, Whoopi is still looking for love. Using Whoopi's aspect grid, we'll look for the symbol for conjunctions ☌, which show focus and shared energy. How many can you find? There are 12. We list three of them here:

- Moon conjunct Mercury ☽☌☿
- Sun conjunct Moon ☉☌☽
- Sun conjunct Saturn ☉☌♄

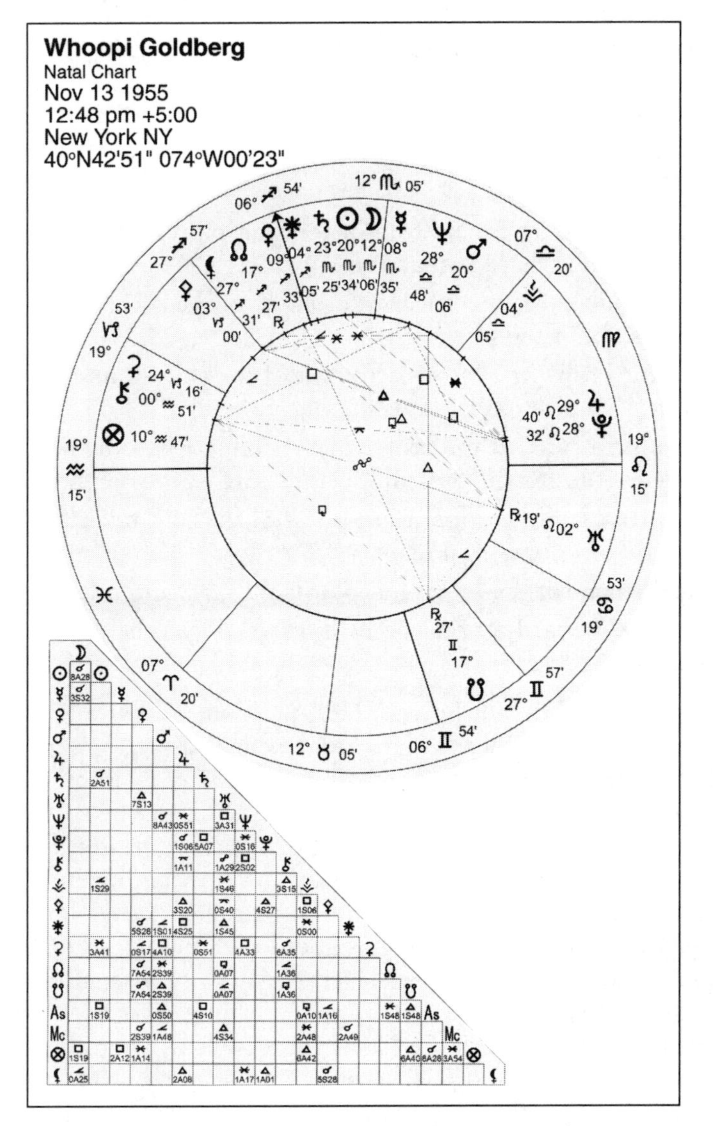

Whoopi Goldberg's birth chart and aspect grid.

Once you have located Whoopi's conjunctions ☌, see if you can do the same for her sextiles ⚹, squares □, trines △, oppositions ☍, and quincunxes ⚻. Take your time. You may want to make some notes in your Intuitive Arts notebook as you do.

Looking for Your Lover in Tarot's Star

Are you ready to discover the lover you've been hoping and wishing for? Let's begin with Tarot's Star Spread, which takes into account both your emotions and your desires. Each of the cards in a Star Spread presents a new "aspect," to borrow a term from Astrology, surrounding your question.

- ☯ The first card, at the bottom of the star, represents you, the querent, and where you are now.
- ☯ The second card, the lower-right point of the star, shares your feelings about the question.
- ☯ The third card, the lower-left point of the star, examines how you feel intellectually about the question.
- ☯ The fourth card, at the center of the star, goes to the heart of the question. It's the most important card in the spread.
- ☯ The fifth card, the upper-right point of the star, reveals your unconscious hopes and fears.
- ☯ The sixth card, the upper-left point, shows your conscious desires.
- ☯ The seventh card, at the top of the star, shows the potential outcome at this time.

Here is Shawanda's Star Spread. Her question: "What qualities do I desire in a potential partner?" Here are the cards that came up for her:

First card, representing the querent: *King of Wands*. Representing the querent, we find an enthusiastic king. Women can be kings, too, and when it comes to this question, the King of Wands indicates the querent has a positive outlook and the confidence to follow her heart. She knows herself, is helpful to others, and has excellent leadership qualities.

Second card, the querent's feelings about the question: *8 of Swords*. Shawanda's card shows that she is fearful or uncertain about finding the love she desires, and what will happen if she receives the love she seeks. The intensity of her desire (she's got 8 swords, after all—the number of achievement and goal setting) is equaled by her fear of the unknown castle on the hill and the delights, or heartbreaks, its prince may provide.

Shawanda's Star Spread: "What qualities do I desire in a potential partner?"

Third card, the querent's thinking about the question: ***5 of Swords R.*** This card reveals that Shawanda is concerned about relationships where conflict and controversy, gossip and innuendo, consume the love dynamic. The 5 of Swords in its reversed position indicates that Shawanda feels equal to any lover's shenanigans, but who needs it? Intellectually, Shawanda has clearly decided to move away from conflict in love.

Fourth card, the heart of the question: ***8 of Wands R.*** At the heart of the matter is a desire to move forward, but as this card is reversed, delays and even conflict and unruly emotions are indicated.

Fifth card, unconscious hopes and fears: ***Queen of Cups.*** But here's the Queen of Cups! In the fifth position of unconscious hopes and fears, the querent desires to be mistress of her own heart. The Queen of Cups will be a good wife, a loving mother, and is devoted to those to whom she's made commitments. This queen trusts her own intuition and is empathetic and caring toward all.

Sixth card, conscious desires: *Empress R.* Once again, Shawanda sees only delays in finding a love partner who has the qualities she seeks. But knowing that the Queen of Cups lies deep in her soul, Shawanda knows she can work to turn this Empress upright, should she make the choice to overcome her fears and look for her love partner.

Seventh card, the potential outcome at this time: *Ace of Wands.* With the message of this spread to guide her, Shawanda is ready to embark on a new search for the committed relationship she seeks with a stable, nurturing love partner whose heart is as steady as her own. Remember, the Tarot's Wands indicate timing within days or weeks, and as this is the Ace, or 1 card, we are pretty sure Shawanda will not waste any time getting out there to find her guy!

Discovering the Love You Are Wishing For

Now it's time for you to discover the love *you* are wishing for in Tarot's Star Spread.

1. Begin by writing down your question: ____________________

   ____
2. Think about your question as you shuffle your cards.
3. Shuffle until you feel the cards are ready. Cut the deck if desired.
4. Lay out the cards in a Star Spread. Record your cards directly on the following spread form.

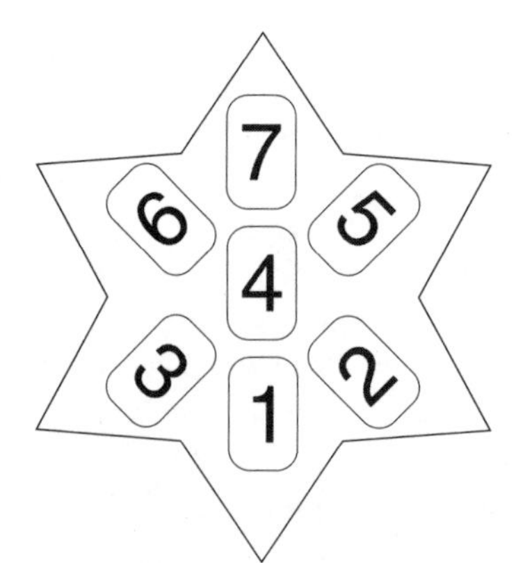

The Star Spread uses seven cards to reveal your emotions and desires about a particular issue.

Record your first impressions here:

First card (you): ____________________

____

Second card (emotions): ____________________

____

Third card (thinking): ____________________

____

Fourth card (heart of the matter): ____________________

____

Fifth card (unconscious hopes and fears): ____________________

____

Sixth card (conscious matters): ____________________

____

Seventh card (outcome): ____________________

____

After you've recorded your first impressions, you can go ahead and look in Appendix B to see what we have to say about each of these cards. Add any of the keywords that seem appropriate to your notes.

Uncover Your Dream Lover

Now let's begin to put it all together. Here you use what you've learned about your unconscious patterns in the quiz that began this chapter, plus what you discovered by looking at your personal planets in their signs and houses. Your Star Spread also comes into play here.

The question that began this chapter is the question with which we end it: How do you attract the love you want? To help you answer this question, we designed a dream meditation so that you can ask your own Psychic Intuition for further guidance. Sigmund Freud called dreams "the royal road to the unconscious." Asking your dreams for guidance is a terrific way to allow the data your conscious mind compiles to be processed and interpreted by your deepest—and truest—awareness.

To perform the dream meditation, follow these steps:

1. Shortly before you are ready to go to bed, gather your quiz responses, birth chart and aspect data, and notes on your Tarot Star Spread reading.
2. On a new page of your Intuitive Arts notebook, write out the question "How can I attract the love I want?"
3. From your quiz results, retrieve your approach to love (extrovert, introvert, logician, or passive/aggressive). Write down your approach to love below the question in your notebook.
4. From your birth chart and aspect grid analysis of your romantic approach, write down the unconscious patterns and conflicts you discovered.
5. Consider the cards in your Tarot Star Spread. Which of these cards seems to connect most with your own particular patterns and conflicts when it comes to love? Keep this card out and return the rest to your Tarot deck. Set the card on the notebook page so that you can see the card along with your approach to love, your astrological data, and the question you wrote at the top of the page.
6. Just before you turn out the light, consider all the data one more time. When you are ready to go to sleep, put the Tarot card under your pillow, close your eyes, and ask your dreams to give you an intuitive dream message that will help you attract the love you want. Be sure to keep your notebook at your bedside. As soon as you wake up from the dream, write down what you remember.
7. Consider what your dream imagery has to tell you about attracting the love you want. Look at all aspects of the dream and your current situation and write your interpretations in your notebook. If the message your dream provides still seems unclear, don't despair. Over time, you will begin to identify your personal dream imagery and become more adept at remembering and interpreting your dreams. Eventually, your dream intuition will tell you what it is you need to know—and do—to set off on a path toward the love you desire!

chapter 5

Love the One You're With

Love styles
What kind of love have you got?
Your love relationship paradigm
Synastry: Astrological aspects of relationships
Exploring your compatibility ratio
The state of a union
Lessons of love, lessons of life
Rediscovering the romance through Feng Shui and the number 9

Although your partnership may have started with flowers (and fireworks), if you've been together for any length of time, you may have begun to wonder where all the flowers (and passion) have gone. However, being in a committed relationship doesn't have to mean the same thing day in and day out—unless that's precisely what you're after. That's why in this chapter we help you discover what kind of love you've got. We introduce you to synastry, a branch of Astrology devoted to relationships and how they work, and show you how to can use synastry to explore your compatibility ratio. Then we provide a Tarot exercise for you to ask about the state of your union. We also provide a karmic Tarot reading that connects with a meditation, so that you can use your Psychic Intuition to help you connect your lessons about love to your lessons about life. Finally, we provide an exercise that can help you relight the fire, find the flowers, and rediscover the romance that got you here in the first place.

What Kind of Love Have You Got?

"All happy families are like one another; each unhappy family is unhappy in its own way." More than 100 years after they were written, the first words of Count Leo Tolstoy's *Anna Karenina* still ring true. As Tolstoy knew, the books we like to read (as well as the films we like to see and the songs we like to listen to) don't tell us about another regular day. We would much rather read about Anna and her lover Count Vronsky; see Rick and Ilsa, the ill-fated lovers of *Casablanca,* play out their story in World War II Paris again and again; and listen to Faith Hill and Patty Loveless sing about faithless love.

In our own lives, however, we much prefer to experience the "happy family" of Tolstoy's equation, with no unpleasant surprises, no confrontations, and no sad songs. Still, to paraphrase singer Lyle Lovett, what's "happy" to us may not be "happy" to you, and that's where the questions arise. It's not just a matter of what kind of love you've got, but what kind of love you thrive with. Do you prefer complementarity or control? Competition or coexistence? The four couples in this chapter, and the Tarot cards we chose to illustrate their stories, show four very different relationship profiles.

Love Styles: From Mundane to Magic

Each of the following four stories illustrates a real relationship paradigm. It's not very likely your own relationship will dovetail exactly with any of these stories, but exactitude is not what you're seeking here. Rather, as you read each story, see if you identify with one or both partners. We've designed these stories so that there will probably be one couple with whom you identify most strongly, several with whom you see some parallels, and one with whom it seems you have nothing whatsoever in common. The Tarot cards that accompany each story may provide further identifications for you as well.

Read all the stories all the way through and study the Tarot card representations before you decide which you identify with most. Make an initial determination about which you identify with most strongly, and then read the stories again—first, the one you felt *least* connected to; next, the one you felt next least connected to; third, the one you felt second most connected to; and last, the one you felt most connected to. After reading the stories and looking at the cards a second time, prioritize them 1, 2, 3, and 4 in the space provided, number 1 being the one with which you identified most strongly. Then read on to see what this identification can tell you about your own relationship.

____ *It's Only Because I Love You.* Justin would follow Kelly to the ends of the earth. He did, in a way: When Kelly transferred from a large Midwestern university to a small liberal arts school in the southeast, Justin did the same. When Kelly got a job, Justin got one a block away. When Kelly's best friend came to visit and Kelly went off without Justin to show her the sights, however, Justin sulked. A few weeks later, he accused Kelly of having an affair with a co-worker. Justin says he does these things because he loves Kelly, and like all of us, Kelly loves to be loved. But lately, she's begun to feel as if Justin may just love her *too* much.

The confusion of the Moon and the chains of the Devil illustrate what can happen with obsessive love.

____ *I Am You as You Are Me.* When Ellen first graduated from college, she went to work as a secretary to put Don through medical school. Once Don graduated and joined a practice, Ellen quit and devoted her time to raising their children, breeding quarter horses, and writing poetry. Don soon began rising through the administrative ranks at the hospital where he worked, and then, shortly after the last of their three children started college, Don was offered a position as CEO at a much larger hospital in another city. Don and Ellen discussed the offer and then agreed they'd give the new city—and the new position—a try. Once they'd moved, Ellen volunteered at the library, started writing articles for a local lifestyle magazine, and quickly made new friends. And every evening, Don comes home from work and they discuss their respective days while they cook dinner together.

Harmony in love through a celebration of partnership appears in the 4 of Wands, and its rewards are illustrated in the 10 of Pentacles.

____ *Mi Casa, Su Casa.* Mark is an architect whose work takes him to cities all over the country; Sarah's position as publicity director for a large corporation means she works long hours. When they decided to get married, each signed a prenuptial agreement, and both sold their condos and bought a house together. They often make what they consider to be minor decisions without the other's input, but both say they discuss the "big stuff" with the other. Mark and Sarah schedule time for each other along with their other appointments. While each maintains separate friendships, and pursues different interests, both consider their marriage—and the home they've created together—a refuge from the rest of the world.

When you live separate lives, you also reside in separate but equal cards, such as those represented by the 9 of Pentacles and the Chariot.

____ *The Fight Club.* It seems as if Harry and Sue fight about everything, from how to raise their children to who takes out the garbage. If Harry says "black," Sue says "blue," and if Sue says "up," Harry says "down." Sue and Harry compete, too—for their children's affections, for the front section of the *Times,* for the bigger paycheck. Harry and Sue are this way at their workplaces, too: He's an investment analyst and she's an editor, and both are quick decision-makers who aren't afraid to take the flak for unpopular decisions. Both Harry and Sue consider their home an extension of their volatile workplaces—and they wouldn't have it any other way.

The excitement of constant change and conflict can become the spark for your passion, as in The Tower; like the woman in the 2 of Swords, however, you may be poised for action but blind to your potential for mutual growth.

Decoding Your Relationship

After you've decided which of these four relationships most closely resembles your own, read on to find out what kind of relationship you are in. Each of these four snapshots reveals a very different kind of relationship. Whether you prefer to live in the slow lane or the fast, the kind of love relationship you and your partner have created can spell the difference between magic and mundane.

Basically, relationships fall into one of four categories:

- "It's Only Because I Love You" is an example of a *controlling* relationship.
- "I Am You as You Are Me" is an example of a *complementary* relationship.
- "Mi Casa, Su Casa" shows a couple in a *coexisting* relationship.
- "The Fight Club" illustrates a *competing* relationship.

The following table lists keywords that help decode the unique nature of each type of relationship. See which of these keywords sound familiar to you.

Relationship	Communication	Sharing	Decision-Making	Values
Controlling	Circumspect	One gives, one takes	Unilateral	Imposed
Complementary	Open, honest	Give and take	Mutual	Similar
Coexisting	As necessary	Separate but equal	Depends on decision	Different but accepted
Competing	Confrontational	A contest	One makes, the other disagrees	Source of friction

No one love paradigm is right or wrong—necessarily! Some people find a complementary relationship boring, while others actually thrive with competition. Some prefer to be in control, while still others are happy to leave the decisions to someone else. Nor does the laissez-faire approach of coexistence work for everyone. Examine your current relationship style and see whether it actually describes the optimal paradigm for your personality and your partner's personality.

If your relationship style is too complicated to fit one paradigm clearly, or if your relationship dynamic is clearly not working and you don't know what to do, consider asking the Tarot to help reveal your love relationship paradigm. Try this Three-Card Love Style Spread.

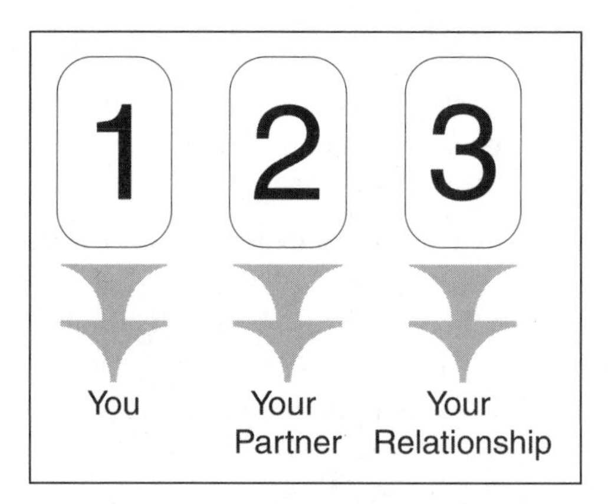

Card 1 represents you, card 2 represents your partner, and card 3 your relationship.

An Astrology of Relationships

Synastry is a branch of astrology that focuses on relationships and how people interact. According to synastric theory, the rhythms of the planets through the signs coupled with our own planetary rhythms create a dynamic cycle that helps explain not only the ups and downs of our lives, but also the nature of who we choose for our partner and the rhythms of that partnership, once we've made that choice. When it comes to loving the one you're with, therefore, synastry is the astrological place to look for answers.

For a relationship analysis of your and your love partner's astrological birth charts, we look at how the aspects between your two charts relate to each other. Is the union harmonious and oh-so-easy, or are there challenges and conflicts you need to work through together?

Let's begin with more information on Astrology's aspects: conjunctions ☌, sextiles ⚹, squares □, trines △, oppositions ☍, and quincunxes ⚻.

- ☯ *Conjunction* ☌ In a conjunction, the planets are placed at the same point in a chart or charts. Conjunctions are considered a focal point, with the interaction of the two planets emphasized.
- ☯ *Sextile* ⚹ In a sextile, the planets are 60° apart. The signs in a sextile share the same energy (*yin* or *yang*), so this is considered to be a favorable aspect.
- ☯ *Square* □ In a square, the planets are 90° apart. Although squares are considered to be chart challenges, they nonetheless often provide the impetus for change and improvement.
- ☯ *Trine* △ In a trine, the planets are 120° apart. This most favorable of the aspects means the planets share both element and energy. Trines indicate positive connections, often made so easily you may not even notice.
- ☯ *Opposition* ☍ In an opposition, the planets are 180° apart. There's little in common with an opposition, but, like squares, their difficult energy can spur us on to meet challenges.
- ☯ *Quincunx* ⚻ In a quincunx, the planets are 150° apart. Quincunxes are interesting—nothing is shared between the two signs, so some adjustment is usually required for them to interact.

When the aspects in two charts are favorable—that is, largely conjunctions ☌, sextiles ⚹, and trines △—a relationship is more likely to proceed smoothly, but there is the danger of boredom because neither of you is spurred on to change. On the other hand, when the aspects are more challenging—squares □, oppositions ☍, and quincunxes ⚻—you may frequently find yourselves on opposite sides of an issue.

In this chapter, we look at two synastric equations. First, understanding your and your partner's particular cycles can help you learn to work with your shared rhythms instead of against them. Comparing your birth charts in a synastry grid can reveal not only what attracted you to each other in the first place, but also how you each deal with conflict, who leads and who follows (and whether you do so willingly), and whether your goals and visions are in synch.

A second feature of synastry involves a relationship analysis of your charts to determine where each of your planets falls in your partner's houses, and vice versa. Taken together, these comparisons can be called your compatibility ratio.

Exploring Your Compatibility Ratio

As you already know, compatibility is about a lot more than *yin* and *yang* and the Elements—Fire, Water, Air, and Earth. While the complementarity shared by the long-married couples we looked at in Chapter 2 is a wonderful thing, it's not a must-have for a marriage that works. To show you what we mean, we've picked one of our long-term couples, Joanne Woodward and Paul Newman, and set up a synastry grid so that we can explore their compatibility ratio.

As you can see, a synastry grid explores the aspects two people's planets make to each other. When we look at a synastry grid, we first look at Sun ☉ and Moon ☽ connections, because these are what will bring about a bonding between people, whether friends or loved ones. That's because these natal luminaries ("luminaries" is astrological shorthand for the Sun and Moon) focus on inner, more personal, aspects.

When we look at the synastry grid for Joanne Woodward and Paul Newman, we notice immediately that Joanne's natal Sun ☉ conjuncts ☌ Paul's natal Moon ☽, while Joanne's natal Mercury ☿ conjuncts Paul's natal Sun. These are excellent aspects for communication and emotional support, as the longevity of this relationship (or any relationship) depends a great deal on openly communicating about any subject that partners feel needs to be worked through. In addition, Joanne's Sun conjuncts Paul's natal Moon, representing their uncanny ability to bond and create their life's goals together.

Next we look at the aspects that *really* make a relationship endure and maintain growth: conjunctions to the North ☊ and South Nodes ☋ of the Moon, and Saturn ♄ connections. To examine these for Joanne Woodward and Paul Newman, let's again look at our synastry grid.

Across
Joanne Woodward
Natal Chart
Feb 27 1930
0:30 am EST +5:00
Thomasville GA
30°N50'11" 083°W58'44"

Down
Paul Newman
Natal Chart
Jan 26 1925
6:30 am +5:00
Cleveland Heights OH
41°N31'12" 081°W33'23"

	☽	☉	☿	♀	♂	♃	♄	♅	♆	♇	⚷	⚶	⚴	⚵	⚳	☊	☋	As	Mc	⊗	⚸
☽		☌ 6A15				□ 5A53			☍ 0A24	⚼ 1A00		⚻ 0A46	∠ 0A43	∠ 1A05		⚹ 2A45	△ 2A45		☍ 1A15	△ 8A50	⚺ 0S16
☉		⚺ 1A53	☌ 8A04		☌ 9A53	△ 1A31		⚹ 3A28			□ 4A20	☍ 3S37			△ 2A59	□ 1S38	□ 1S38			□ 4A28	☌ 4S38
☿			⚺ 0A47	⚹ 0S25			☌ 3S40	□ 3S49		☍ 4A20	△ 2S57		□ 4A03	☌ 4A25		△ 8S55				⚹ 2S49	
♀			⚺ 0S19	⚹ 1S31	⚺ 1A30		☌ 4S46	□ 4S55	⚼ 2A39	☍ 3A15	△ 4S03		□ 2A57	☌ 3A20							
♂	⚹ 0S31	∠ 0S44				∠ 1S06			△ 8A25	□ 5S59			☌ 6S16	□ 5S54	∠ 0A22			⚻ 1A38	△ 9A16		
♃	∠ 0S45	⚹ 0S58				⚻ 1S20	☌ 0A47	□ 0A37	△ 6S49	☍ 8A47	△ 1A29			☌ 8A52	⚻ 0A08	△ 4S28		∠ 1A25	△ 5S58	⚹ 1A38	
♄		△ 5S48	□ 0A24	△ 0S48	□ 2A13					△ 3A57	☍ 3S21									☌ 3S13	
♅				☌ 6S10						△ 1S25		⚼ 1S39		⚹ 1S20		∠ 0A20	⚼ 0A20	△ 6A13		△ 8S34	
♆	☍ 1S30		☍ 7A32		☍ 5A43								△ 4A16					□ 3S39			
♇		△ 4A07		△ 0S52			☍ 2A22	□ 2A32		☌ 5S38	⚹ 1A40		□ 5S20	☍ 5S43			△ 7A37	⚼ 1A45		△ 1A32	
⚷	⚹ 2A43	∠ 2A30				∠ 2A08				□ 2S46			☌ 3S03	□ 2S41							
⚶	⚺ 0A01									△ 5S28	∠ 2A15	△ 9A18						△ 2A10		⚼ 2A23	
⚴				☌ 5S04						△ 0S18		⚼ 0S32	⚺ 0S35	⚹ 0S13		∠ 1A27	⚼ 1A27	△ 7A19		△ 7S28	∠ 1S34
⚵		□ 1S00		□ 4A00		☍ 1S22	⚺ 0A45	△ 0A35			⚻ 1A27	△ 6S29	△ 8A28		☍ 0A06				□ 6S00	⚺ 1A35	
⚳							△ 8A22		△ 0A46		☌ 9A04	□ 1A08				☌ 3A07	☍ 3A07		△ 1A37		□ 0A06
☊			☍ 0A23	⚻ 0S49	☍ 2A12			△ 4S13			□ 3S21		△ 3A39							□ 3S13	
☋	☌ 9A25		☌ 0A23	⚺ 0S49	☌ 2A12	△ 6S10					□ 3S21		⚹ 3A39		△ 4S42					□ 3S13	
As			⚺ 0A54	⚹ 0A19			☌ 3A33	□ 3A43		☍ 4A27	△ 2A51		□ 4A10	☌ 4A32		△ 8A48		∠ 2A56		⚹ 2A43	
Mc		△ 0A40	□ 5A32	△ 4A19		⚻ 1A02	⚹ 1A05	⚻ 0A55		△ 9A05	☍ 1A47	□ 6A09			⚻ 0A26	☍ 4A10	☌ 4A10			☌ 1A55	
⊗		⚺ 0A56	☌ 5A16		☌ 7A05	△ 1A17	⚺ 0A49	⚹ 0A39			□ 1A31	☍ 6A25			△ 0A10	□ 4A26	□ 4A26			□ 1A40	☌ 7A26
⚸		△ 3A20		△ 8A20			☍ 5A05	□ 4A55	⚹ 2S31							⚹ 0S10	△ 0S10		⚹ 1S40	△ 5A55	

Across: Joanne Woodward; down: Paul Newman.

We note first that Joanne's Moon conjuncts Paul's South Node ☽☌☋. And Paul's Moon is trine Joanne's South Node ☽△☋—and sextile her North Node ☽⚹☊. Nodes are about karmic duties, so karmic duties are clearly being fulfilled between these two. In addition, because the Saturn ♄ in each chart is connected by conjunctions ☌, trines △, and squares □ to the other's, an amazing endurance and strong devotion to each other is indicated. When we look at the rising signs for Joanne and Paul, we also note strong aspects.

Finally, we look at the relationships between retrograde planets (represented by ℞ on a birth chart). In the case of these two charts, we find the following retrogrades:

Retrogrades ℞	**Joanne Woodward**	**Paul Newman**
	Pluto ♇	Pluto ♇
	Neptune ♆	Neptune ♆
	North ☊ and South ☋ Node	

When we look at both retrograde Plutos ♇℞ on the synastry grid, we find they are conjunct ☌. Because Pluto is often thought of as energy that breaks down the usual patterns and insists on change, when Pluto is retrograde in someone's chart, that person is likely to be even more focused on transformation—in order to transform the world. Imagine someone who wants to change the world living with someone who is more inward looking, and you begin to see yet another reason why this relationship has survived the test of time. Strong aspects like this assure compatibility and attraction on a very deep level.

While astrologically this couple's longevity is a sure thing, this isn't a love relationship without its share of trial and error. What's important is that these two have the types of aspects between their charts that mean they will *work on* troubles when they arise, rather than allow them to either get blown out of proportion or come between them.

Let's review the key points of a synastry chart for relationship longevity:

- Aspects between the planets and the North ☊ and South ☋ Nodes
- Saturn ♄ and ascendant (rising sign) aspects
- Retrogrades ℞ that make connections to the Nodes, Saturn, and the ascendant

The second half of a compatibility ratio is a relationship analysis. For this, we look again at Joanne Woodward's and Paul Newman's birth charts.

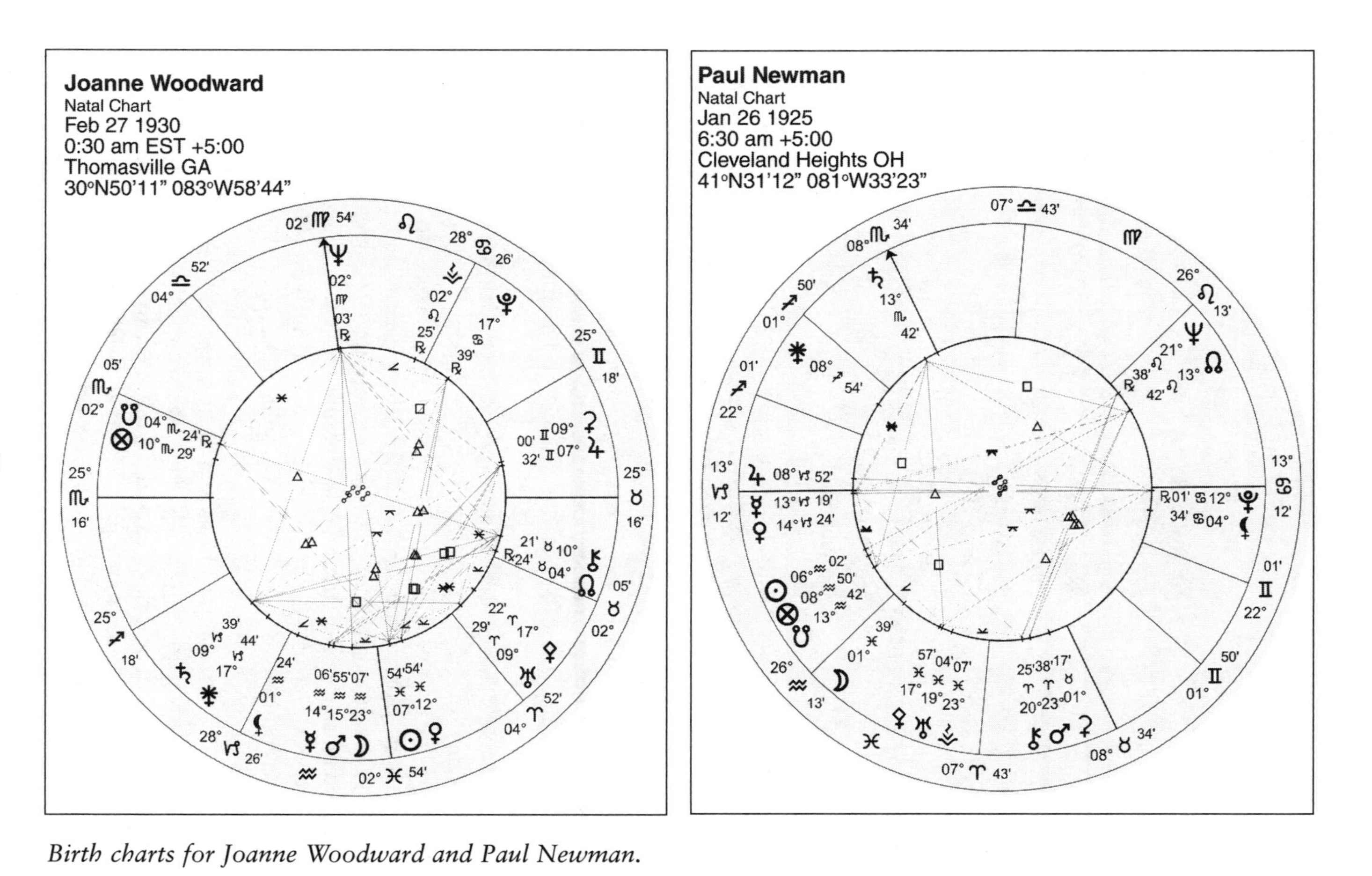

Birth charts for Joanne Woodward and Paul Newman.

A relationship analysis begins by listing each planet's sign for each person. We've done that for both Joanne and Paul in the following table.

Planet	Joanne's Astro Sign	Paul's Astro Sign
Sun ☉	Pisces ♓	Aquarius ♒
Moon ☽	Aquarius ♒	Pisces ♓
Mercury ☿	Aquarius ♒	Capricorn ♑
Venus ♀	Pisces ♓	Capricorn ♑
Mars ♂	Aquarius ♒	Aries ♈
Jupiter ♃	Gemini ♊	Capricorn ♑
Saturn ♄	Capricorn ♑	Scorpio ♏
Uranus ♅	Aries ♈	Pisces ♓
Neptune ♆	Virgo ♍	Leo ♌
Pluto ♇	Cancer ♋	Cancer ♋

The next step in a relationship analysis is to determine in which house of the *other person's chart* that planet falls, to look at how the energies balance or challenge each other. We do this by matching the astrological sign the planet is in with the house containing that sign in the other person's chart. This requires us to delve a little deeper into Astrology and consider the *degree* of the sign for the planet in the one chart and the house in the other; signs and houses don't always start in the same places. Let's look at the Moons ☽ of Joanne and Paul as an example.

In Joanne's chart we find her Moon ☽ in the 3rd house, at 23 degrees into the sign of Aquarius ♒. So we go to the outer ring of Paul's chart to locate the sign of Aquarius ♒. There it is, on the cusp of the 2nd house. Notice the numbers: 26° ♒ 13'. This tells us that Paul's 2nd house starts 26 degrees and 13 minutes into the 30-degree segment of the Zodiac that is Aquarius. Now, Joanne's Moon is at *23* degrees and 7 minutes Aquarius—*earlier* than the start of Aquarius at *26* degrees in Paul's 2nd house. So Joanne's Moon in Aquarius falls in Paul's 1st house.

In Paul's chart we find his Moon ☽ at 1 degree Pisces ♓ in his 2nd house. When we go to Joanne's chart, we see that Pisces is on the cusp of her 4th house, at 2 degrees and 54 minutes. Joanne's 4th house at 2 degrees Pisces is later than Paul's Moon at 1 degree Pisces, putting his Moon in her 3rd house. Got it? It's not so complicated once you get the knack of it. As we add this dimension to our relationship analysis for Paul and Joanne, we've included the degrees of the signs so you can see how we made our determinations.

Planet	Joanne's Sign	Paul's House	Paul's Sign	Joanne's House
Sun ☉	Pisces ♓ 07°♓54'	2nd (int)	Aquarius ♒ 06°♒02'	3rd (int)
Moon ☽	Aquarius ♒ 23°♒07'	1st	Pisces ♓ 01°♓39'	3rd
Mercury ☿	Aquarius ♒ 14°♒06'	1st	Capricorn ♑ 13°♑19'	2nd
Venus ♀	Pisces ♓ 12°♓54'	2nd (int)	Capricorn ♑ 14°♑24'	2nd
Mars ♂	Aquarius ♒ 15°♒55'	1st	Aries ♈ 23°♈38'	5th
Jupiter ♃	Gemini ♊ 07°♊32'	5th	Capricorn ♑ 08°♑52'	2nd
Saturn ♄	Capricorn ♑ 09°♑39'	12th	Scorpio ♏ 13°♍42'	12th
Uranus ♅	Aries ♈ 09°♈29'	3rd	Pisces ♓ 19°♓04'	4th
Neptune ♆	Virgo ♍ 02°♍03'	8th (int)	Leo ♌ 21°♌38'	9th (int)
Pluto ♇	Cancer ♋ 17°♋39'	7th	Cancer ♋ 12°♋01'	8th

Notes: (int) An intercepted sign occurs wholly within a house but is not the sign on the cusp of that house.

To help begin to assess the interconnection between these signs and houses, let's first refine our sign keywords from Chapter 1.

Sign	Keyword	Sign	Keyword
Aries ♈	Energy	Libra ♎	Balance
Taurus ♉	Grounding	Scorpio ♏	Power
Gemini ♊	Communication	Sagittarius ♐	Enthusiasm
Cancer ♋	Emotion	Capricorn ♑	Responsibility
Leo ♌	Confidence	Aquarius ♒	Idealism
Virgo ♍	Resourcefulness	Pisces ♓	Spirituality

Next, we assign a verb to each planet. You'll see where we're going with this in a moment.

Planet	**Keyword**
Sun ☉	Explores
Moon ☽	Senses
Mercury ☿	Communicates
Venus ♀	Enjoys
Mars ♂	Engages
Jupiter ♃	Benefits
Saturn ♄	Cooperates
Uranus ♅	Innovates
Neptune ♆	Dreams
Pluto ♇	Transforms

Finally, we give each house a key term.

House	**Key Term**
1st	Identity
2nd	Self-worth
3rd	Knowledge
4th	Home and family
5th	Creativity
6th	Work and service
7th	Relationships
8th	Transformation
9th	Beliefs
10th	Ethics and career
11th	Community
12th	Spirituality

We've assigned all these keywords to make relationship analysis not only easy, but also fun! Here's an example: Joanne Woodward's Pisces ♓ Sun can be found in Paul Newman's 2nd house. Using our keywords, we would say that Joanne *explores* (Sun ☉ keyword) her *spirituality* (Pisces ♓ keyword) in *self-worth* (2nd house keyword). This means that Joanne can discover enlightenment through Paul's values and humanitarian efforts.

Let's try another. Paul Newman's Aries Mars can be found in Joanne Woodward's 5th house, or Paul *engages* (Mars ♂) his *energy* (Aries ♈) in *creativity* (5th house). This means that Paul can discover his connection with the larger world through Joanne's artistic endeavors.

Go ahead and try to make your own assessments of this couple's relationship analysis by using these keywords. Take your time—this is meant to be fun as well as enlightening!

In addition to these keyword analyses, we can make a number of observations about this couple's relationship table. For example, the sign of each of their Saturns ♄ appears as the other's rising sign. As Saturn is the planet of rules and regulations, and the rising sign is how one appears to the world, it's clear that these two are in synch when it comes to the picture they present to others.

We also noted intercepted signs in both charts. Intercepted signs are contained wholly within houses without being on a house cusp. When this occurs, the person will need to work extra hard on those particular areas of his or her life. For this reason, these can be areas where the right marriage proves particularly helpful. When we compare Joanne Woodward's intercepted Aquarius ♒ and Leo ♌ to Paul Newman's, we find his Aquarius on the cusp of his 2nd house of self-worth, and his Leo on the cusp of his 8th house of transformation. Similarly, Paul Newman's intercepted Pisces ♓ and Virgo ♍ are more than offset by Joanne Woodward's strongly rooted Pisces on the cusp of her 4th house of home and family and her Virgo standing at the midheaven of her chart on the 10th house cusp of ethics!

Now that you've seen how a compatibility ratio works for Joanne Woodward and Paul Newman, you can try it with your own birth charts. Remember that you can order synastry grids online; there's more information on how to do so in Appendix A.

First, list each planet's astrological sign and keywords for each person.

Planet	Your Astro Sign and Keyword	Your Partner's Astro Sign and Keyword
Sun ☉ *Explores*	____________	____________
Moon ☽ *Senses*	____________	____________
Mercury ☿ *Communicates*	____________	____________
Venus ♀ *Enjoys*	____________	____________

Planet	Your Astro Sign and Keyword	Your Partner's Astro Sign and Keyword
Mars ♂ *Engages*	____________	____________
Jupiter ♃ *Benefits*	____________	____________
Saturn ♄ *Cooperates*	____________	____________
Uranus ♅ *Innovates*	____________	____________
Neptune ♆ *Dreams*	____________	____________
Pluto ♇ *Transforms*	____________	____________

Using both birth charts, find which houses of your partner's chart your planets' signs fall in, to discover how your partner helps fulfill your needs. (Feel free to review how we did this for Joanne Woodward and Paul Newman, to make sure you get it right.) When you've completed the table for yourself, do the same for your partner. We've provided space for both in the following tables:

Planet	Your Astro Sign and Keyword	House in Your Partner's Chart and Keyword
Sun ☉ *Explores*	____________	____________
Moon ☽ *Senses*	____________	____________
Mercury ☿ *Communicates*	____________	____________
Venus ♀ *Enjoys*	____________	____________
Mars ♂ *Engages*	____________	____________
Jupiter ♃ *Benefits*	____________	____________
Saturn ♄ *Cooperates*	____________	____________
Uranus ♅ *Innovates*	____________	____________
Neptune ♆ *Dreams*	____________	____________
Pluto ♇ *Transforms*	____________	____________

Planet	Your Partner's Astro Sign and Keyword	House in Your Birth Chart and Keyword
Sun ☉ *Explores*	___________	___________
Moon ☽ *Senses*	___________	___________
Mercury ☿ *Communicates*	___________	___________
Venus ♀ *Enjoys*	___________	___________
Mars ♂ *Engages*	___________	___________
Jupiter ♃ *Benefits*	___________	___________
Saturn ♄ *Cooperates*	___________	___________
Uranus ♅ *Innovates*	___________	___________
Neptune ♆ *Dreams*	___________	___________
Pluto ♇ *Transforms*	___________	___________

Finally, using these keywords, create sentences that show how you and your partner fulfill each other's needs:

____

____

____

____

The State of Your Love Union

If your synastry grid doesn't provide all the answers you're seeking, don't despair. The Tarot can help you explore the state of your union, too.

For this reading, we chose a Celtic Cross Spread. The Celtic Cross is the most commonly used Tarot spread. Its 10 cards not only lay out the past, present, and future about a question, but also reveal where the querent stands with regards to the question and how others feel about it as well.

Each card position in a Celtic Cross has a specific meaning.

First card: ***The Querent.*** This card represents the person asking the question. Its image will begin the story about the question.

Second card: ***Cross Card.*** This card represents the energy surrounding the question. In its position crossing the first card, it quite literally supports the person asking the question.

Third card: ***The Basis of the Question.*** Here we find the real reason the question was asked. Even if the querent says otherwise, this will represent the question's roots.

Fourth card: ***Passing Away.*** The energy represented by the image on this card is already beginning to fade at the time of the reading.

Fifth card: ***Free Will Future.*** This card, at the top of the reading, can be thought of as the top of the matter. What happens with this card's energy's, however, is up to the querent.

Sixth card: ***Fated Future.*** The energies of this card *will* occur, so you'll want to pay special attention to the image on this sixth card.

Seventh card: ***Hopes and Fears.*** Here you'll find the querent's highest hopes and most terrifying fears about the question. Even if the querent hasn't dared confront these hopes and fears, they will appear here for the querent to see.

Eighth card: ***Others.*** Others' attitudes to the question matter very much—especially when you're asking about love relationships. This card reveals what those attitudes are, and how they might affect the question's outcome.

Ninth card: ***Energy at Work.*** Here we find the rest of the story, the hurdles to leap over, the hoops to jump through, before we arrive at the …

Tenth card: ***Outcome.*** How it will all end up is revealed in this final card of the Celtic Cross. This card represents the end of this particular story.

Are you ready to try a Celtic Cross Spread of your own? Begin by writing down your question here:

Shuffle your Tarot deck until you feel it is ready. Cut the deck if you'd like. Then lay out the cards in the Celtic Cross. Take the time to look at your spread to reveal the story about your question. Rather than think in terms of absolute meanings for each card, let the images "speak" to you about your relationship. Record your notes here, right on the spread, before you go on to look up each card's suggested meanings in Appendix B.

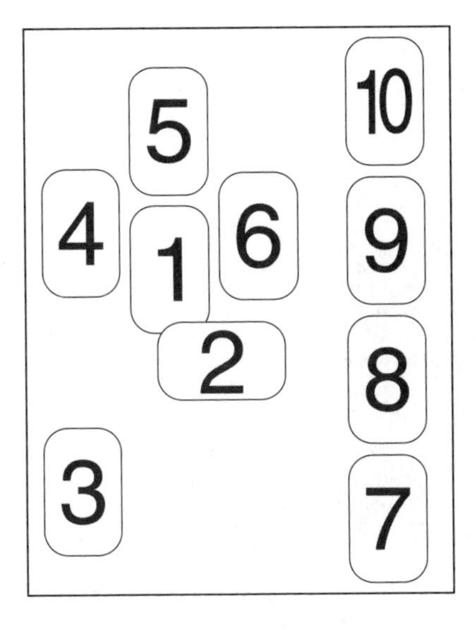

The Celtic Cross Spread tells a story about your question in 10 cards.

Lessons of Love, Lessons of Life

The lessons that we need to learn about love are often closely connected to the lessons we need to learn about life. For this reason, a good way to discover the lessons you are learning now is just to ask the Tarot what those lessons are, and then ask your Psychic Intuition for guidance in helping you learn those lessons.

We begin with a Karmic Spread to discover your life lessons. This simple spread is a marvelous way to discover why it seems you go through the same sorts of situations again and again. The question for a Karmic Spread is always the same: "What are the karmic lessons I am learning now?" The key word here is "now," as our karmic lessons change as we learn some and acknowledge others.

Thinking about this question, shuffle your Tarot deck, and then cut it if you desire. When you are ready, lay out the cards as shown in the illustration.

The Karmic Spread consists of four cards lain out as shown.

To show you how one person's Karmic Spread works, we had Sharon shuffle the cards and then deal them as shown. Here are the cards that came up for Sharon:

Sharon's Karmic Spread: "What are the karmic lessons I am learning now?"

First card: 5 of Cups R. Like all reversed 5s, the 5 of Cups indicates that you have learned from the past, so for this reading, this card suggests that Sharon has learned how to accept loss and sorrow and move on. Like many Cancers, Sharon has accumulated a lifetime of well-remembered sorrows (and joys!). This card shows that she has finally learned that even sorrows are a part of the person we are.

Second card: 7 of Cups R. Here is another emotional lesson that Sharon has mastered: learning how to make a decision. Sharon let life make decisions for her, instead of actively choosing from among the many options open to her. Here we see that Sharon has learned to consider all her options and decide which one to pursue.

Third card: The World. This is a wonderful card to have in a Karmic Spread (or any spread, for that matter!). It suggests that Sharon has completed her present karmic lessons and can move on to the next cycle in her life. There will, of course, be new lessons in the next cycle, but remember, the word "now" is key to this reading. Receiving this card tells Sharon that she has become well mastered in her relationships. Karmic rewards follow after we accept the lessons of our past.

Fourth card: 8 of Pentacles. Finally, the 8 of Pentacles shows a craftsman hard at work, able to move ahead quickly because he's honed his craft and worked hard on developing his skills. This card indicates that Sharon is willing to work hard to create objects of beauty and skill—and this can be taken literally, the creation of physical objects, or figuratively, the creation of well-crafted relationships.

For the meditation portion of this exercise, you work with one card at a time. Select the card that seems to be the most important karmic issue for you now. Sharon, for example, selected the 5 of Cups, placing the card once more in its upright position to make certain she had learned this karmic lesson as well as what its reversed position indicates.

Sitting comfortably, study the image on the card you have selected. As you study the image, consider the following questions:

- What does the card have to tell you about your karmic lesson?
- How does this card connect to recurring issues that come up in your love relationship?
- What might you do now in your life to begin to learn this karmic lesson?
- Does this issue seem to connect to a karmic lesson your love partner has as well?

Listen to the messages you give yourself as you explore these questions. You'll likely want to make some notes on what you discover. You may find it helpful to make your own sketch of the image on the card, or to make a drawing of your own to represent this lesson.

Perform this same meditation with each of your four karmic lesson cards. Don't do them all at once: It's best to spread this exercise over a number of days, or even weeks. You may decide to do a reading for your partner as well, and see how your karmic lessons connect (and disconnect). As with all meditations, take your time. Your Psychic Intuition will work with you to help you find the answers you seek.

Rediscovering the Romance

Sometimes your relationship just needs a good jump-start. If that's the case, you may want to try this transcendental cure, which has been adapted from the Black Hat Sect of Feng Shui. There are two parts, and parts within the two parts, but friends who have used this cure in its entirety swear by it. The particular beauty of this cure is that it can be performed in sections or as a whole. The key here is the number 9 and its multiples. As the ninth card of the Major Arcana, the Hermit, and all of the 9s of Tarot's Minor Arcana show, meditation can be key to rediscovering the romance in any relationship.

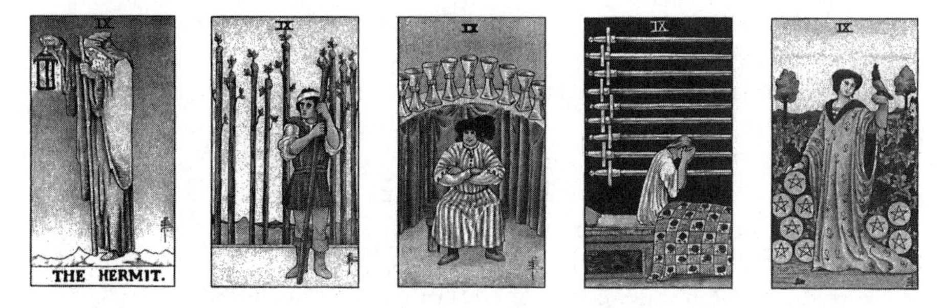

The number 9 and the Tarot cards associated with it remind us that listening to our inner voice can help us with life's difficulties—and its successes.

Part One: Picture Yourselves

Begin by finding a photo of yourself and one of your partner. Ideally, these should be photos that you both like.

1. Write your name on the back of your partner's photo.
2. Write your partner's name on the back of your photo.
3. Write the same message on the back of each photo. If you are doing this transcendental cure for your marriage, you might write, "This is for a good marriage," or simply the word, "marriage." Or you could write "loving relationship" if that's the message you're seeking.
4. Wait until the next Full Moon, and take the photos outside so that the full light of the Moon shines on both you and them.
5. Place the photos face to face and, using red string, wrap them 99 times. While you are wrapping them, visualize what you want for the two of you.

6. After you have wrapped the photos and done your visualization in the moonlight, place the wrapped photos under the mattress in the upper-right sector of your bed, which corresponds to the marriage and family *gua* in Feng Shui's *baguas*. You will sleep with the photos here for 9 nights.
7. Each night before you go to bed, perform the Three Secret Reinforcements revealed in the following section.
8. After the 9th night, you have two choices: You can toss the still-tied photos into moving water, or you can "plant" them in your yard and set a beautiful plant to grow over them.
9. Perform the Three Secret Reinforcements one more time afterward.

The Three Secret Reinforcements

You can perform the Three Secret Reinforcements together or separately. Although it is recommended that you perform them as suggested in Part One and Part Two, the transcendental cure will work without them. However, performing the Three Secret Reinforcements as recommended enhances the effectiveness of the cure.

The First Reinforcement is the Body Secret, and consists of a *mudra,* or hand position that channels energy. Designed to calm the spirit and oust bad things, this *mudra* is best performed when you are sitting comfortably.

With both palms face up, place your left hand over your right so that the pads of your thumbs are touching. Keep your hands relaxed and comfortable.

The Second Reinforcement is the Speech Secret, and consists of the heart *sutra.* To perform the Speech Secret, say the following words, either in Sanskrit or English: *Om ma ni padme hum.* This loosely translates to "I vow to the jewel in the lotus blossom," but closer English approximations of the sentiment include "I acknowledge the good in you" or "I acknowledge the beauty of our relationship." For maximum effect, speak the Speech Secret 9 times while performing the hand *mudra.*

The Third Reinforcement is the Mind Secret. Before you begin this reinforcement, come up with 9 steps toward fulfillment of your intentions. Designing these steps in three sets of three will help you memorize them. For example, if you are seeking a loving marriage, you might begin with love, respect, and sharing; move on to giving, receiving, and equanimity; and conclude with compassion, sympathetic joy, and understanding. After you have determined and memorized these 9 steps, while sitting in the *mudra* position, *visualize* each of these steps 9 times. Ideally, you will also be reciting your 9 repetitions of the Speech *sutra* at the same time, but this last addition isn't easy, and you may choose to perform it separately.

Part Two: Adjustment for the Home

If you want to make triple sure your transcendental cure takes hold, you can also make a simple Feng Shui adjustment in the room where you sleep.

1. Find a small crystal, wind chime, or mirror.
2. Tie this on a 9- or 18-inch red string.
3. Hang your object in the marriage *gua* of your bedroom. (Standing in your bedroom's doorway, the marriage *gua* will be to your upper right.)

You can reinforce this adjustment by doing the Three Secret Reinforcements as you hang it, after you hang it, and/or for 9 nights after you hang it.

Again, you can perform these parts separately. You may choose to adjust the home without performing the photo portion, or vice versa. You may find that certain steps are more effective for you than others. And the Three Secret Reinforcements may be used separately or together—and for far more than rekindling the romance in your relationship.

This meditation takes some time and effort, but rekindling the romance that brought you together in the first place is worth it. Learn it and you can use it in other aspects of your life!

chapter 6

The Green-Eyed Monster and Other Problems in Romance

When love relationships become challenging
Push me ... pull you
Mooning around
Astrological cycles great and small
Traveling your Saturn returns with confidence
Taking the plunge with Pluto
Psychic Intuition prompts change for the better
Tarot's Cups reveal the ups and downs of love
Your love fortune in a Cup

As Shakespeare (and others both before and after him) noted, the course of true love is seldom smooth. What do you do when the going gets tough? Do you look for blame outside yourself—or your relationship—or do you find fault with yourself or your partner? In this chapter, we explore how love relationship issues can be connected to planetary cycles, from the monthly cycles of the Moon to even larger planetary cycles, such as Saturn returns that take place over many years and the demanding transits of distant Pluto. We show you how you can learn to work with your planetary cycles instead of against *them, and we provide an exercise to help you work through your problems together. Finally, we take a journey through Tarot's Minor Arcana Cups to see how the images on these cards mirror the ups and downs of romance. Working toward a more loving union takes two—but the tools of Astrology, Tarot, and Psychic Intuition can make this work fun as well.*

When the Going Gets Tough in Love

Even in the best of relationships, there are moments of anger or frustration. The monthly cycles of the Moon ☽, the periodic demands of Saturn ♄ returns, and the vagaries of Pluto ♇ are just three of the planetary astrological cycles that can wreak havoc with your love life. Couples who have been together for any length of time have learned that there are times to avoid each other and times meant to cozy up. They've also learned which issues are hot buttons for each other, and, depending on the nature of their relationship, either take care to avoid these issues or use them for more destructive purposes.

Chances are you've encountered the relatively simple relationship issues of disagreement or jealousy—or more difficult problems, such as codependence or abuse. One of the keys to a successful love relationship is in understanding the roots of these issues, whether in one's own birth chart or because of planetary cycles. Learning how to work with both your own and more global planetary rhythms could mean the difference between your love relationship's failure and success.

Push Me ... Pull You

Have you ever noticed that you seem to feel a certain way at certain times of the month? (No, we aren't talking about menstrual cycles here—although they are related: The Moon has a pull on all earthly fluids.) Or have you noticed how you seem to have highs and lows throughout the year? You may have thought it was just the weather, or you may have even thought it must be you, but the secret to your ups and downs can more likely be found in the cycles of the Moon.

The Moon card of Tarot's Major Arcana reflects both the confusion and the intuitive insight that is possible with the Moon's push me ... pull you energy.

From small disagreements like where to go for dinner to larger control issues like jealousy and frequent fighting, much can be discovered in lunar cycles, because that's where the push me ... pull you of control issues often originates. The Moon ☽ goes through a full cycle—from New Moon to Balsamic Moon—every 29½ days. During that time, it passes through each of the 12 signs of the Zodiac, "resting" between astrological signs in a period called a void of course Moon. It's generally best to not begin something new, make any decisions, or chart definitive courses during a "void of course" Moon. The void Moon provides a rest period every two days or so—ranging from a few minutes to all day, depending on the void of course period's length.

Just as the pull of the Moon affects the tides, it affects the way humans feel as well. (After all, our bodies are mostly water.) This means that, depending on your own Moon sign, how you feel when the Moon is in a particular sign will vary. Someone with a Moon in Cancer ♋, for example, will feel very comfortable with the emotional flow of a Cancer Moon because Cancer is ruled by the Moon, and so is naturally Moon-y. However, someone with a more aloof Moon, in Aquarius ♒ for instance, might feel out of his or her element during a Cancer Moon—because that's precisely how an Air Moon sign feels when the Moon is in watery Cancer.

Knowing how someone with your—and your sweetie's—Moon sign will feel when the Moon is in a particular sign can help you plan ahead for possible relationship issue flare-ups, as well as realize why you're feeling a certain way on a certain day. We've developed these descriptions to help you see that you don't necessarily have to be jealous of your partner's devotion to his or her job; after all, maybe it's the current sign of the Moon that's got you feeling less worthy.

Mooning Around: Know Your Love Relationship Moon Signs

To use these tables, simply find your—and your sweetie's—Moon sign. Read the thumbnail description of your approaches to feeling, along with the "if you're looking for a lover" tag for a thumbnail description of a lover with that Moon sign. If your—or your sweetie's—description "feels" wrong to you, you may want to ask an astrologer about having your chart rectified. That's because, along with your ascendant (rising sign), your Moon sign is one of those indicators that you yourself will be able to sense.

To locate your Moon sign, simply find where the symbol ☽ appears on your birth chart.

Like the King of Wands, an Aries Moon is a confident lover.

If your Moon ☽ is in Aries ♈, you feel with your head first, aggressively and directly. You don't like to dilly-dally when it comes to feeling, and you don't have much patience for those who can't make up their minds. Your mind arrives already made up—why can't everyone else's mind be made up? If you're looking for a lover who takes the lead, an Aries Moon is your ride. Just be sure you hang on tight.

Like the King of Pentacles, a Taurus Moon is an easygoing lover.

If your Moon ☽ is in Taurus ♉, you feel most comfortably with your senses. After you've made a commitment to a something or someone, you're in it for the long haul—whatever that long haul may be. Warm and affectionate, you're a great believer in the finer things in life, and nothing is too good for the one(s) you love—including yourself! If you're looking for a lover who knows how to build a comfortable and secure love nest, look no further than a Taurus Moon.

Like the Knight of Swords, a Gemini Moon is a quicksilver lover.

If your Moon ☽ is in Gemini ♊, you feel with your quick mind. "Quick" is a byword for Gemini—hurry here, hurry there—and you may not slow down long enough to see if your loved one is keeping up. People with Gemini Moons need continual romantic excitement the way that we all need to breathe, and they're not afraid to try new things—or to discard the old ones. If you're looking for a lover who will be the life of the party, latch on to a Gemini Moon and go, go, go!

Like the King of Cups, a Cancer Moon is a heart-centered lover.

If your Moon ☽ is in Cancer ♋, you feel with your feelings, and if that sounds like a lot of mush, well, take it from one Cancer Moon, "mush" is "gush." Receptive, empathetic, moody Cancer Moons wear their hearts on their sleeves—and wipe their noses there a lot, too—and they're emotionally in tune with the universe. If you're looking for a lover who understands the absolute meaning of "true romance," a Cancer Moon will be your dream come true.

Like the Queen of Wands, a Leo Moon is an enthusiastic lover.

If your Moon ☽ is in Leo ♌, you feel with your heart. No small gestures for you—Leo Moons love grandly and broadly. Affectionate and warm, you give your love as if assuming it will be returned—so you may be surprised if it's not returned as dramatically as you've given it. If you're looking for a lover whose heart is as strong as a lion's, a Leo Moon will give you all the love you've ever wanted.

Like the Queen of Pentacles, a Virgo Moon is a generous lover.

If your Moon ☽ is in Virgo ♍, you feel with your generosity. Precisely aligning with someone who understands the rationale of a well-planned love will send your romance Geiger counter off the graph. But you may run less-efficient sorts off your romantic roadmap—much to your relief. If you're looking for a lover who will plan that perfect romantic getaway down to the smallest detail, a Virgo Moon will take the checklist over.

Like the King of Swords, a Libra Moon is a well-balanced lover.

If your Moon ☽ is in Libra ♎, you feel with your charm and social skill. Perfect partnership is paramount to a Libra, and creating an atmosphere where everything will look and feel just right for romance is a Libra Moon's expression of true love. If you're looking for a lover for whom harmony is the guiding grace, a Libra Moon will set your chimes ringing in perfect pitch.

Like the Queen of Cups, a Scorpio Moon is a devoted lover.

If your Moon ☽ is in Scorpio ♏, you feel with your intuition. Deep and powerful—even obsessive—love is a hallmark of a Scorpio Moon. When you know who you love, you are capable of compelling emotional attachment. If you're looking for a lover who will love you to the ends of time—and beyond—look no further than a Scorpio Moon.

Like the Knight of Wands, a Sagittarius Moon is a dynamic lover.

If your Moon ☽ is in Sagittarius ♐, you feel with your enthusiasm. Spontaneous, fun-loving, adventurous, Sagittarius Moon loves the excitement of the chase as much as the thrill of victory. Stay-at-home love is definitely not your style—nor is a mushy romantic your idea of a fun date. If you're looking for a lover who will make your lives together a continual adventure, hand the keys to a Sagittarius Moon—and fasten your seatbelt.

Like the Knight of Pentacles, a Capricorn Moon is a trustworthy lover.

If your Moon ☽ is in Capricorn ♑, you feel with your determination. Once you set your sights on someone, you'll make damned sure he or she will be yours—and stay yours—but you'll approach cautiously just to be on the safe side. If you're looking for a lover who has self-discipline and determination for far more than just the two of you, sit back and let a Capricorn Moon drive.

Like the Queen of Swords, an Aquarius Moon is a humanitarian lover.

If your Moon ☽ is in Aquarius ♒, you feel to the tune of a different drummer. Unconventional and progressive, Aquarius Moons often think marriage is for fuddy-duddies and conventions for the birds. Although your very aloofness may attract those less self-assured in droves, you're not likely to notice—and you'll be surprised if it's pointed out to you. If you're looking for a lover who will never question your need for your own space, an Aquarius Moon will give you the key.

Like the Knight of Cups, a Pisces Moon is a dreamy lover.

If your Moon ☽ is in Pisces ♓, you feel with your imagination. "Reality?" you say. "That's for the faint of heart." With a Pisces Moon, you love to live in the land of dreamy dreams, where all dreams are in Technicolor and all dreams come true. Easily compassionate—and easily hurt—Pisces Moons are sensitivity at its most highly tuned. If you're looking for a lover who will always believe the best of you, a Pisces Moon will worship you to your heart's desire.

The intuitive Moon has many moods, three of which are represented here by the psychic High Priestess, solitary Hermit, and hopeful Star.

Where's the Moon Today?

For this Moon sign exercise, use a lunar calendar to discover where the Moon ☽ is today. (You can find a lunar calendar either online or in most bookstores.) Then find the corresponding astrological Moon sign in the first column of the following table. In the second column, you'll find that how you're feeling today can be easily connected to the glow of today's Moon sign. In the third column, we've provided each Moon sign's "Moon shine challenges"—the areas most likely to cause friction or dissension in love relationships when the Moon appears in a particular sign. In other words, your "irrational" jealousy may not be irrational after all, but rather the "Moon shine" of a Taurus Moon.

When the Moon ☽ Is In	Today's Moon Sign Glow	Moon Shine Challenges
Aries ♈	Direct and assertive	Impatience, irritability
Taurus ♉	Peaceful and calm	Stubbornness, jealousy
Gemini ♊	Clever and communicative	Restlessness, irrationality
Cancer ♋	Sensitive and sentimental	Depression, insecurity

When the Moon ☽ Is In	Today's Moon Sign Glow	Moon Shine Challenges
Leo ♌	Sunny and warm	Arrogance, self-absorption
Virgo ♍	Logical and certain	Fault-finding, boredom
Libra ♎	Cooperative and charming	Indecision, exploitation
Scorpio ♏	Powerful and passionate	Ruthlessness, abusiveness
Sagittarius ♐	Restless and optimistic	Irresponsibility, tactlessness
Capricorn ♑	Determined and dignified	Inflexibility, humorlessness
Aquarius ♒	Innovative and altruistic	Unpredictability, instability
Pisces ♓	Compassionate and mystical	Helplessness, paranoia

Is It Love or Just a Phase?

While the Moon ☽ is passing through the signs on its 29½-day journey, how it looks to us earthbound sorts changes. But looks aren't all that are affected: The lunar cycle affects how we feel at certain times of the month both physically and mentally. This means that just as knowing which sign the Moon is in can help you head off romantic difficulties before they get out of hand, knowing which *phase* the Moon is in can alert you to love's mood swings that are, quite literally, out of this world.

We're all familiar with Full Moon Madness: It's even been scientifically documented. While other phases of the Moon are less dramatic, the overall sweep of Moon phases can potentially take you from the highest high to the lowest low—every single month! If Cancer ♋ is prominent in your chart, chances are you'll notice this even more. When it comes to your love life, the theme song of lunar cycles is "Feelings." Let's look at the lunar cycle more closely to see specifically what might happen when the Moon is in a certain phase.

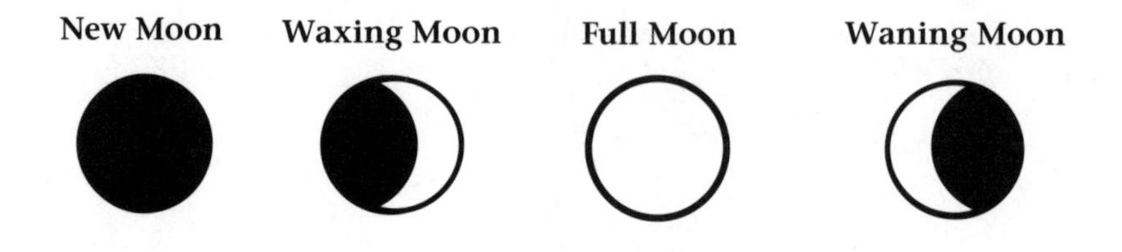

New Moon. Let's fall in love all over again! The New Moon signals new beginnings, so anything begun in a New Moon has a far better chance of success. Everyone feels more optimistic during a New Moon, even those naysayers we all try our best to avoid. No matter how angry you became with each other during the previous lunar cycle, you'll be inclined to give it another go during a New Moon. The New Moon is associated with the astrological sign Aries ♈ and its full-speed-ahead surge of energy. New Moons are a great time for first dates, getting engaged, or celebrating your love with a wedding.

First Quarter (Waxing) Moon. The challenges of a First Quarter Moon can be easily met if you understand their nature, because it's here the dreams of the New Moon come face to face with reality. It's important to not think in terms of "good" and "bad" when it comes to things that happen easily and things that are challenging: After all, it's the challenges that spur us on to work harder on a relationship that up until now seemed perfect. The First Quarter Moon is associated with the astrological sign Cancer ♋ and its nurturing and concern about the things that matter to us most.

Full Moon. When the Moon is full, we can all see quite clearly—and what we see isn't always what we expected to see. Flare-ups of all kinds can occur during a Full Moon, and in its light you may see someone you thought you knew well in a new light, so breakups are more likely to occur during a Full Moon, too. The Full Moon is associated with the astrological sign Libra ♎ and the ability to see things from all sides.

Last Quarter (Waning) Moon. The Last Quarter Moon is the wisest Moon—it has the knowledge of experience it gained throughout its cycle. It is here we can stand back to see what's working and what's not, and because we are standing back, we're far less likely to take things personally. For relationships that were at the brink of disaster at the Full Moon, the Last Quarter Moon can mean all is not lost. The Last Quarter Moon is associated with the astrological sign Capricorn ♑ and the deep knowledge available to us when it is dark.

All Cycles Great and Small

The Moon isn't the only planet with far-reaching effects. Each planet's push and pull has a corresponding push and pull in each of us, and when it comes to love relationship difficulties, much can be traced to transits such as Saturn ♄ returns and the transformative upheavals of Pluto ♇ square □ Pluto ♇. Let's begin with Saturn returns—most of us have been there before, and all of us will be there again.

Traveling Your Saturn ♄ Returns with Confidence

Saturn ♄ returns, which occur approximately 30 years and 60 years after you were born, are all about knowing when to fold, and knowing when to hold on. Saturn returns insist we change in some dramatic way, and if we try to hold on to something we need to let go of, a Saturn return can go to great extremes to make sure we let it go. There are major adjustments when you are entering your Saturn return cycle, because Saturn returns back to its original position of birth to allow you to enter yet another level of your growth.

Stern Saturn demands that you review and revamp your life to his specifications.

Marriage and divorce are common during Saturn returns. People also change jobs, relationships, cities, houses, and careers. Lisa went back to college to finish her undergrad degree during her Saturn return—plus she changed jobs, and her first marriage ended! During *her* Saturn return, Arlene started a new career—teaching the Tarot, even though she had only recently gotten started reading the Tarot publicly and professionally. At the same time, Arlene realized that

Seattle would become her home. Previous to that good ol' Saturn cycle, she had never felt quite rooted in the Northwest. Even after four years, Los Angeles (and California) still tugged at Arlene's heart. But when Saturn hit its return, Arlene realized Seattle *was* home, and that she could have California, too. LA waited only a short plane ride away—and she could finally afford the ticket price!

Basically, you can expect a Saturn return to include certain elements:

- Acknowledgment of certain things losing importance in your life, including dreams or goals that you now realize no longer matter to you.
- Commitment to a new and exciting endeavor, some major change in your life that will affect you for years to come. "I'm not getting any younger," you might think. "I'd better (fill in the blank) before it's too late." Saturn returns bring out our serious sides (Saturn's a sober old planet), and you will approach this change cautiously and carefully.
- After a few years of feeling responsible and grown up, you'll start having fun again. A Saturn return is as much about building a new firm foundation as it is about letting go of the old ones, and once that foundation is in place, you'll feel comfortable relaxing again.

Just so you understand how much a Saturn return means business when it comes to your relationships, here are just a few well-known couples whose marriages ended during the women's Saturn returns:

- Princess Diana and Prince Charles
- Sonny and Cher
- Sylvia Plath and Ted Hughes
- Courtney Love and Kurt Cobain

Here, for example, is Courtney Love's birth chart for her exact Saturn ♄ return on June 9, 1994. Kurt Cobain died in April 1994—but it's believed that he was planning to divorce Courtney had he lived. Clearly, Courtney's marriage was going to end during her Saturn return—one way or another.

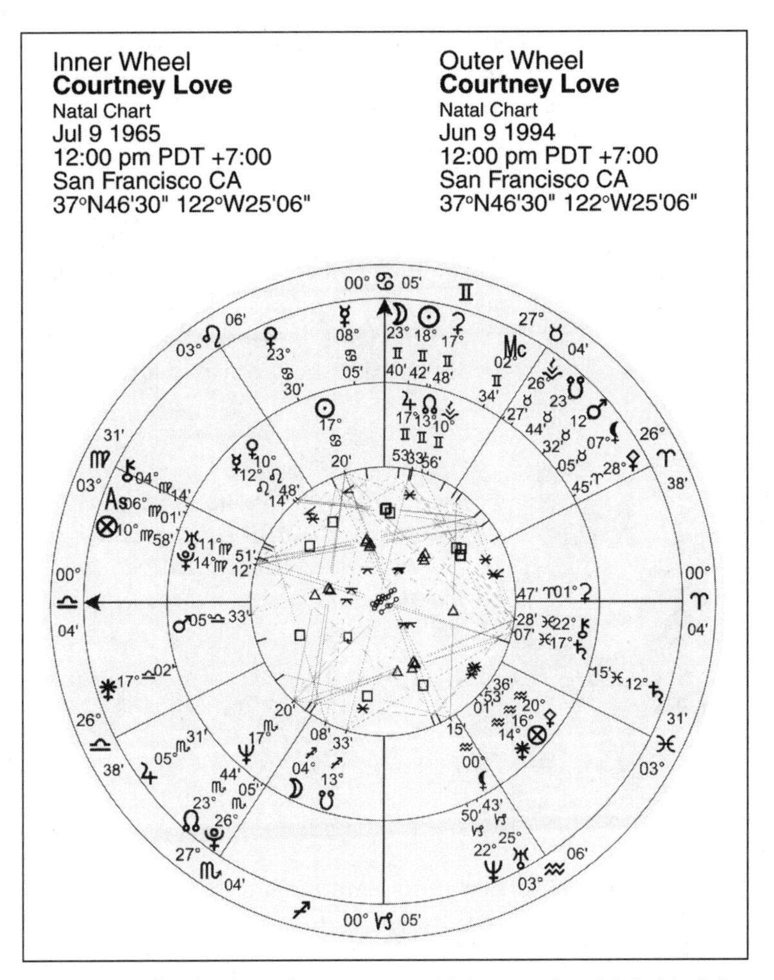

Courtney Love's birth chart for June 9, 1994, near her 30th birthday.

Of course, just as many people get married—or remarried—during a Saturn return. Hillary and Bill Clinton married during her first Saturn return. Melanie Griffith and Don Johnson remarried during hers. And Elizabeth Taylor married her seventh husband, Larry Fortensky, during her second Saturn return! Sure, a Saturn return is challenging, but its challenges spur us to learn and change—and ultimately, to start anew.

Saturn ♄ returns to its natal position in your birth chart every 28 to 32 years. This means that your first Saturn return occurs between the ages of 28 and 30, your second between the ages of 58 and 60, and your third between the ages of 88 to 91. No wonder there are so many weddings in nursing homes! That's old Saturn at work, all right!

Taking the Plunge with Pluto ♇

Every planet transits your chart in its own way, and every planetary transit feels like a literal "hit," but nothing hits us quite so hard as our Pluto ♇ transits. That's because Pluto is the planet of transformation, and won't take no for an answer when it comes a-knockin'. When Pluto swings around to square your natal Pluto, ♇□♇, sometime between the ages of 36 and 48, you can't help but pay attention, because it's midlife crisis time.

Don't be frightened by the figure of Death: The transformation promised by a Pluto ♇ transit can signal the new beginnings associated with the new dawn rising beyond the hills in this image.

This Pluto transit lasts two years, and during this time, you may feel as if you're someone entirely different from who you were up until then. Buying a jazzy new sports car is a mild Pluto transit occurrence compared to the far more common one of having an affair or leaving a spouse (who you loved just fine till old Pluto rolled around) behind. The Pluto plunge literally takes you by storm; you'll be so wrapped in its drama that you won't even stop to consider how radically different everything suddenly seems to you—until two years later when the whirlwind subsides and you're standing in the quiet left behind. "How did this house end up in Oz?" you may wonder. "Why did I leave the partner I loved all those years?" (Or "Why did my partner leave me?") Too late now—your Pluto transit's made you transform. Unless …

You're reading this *before* a Pluto square Pluto transit. If you're aware that it's Pluto wreaking havoc with your status quo, you may be able to convince your partner that it's just a phase. (Well, it's worth a try …) Or you could sign up at a monastery for a year or two or sail solo around the world. Pluto transits are demanding, though: Your old behaviors may well be outmoded, and if that's the case, Pluto just won't let them remain with you any longer.

To show how you can find a Pluto square Pluto ♇□♇ transit, we've provided Denzel Washington's birth chart with transits to a date revealing his Pluto square Pluto ♇□♇: September 28, 1994. In January of that year, the controversial—and brilliant—movie *Philadelphia* was released, with Denzel co-starring in his Oscar-nominated role as a homophobic attorney whose compassion and tolerance evolve while representing a colleague with AIDS.

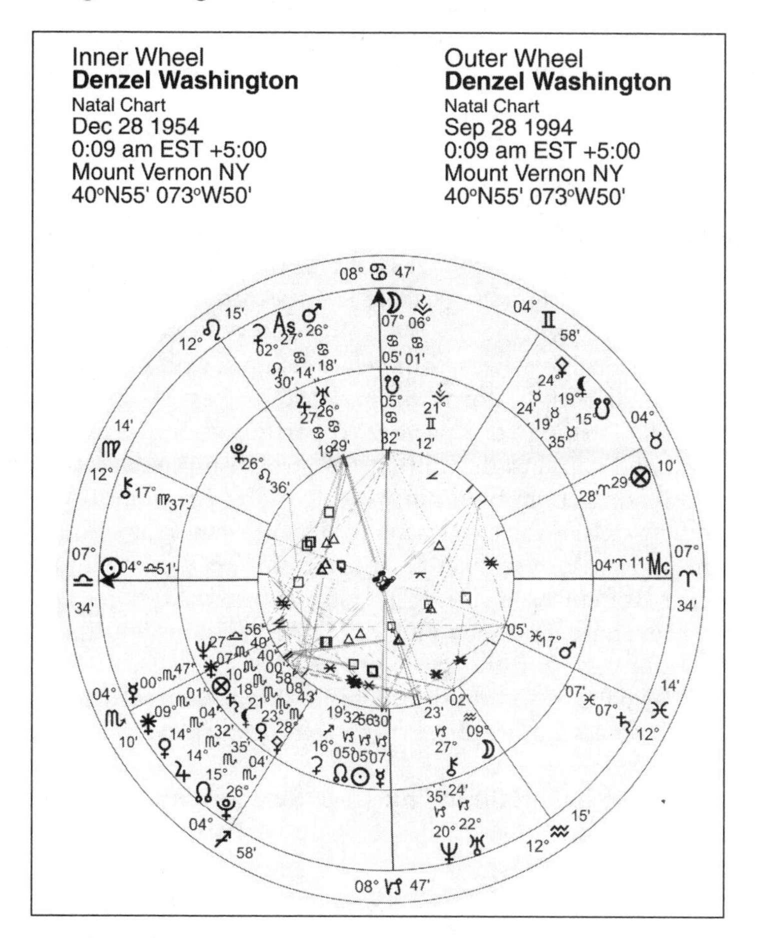

Denzel Washington's birth chart with transits to September 28, 1994, very close to his 40th birthday, revealing his Pluto square Pluto ♇□♇ for you.

Finding Your Pluto ♇ Transits

It takes Pluto ♇ 240 years to go all the way around the Zodiac; so, although a Pluto return isn't very likely (unless you're the 6,000-year-old man), Pluto's transits over the angles of your chart—the 1st (identity), 4th (home and family), 7th (relationships), and 10th (ethics and career) astrological houses—are true turning points in your life. When Pluto transits over your natal Sun ☉ and Moon ☽ (the luminaries), it's another signature of transformation and rebirth.

If, like us, you know the precise date of a life-changing event or decision that occurred sometime around your 30th or 40th birthday, you can ask an astrologer for a transited chart for that date. Just don't be surprised when you find Pluto square Pluto, ♇□♇, around your 40th birthday!

Change in Love for the Better

While you may think change is just what you need to add some spice to your relationship, your partner may prefer things just as they are. That's when it's time to call in your Psychic Intuition to do some detective work, and discover whether there's a problem with you, a problem with your partner, a problem with your relationship, or no problem at all.

Ideally, you'll both perform this exercise for best results; if you don't feel comfortable asking your partner to participate, however, you can ask a friend and gain insights about your friendship, which is perhaps a less-intimidating context within which to start your intuition exploration. The first step in the exercise is to decide what is most important for you in your love relationship, or friendship. Is it companionship? Excitement? Romance? Security? The list of possibilities goes on and on, but for this exercise, you may pick only one. Without your partner seeing, write your choice in the space provided.

Now your partner should do the same thing. You partner writes her or his choice on a separate sheet of paper, and then records it here as well.

What's Most Important in Our Love Relationship or Friendship?

You	Partner
____________________	____________________
1 2 3 4 5	1 2 3 4 5

Now consider how you feel about what's most important to your partner. Is it also important to you? Or is your reaction "You've got to be kidding?" Or is it somewhere between those two extremes? Select a rating, 5 being the highest, for your partner's priority and circle it below his or her choice. Have your partner do the same for your priority.

Next comes the intuition part. You're going to proceed as if what matters to each of you matters just as much to the other—as if you both circled 5 under each other's priority.

Sitting together in the same room, close your eyes and focus your mind on your breathing until you are relaxed. When you are ready, you should each ask yourself how you may best meet your partner's most important need. This is no longer about what *you* want; it's about what your partner wants. Your partner is thinking about what you want, so you don't have to. If your partner wants security, for example, think about five changes you can make that would make your partner feel more secure. If your partner desires romance, think about five romantic possibilities.

Picture the changes in your lives, one at a time. If they're pure fantasy, discard them and replace them with changes you can actually make. When you have come up with five changes you can make to address what's most important to your partner, write them down on a separate sheet of paper.

Now give each other your lists. Suppose your partner wanted some affection. You hand her a list that says, "Kiss her good morning. Kiss her goodnight. Hug her hello. Hug her good-bye. Hold her hand when you go for a walk." Ask her whether those changes would fulfill her desire. If she says yes, agree to practice each change at least once a day. Each partner should agree to practice the changes if they're what the other wants.

The beauty of this exercise is that these changes will soon become second nature. They'll be so much a part of your daily lives that you'll no longer remember that they originated in an exercise. But if, down the road, you find you need another set of changes for the better, feel free to do this exercise and tap into your love partnerships powers of Psychic Intuition again!

Tarot's Cups: The Ups and Downs of Love

The lessons of our lives have a way of coming up again and again. How, for example, do you feel when your partner's old lover calls? How does your partner feel when your ex sends you a birthday card? Some women swear their best friends are their partner's old lovers (which says as much about the women he's loved as it does about him); others insist every memento of the former love be destroyed at once. Some men are flattered that their partner's old lovers still care about her; others feel threatened and jealous.

One good way to explore the lessons of love (and life) is to take a journey through Tarot's Cups. Cups are the cards of romance and emotion, and by traveling through these 10 cards, we can see love from every angle there is. Take a moment now to remove the Ace through 10 of Cups from your Tarot deck and lay them in a row in front of you. Let's look at these cards one at a time to see what they can tell us about old love and new.

When we have the Cups all laid out, we can visualize what the pictures show us. No matter which Tarot deck you choose, love and joy and emotional connections are evident in these images. The Ace of Cups is the beginning of new romance or a new attachment. Then, as we go through the 2, 3, and 4 of Cups, we see our feelings grow. In the 5, 6, and 7 of Cups, we are evaluating love and the emotions that are inside of us. The 8, 9, and 10 of Cups represent the ultimate expression of emotional depth and commitment.

The higher the numbers on the card, the more attached you have become to the situation, person, or idea of love. From 1 through 10 in this suit, we grow in emotional attachment and intimacy; in other words, we evolve emotionally through the Cups. As we move through each card, our hearts become more open and receptive.

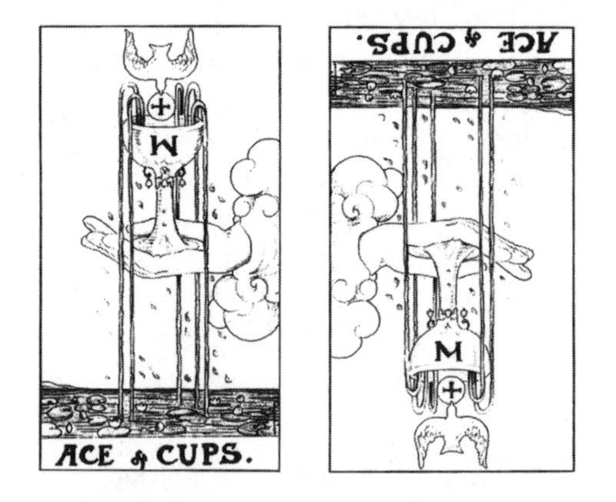

The Ace of Cups resonates to the number 1, the number of new beginnings.

The Ace of Cups is the card of new love. "Once upon a time," the story begins. Even if you're in a relationship already, this card can bring a breath of fresh romance, or the possibility of new romance.

When the Ace of Cups is reversed, however, all the love is pouring out. You may want a new romance so much it's all you can think about, and you're becoming more and more insecure. It's been our observation that love comes to those who are secure in themselves. So the best approach with the Ace of Cups R is often to quit thinking about someone else to complete you, and instead focus on what makes *you* happy, and just do it! We can't tell how many times our friends have done just that, only to discover the Ace of Cups upright—that's right, new love—the day they said they were happy with their lives!

The 2 of Cups resonates to the number 2, the number of partnerships.

"Getting to know you" is the theme of the 2 of Cups. Here's that first date, that get-acquainted talk at a party. New friendship may be boded by the 2 of Cups, too. While in the Ace of Cups love is coming, with the 2 of Cups, the other person has arrived.

With the 2 of Cups R, negative emotions get in the way of what could be a beautiful friendship. The connection boded by this card in its upright position isn't made, because each person is thinking about himself or herself rather than the other person. A loss of balance is indicated by the 2 of Cups R, and it can take the form of everything from jealousy to possessiveness. Don't let your passions rule you; step back and take a more objective look at your own feelings about your relationship before it's too late.

The 3 of Cups resonates to the number 3, the number of joy.

It's time to celebrate with the 3 of Cups. In the story of any relationship, there's the "honeymoon" phase where neither of you can do any wrong in the eyes of the other, and the 3 of Cups is about that time. You're happy with yourselves, happy with each other, snuggling in both private and public, and just generally basking in the love you share.

When the 3 of Cups is reversed, not everything is as out in the open as it is when this card is upright. You may be unhappy with your partner, but with this card, you're likely communicating your unhappiness to your friends rather than to your partner. You know the routine: "I hate when he or she does this" or "If he or she does this one more time, I'm leaving," and yet you've yet to tell your partner that you feel this way! The 3 of Cups R suggests you quit your complaining and face your issues head on. Tell your partner your feelings instead of everyone else, and see if you can turn this card upright again.

Uh-oh. Our young man's getting bored. "Look what I brought you," says the magic hand, but once the flush of new love has worn off, there may not be anything of substance to replace it. Dreams of what was, dreams of what might be, and not a whole lot going on in realityville—that's the 4 of Cups. The thrill is gone with this card.

The 4 of Cups resonates to the number 4, the number of security.

When the 4 of Cups is reversed, you'll be refocused and ready to give your relationship another go from this new direction. Or you may begin an entirely new relationship, having discarded the one that left you unsatisfied. In its reversed position, the 4 of Cups R bodes far better than its upright position.

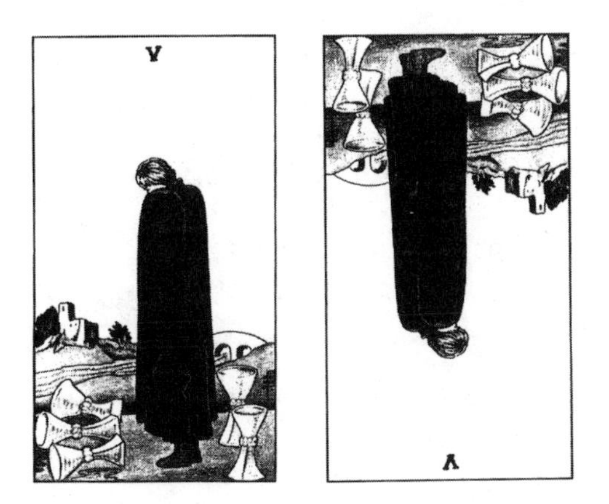

The 5 of Cups resonates to the number 5, the number of change.

Sorrow and heartbreak come to all relationships, and the 5 of Cups represents love's sadder moments. Sometimes we break out soon after the thrill is gone; sometimes we hang on but seem to fight about everything. Both of those relationship difficulties are represented by this card, as well as other problems we encounter in our love lives.

Just like the 4 of Cups R, the 5 of Cups R is this card's more positive position. Reversed, this card means you have new hope, whether for a relationship that up until now has been difficult, or a potential new relationship on the horizon. With the 5 of Cups reversed, you've learned from the past and have incorporated your new knowledge into how you will approach romance. It's not the end of your journey; it's a brand-new day!

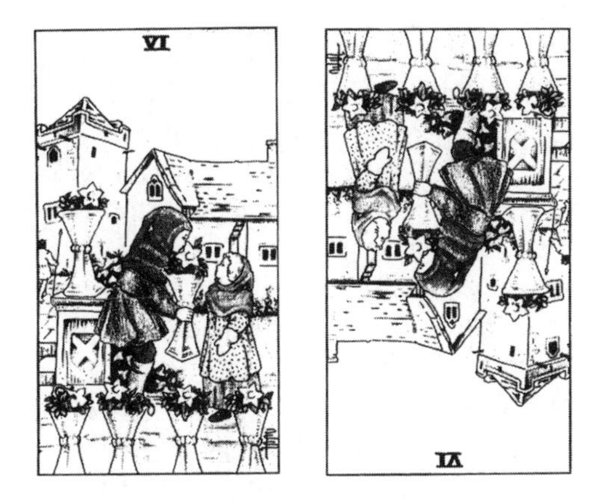

The 6 of Cups resonates to the number 6, the number of family.

Nostalgia has its place, and sometimes it's a good place for us to begin our healing process, too. In the 6 of Cups, we remember how first love feels and long for that feeling again. Sometimes an old lover will actually appear when this card shows up, but either way, this is a card about love gone by.

In its reversed position, 6 of Cups memories are not so sweet. Perhaps you recall another time when someone else hurt you, or you may be wallowing in the pain you feel your partner's inflicted on you instead of trying to move past it. The 6 of Cups R is about disappointment because your expectations weren't met, but this may be because you need to let go of those old ideas about how things ought to be, anyway. You might want to consider your own role in getting to this point, and see if you may have been at least partially responsible for hurting yourself so badly.

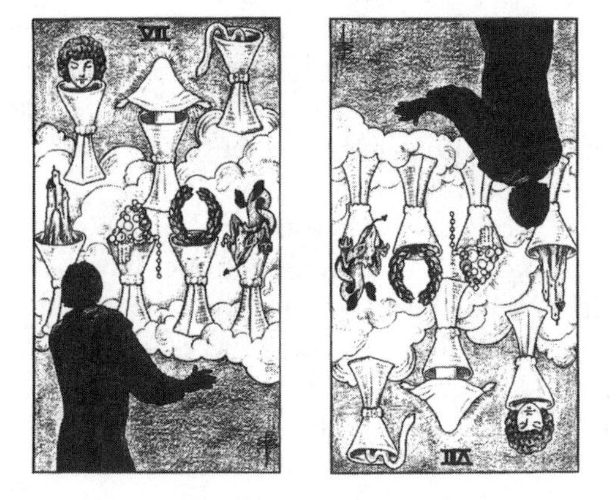

The 7 of Cups resonates to the number 7, the number of meditation.

So many choices! How do you choose between love, fame, and fortune? Or between castles, surprises, and baubles of gold? If your love's gone awry, one of you may be trying to woo the other back by putting everything on the table. Or maybe you've got a choice between two lovers—it's not the enviable position others see it for, as you know.

When the 7 of Cups is reversed, you're ready to make a choice. The options become clear, and as they do, the one you should choose becomes obvious. You may choose to work harder on your relationship, or you may decide it's no longer worth the effort. An entirely different choice may appear with the 7 of Cups R, one you couldn't see for all the choices that were there when this card was upright. Indecision is a thing of the past when this card is reversed, and you'll be eager and happy to go forward again.

The 8 of Cups resonates to the number 8, the number of achievement.

Sometimes the only thing to do about love is to set your cups in order and walk away. In this card, there's nothing left to save but the memories represented by the 8 neatly stacked cups. It's not easy to walk away from something you've invested so much time and energy in, but sometimes that's the best choice of all.

With the 8 of Cups R, you have a renewed interest in others, including your partner. There may be a new love interest in the picture, or you may discover renewed passion where you thought none remained. This card usually appears after you've taken some time to contemplate your choices, and when it does, you'll be ready to take the road you've chosen.

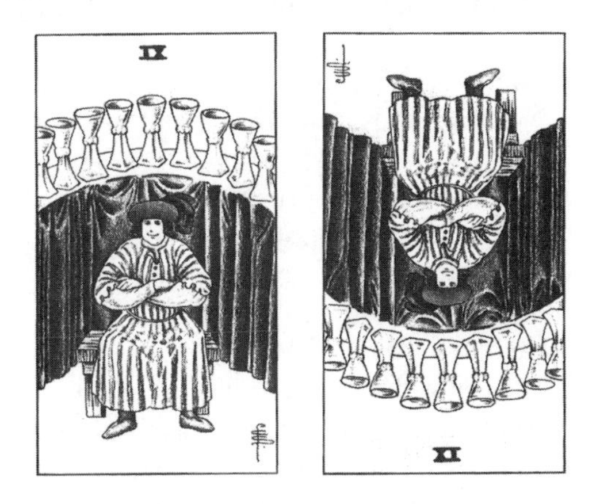

The 9 of Cups resonates to the number 9, the number of transformation.

Sweet dreams are made of this—the Wish Card! The 9 of Cups is like a magic lamp with a genie inside it. When this card appears, your wishes will come true—and happily ever after is just one card away.

When the 9 of Cups is reversed, you may be wishing for something that can't possibly happen. "What? George Clooney's *not* gonna call? Julia Roberts is *not* gonna come riding up on a white horse?" Set your sights more realistically, says the 9 of Cups R. Spending all your time wishin' and hopin' on stars is not going to make your wish come true. Come down off your cloud, quit pushing the cosmos, and, as Arlene would put it, "Cool your jets." Good things will happen when the 9 of Cups appears upright or reversed, but when it's reversed, you need to take a deep breath and step back.

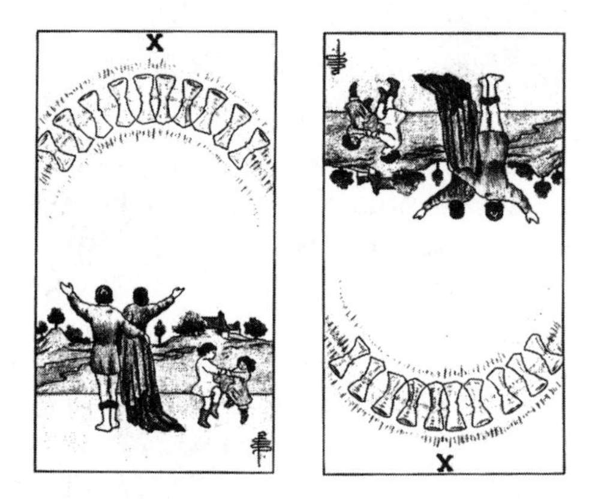

The 10 of Cups resonates back to the number 1, the number of new beginnings—and happily ever after!

This is the card of a long-lasting, secure relationship. You've traveled the sometimes rocky path from the Ace of Cups to get here, and you're now at a point in your life together where you appreciate each other, your differences and your similarities, and your life together. The 10 of Cups truly is the happily ever after card. Go ahead and enjoy it—you've earned it!

When the 10 of Cups is reversed, you're just not quite there yet. Maybe circumstances are intervening with your happily ever after—or maybe you and your partner aren't quite ready for the quiet contentment promised by this card in its upright position. Could it be there are still things you haven't told each other? Or are you finding yourself arguing more and more as your wedding date approaches? In its reversed position, the 10 of Cups R suggests you reassess whether you're rushing toward happily ever after so fast that you may be holding the wrong person's hand. That's not always the case, but maybe you should slow down and see whether you're both ready for this big step.

Your Fortune in a Cup

Cups can help you with romantic problems even without doing a Tarot spread. If you're having a specific problem in your love life, reread the previous descriptions and see which Cup, upright or reversed, represents your situation most clearly. Then remove that card from your Tarot deck and set it in front of you in its upright or reversed position.

Take a few minutes to study the image, thinking all the while about the situation you're having with your partner. Here are some questions to ask yourself:

- What does the image tell me about my specific love challenge?
- Who is who in this image?
- Is a solution offered in this image?
- How might I effect this solution with my partner?

Make some notes about your responses to these questions, as well as what the image has to tell you about your situation. The images of the Tarot have an uncanny way of mirroring our own difficulties, enabling us to see them far more clearly than when they are muddling around in our heads. See if this exercise helps you get to the root of your romantic challenge. Your love fortune really may be as close as a Cup!

chapter 7

Do You Believe in Life After Love?

Can this relationship be saved?
Everyday goddesses
Falling in and out of love
Mothers, lovers, and others
Chiron heals all wounds
Breaking up is hard to do
Learning to love yourself
Is there life after love?

Sometimes, we have no choice but to move on. While the main issues in our love relationships seem to be money, mothers-in-law, and monkey business, how each couple handles these issues depends on how they each communicate and handle conflict, and for some couples, in the end, breaking up may be the best thing to do. In this chapter, we look at how your astrological charts can help you determine whether it's time to say good-bye. We introduce you to the asteroids—Ceres, Juno, Pallas Athene, and Vesta—and Chiron, the wounded healer, all astrological shorthand for various aspects of your approach to love relationship issues. We show you the connection between the asteroids and the Tarot, and how you can use this connection to help you learn to have faith in yourself again. Finally, using a combination of Astrology, the Tarot, and Psychic Intuition, you learn how to chart your own path toward life after love.

Can This Relationship Be Saved?

Most women have at one time or another been enthralled with the "Can This Marriage Be Saved?" stories in magazines such as *Ladies*

Home Journal. Even in our youths, when we both first came across this column in our mothers' magazines, or as young women on the dating scene, we couldn't help but notice that certain patterns seemed to emerge in the "his" and "her" versions, as well as in the professional advice that followed. And for you men, if a woman in your life hasn't waved one of these articles in front of your face, then, believe us, she's wanted to!

Well-known novelist Lois Duncan (*I Know What You Did Last Summer*), one of the writers responsible for these columns in the late 1980s, agreed. When asked, Lois broke down the trends this way: "The cases for that series generally involved problems having to do with money, in-laws, sex (the frequency of marital sex, or one member of the couple having an affair), stepchildren, boredom, one partner outgrowing the other—especially when the wife's career outdistanced the husband's—and division of chores within the home, especially after the birth of a child. Of course, a 'lack of communication' was the catchall term for the therapist. To me, that seemed like putting the cart before the horse, because it's natural not to want to discuss uncomfortable subject matter."

Lois is right. Statistically, most love relationship problems stem from one of four problem areas:

- Parenting (children, stepchildren, and in-laws)
- Partnership (trust, sharing, cooperation, communication, fun)
- Control (money, work both inside and outside the home)
- Sex (or lack of it)

When we began to consider these areas, we noticed that each has both its corresponding astrological sign and planet, as well as a Tarot card whose images can serve as a starting point for considering these love relationship difficulties in more depth. In addition, we were struck by how much these problems connect to the issues associated with the asteroids—a crew of fly-by-nights who've been astrologically anointed to deal specifically with women's issues: Ceres ⚳, Juno ⚵, Pallas Athene ⚴, and Vesta ⚶—and Chiron ⚷, the planetoid that governs healing.

We begin our exploration of these relatively new additions to the world of the Intuitive Art of Astrology with the asteroids, and explore how the areas they cover can help you determine whether it's time to put this particular love relationship behind you.

Everyday Goddesses

The asteroids, part of a belt of planetoids that orbit together in a belt between Mars ♂ and Jupiter ♃, have been given the names of various goddesses, no surprise when you consider their connection to the feminine side of issues. Like the goddesses for whom they're named, each asteroid covers a specific realm of womanhood.

Asteroid	Realm	Areas of Influence
Ceres ⚳	Motherhood	Natural cycles, fertility, crops, relationships to parents and children
Juno ⚵	Marriage	Partnerships, contracts and agreements, social obligations
Pallas Athene ⚴	Wisdom	Intelligence, knowledge, understanding, equality
Vesta ⚶	Power	Sexuality, devotion, health, service to others

When we set out to connect the four relationship problem areas to one of these four asteroids, we found that, because each asteroid is associated with both an astrological sign (or signs) and planet (or planets), this became a surprisingly easy assignment. In the following table, we've also assigned a Tarot card to each sign, something we'll come back to in a moment.

Issue	Asteroid	Astro Sign(s)	Planet(s)	Tarot Card
Parenting	Ceres ⚳	Cancer ♋	Moon ☽	The Moon
Partnership	Juno ⚵	Taurus ♉, Libra ♎	Venus ♀	The Empress
Control	Pallas Athene ⚴	Aquarius ♒	Uranus ♅,	Justice
Sex	Vesta ⚶	Virgo ♍, Scorpio ♏	Pluto ♇	The Lovers

Before we show you how you can work with the asteroids to learn more about your own relationship, we want to introduce you to each of the goddesses associated with them. Let's start with Ceres (Demeter in Greek), the goddess of fertility.

According to myth, Ceres is responsible not only for women's fertility, but also for all things that grow. When the god of the underworld, Hades, fell in love with Cere's daughter and took her away to his kingdom, Ceres found herself so distraught that all crops ceased to grow. Hades and Ceres reached a compromise—Proserpina (Persephone in Greek) would spend six months in the underworld with her husband, and six months with her mother, which created the seasons of abundant summer growth and fallow winter waiting.

Ceres ⚳ is associated with Cancer ♋, the most nurturing of the astrological signs, and its associated planet is the Moon ☽, responsible for natural cycles here on earth. The Tarot card associated with Ceres is the Major Arcana card, the Moon, which represents both those cycles and the intuition that's in tune with them.

The Moon represents the asteroid Ceres ⚳.

Juno (Hera in Greek) reigns as Juno Regina, queen and wife of Jupiter (Zeus in Greek). Juno ruled over marriage, and Romans called her union with Jupiter the Sacred Marriage. Often jealous of her husband's many philanderings, Juno wreaked a variety of havoc on Jupiter's conquests. "Hell hath no fury like a woman scorned," was likely first written about Juno.

Juno ⚵ is associated with Taurus ♉, the sign of making a comfortable home, and Libra ♎, the sign of partnerships. Their associated planet, Venus ♀, is responsible for all things related to love and the home, and the Tarot card associated with Juno is the Empress, which represents both Juno's mother aspect and her role as queen.

The Empress represents the asteroid Juno ⚵.

Pallas Athene, in Greek mythology the daughter of Zeus and Metis, arose full-grown in warrior dress from her father's head—Zeus had eaten Metis when he learned she was pregnant! Athene, the goddess of wisdom and justice, was often prayed to when men sought victory in battle. Not surprisingly, Athene was the favorite of her father's many children, and the only one he let carry his aegis, buckler, and thunderbolt.

Athene ⚴ is associated with Aquarius ♒, the sign of the wise and detached observer, and the planet Uranus ♅, the innovator. The Tarot card associated with Athene is Justice, dispenser of celestial wisdom and balancer of the celestial scales.

Justice represents the asteroid Pallas Athene ⚴.

The last of the major asteroids is Vesta (Hestia in Greek, the oldest Olympian). In mythology, Vesta was the guardian of the hearth. Peaceful and stable, Vesta protected the stability of the family and social order, and was sometimes called the Virgin Goddess. Unlike in our more puritanical Western culture, in Greek and Roman mythology, virginity and sex were always paired.

Vesta ⚶ is associated with Virgo ♍, the sign of service and order, and Scorpio ♏, the sign of power not always visible on the surface. Her planet is transformational Pluto ♇, and her Tarot card is the Lovers, where the angel Raphael reminds us that to love is also to serve.

The Lovers represents the asteroid Vesta ⚶.

Falling In and Out of Love

Every love relationship has its own hot-button issues, and now that you've met the asteroids and their associated Tarot cards, you can use the Tarot to help you understand some of your own love relationship difficulties.

Begin by selecting all four of these cards from your Tarot deck: the Moon for Ceres ⚳, the Empress for Juno ⚵, Justice for Pallas Athene ⚴, and the Lovers for Vesta ⚶. Lay all four cards in front of you and consider their images, both individually and as a group, for a few minutes before you begin. Meditate on the stories of the goddesses. If you'd like, make some notes about what you notice about the cards when you meditate on them as representations of Ceres, Juno, Pallas Athene, and Vesta.

Ceres ⚳ *Juno* ⚵ *Pallas Athene* ⚴ *Vesta* ⚶

When you're ready, think about the biggest problem in your own love relationship right now. Are you arguing about where to live? Does one person want to get married while the other is not ready to commit? If you are married, are you in disagreement over areas from who handles the bills to whether you'll have children? If you do have children now, do you argue about how best to raise them? Are your in-laws or other relatives driving you mad? Are you bored with your partner? Do you feel like you're holding up far more than your end of the bargain?

Write down your biggest love relationship issue here:

____

Now look again at the four Tarot cards representing the asteroids. Which of these cards seems to speak most eloquently to your issue? Is your problem surrounding Ceres's realm of parenting, Juno's realm of partnership, Pallas Athene's realm of control, or Vesta's realm of sex? Select the card for that goddess and put the others away.

For the next part of this exercise, imagine yourself into the world of this card. If you selected the Empress, for example, put yourself on Juno's red-velvet throne, draped in a flowing robe adorned with pomegranates. If you are a guy, imagine yourself taking the Empress's hand and joining her. Notice your kingdom, the wheat and trees that grow around you, and the water that flows to give them life. You'll likely want to make some notes in your journal about how this feels.

After you've imagined yourself in the Tarot landscape of the goddess of your choice, in your mind, step away from the card. Meditate now on the goddess whose world you have just inhabited. Ask her what *she* would do if she stood on your ground, as you have just stood on hers. Remember these goddesses' stories—they are not passive, shy types! What would your goddess have to offer for the conditions surrounding you now? Would she walk away, knowing that she has within her the power to sustain or end a relationship? Would she initiate a conversation with her partner, or suggest changes she herself might make? Consider carefully what your meditation with the goddess yields, and write down your notes and impressions in your journal.

Mothers, Lovers, and Others

Where your and your partner's asteroids are located in your astrological birth charts can help you understand how your particular approaches in these areas of your lives may clash with the other's expectations. Begin by finding the symbol for each of the asteroids in each of your birth charts. Then make a list of the sign and house for each asteroid for each of you. Use the following form, if you'd like.

	Name: ________		**Name: ________**	
Asteroid	**Your Sign**	**Your House**	**Your Partner's Sign**	**Your Partner's House**
Ceres ⚳ in	________	________	________	________
Juno ⚵ in	________	________	________	________
Pallas Athene ⚴ in	________	________	________	________
Vesta ⚶ in	________	________	________	________

After you have compiled your list, use the following tables to discover what your asteroid's sign can reveal about your mothering, partnering, strength, and capacity for giving.

Ceres ⚳ Through the Signs

Ceres ⚳ In	**How You Mother**	**The Mothering You Expect from Others**
Aries ♈	Enthusiastically	Demonstrative—but not for long!
Taurus ♉	Steadfastly	Stable

Ceres ⚳ In	How You Mother	The Mothering You Expect from Others
Gemini ♊	Intellectually	Lighthearted
Cancer ♋	Empathetically	Nurturing
Leo ♌	Warmly	Generous
Virgo ♍	Generously	Self-sacrificing
Libra ♎	Judiciously	Concerned
Scorpio ♏	Deeply	Powerful
Sagittarius ♐	Adventurously	Expansive
Capricorn ♑	Carefully	Dedicated
Aquarius ♒	Innovatively	Detached
Pisces ♓	Intuitively	Unconditional

Juno ⚵ Through the Signs

Juno ⚵ In	How You Partner	The Partnering You Expect from Others
Aries ♈	Impulsively	Fiery
Taurus ♉	Committedly	Secure
Gemini ♊	Casually	Interesting
Cancer ♋	Cautiously	Devoted
Leo ♌	Dramatically	Adoring
Virgo ♍	Practically	Perfect
Libra ♎	Romantically	Balanced
Scorpio ♏	Magnetically	Powerful
Sagittarius ♐	Excitedly	Adventurous
Capricorn ♑	Steadily	Steady
Aquarius ♒	Independently	Hands-off
Pisces ♓	Idealistically	Soulful

Pallas Athene ⚴ Through the Signs

Pallas Athene ⚴ In	How You Find Strength	The Strength You Expect from Others
Aries ♈	In leading	Acquiescence
Taurus ♉	In building	Dependability
Gemini ♊	In communicating	Versatility

Pallas Athene ⚴ Through the Signs (continued)

Pallas Athene ⚴ In	How You Find Strength	The Strength You Expect from Others
Cancer ♋	In empathy	Protection
Leo ♌	In creativity	Adoration
Virgo ♍	In sacrifice	Organization
Libra ♎	In harmony	Judiciousness
Scorpio ♏	In power	Magnetism
Sagittarius ♐	In adventure	Enthusiasm
Capricorn ♑	In achievement	Structure
Aquarius ♒	In uniqueness	Freedom
Pisces ♓	In compassion	Connection

Vesta ⚶ Through the Signs

Vesta ⚶ In	How You Give	The Giving You Expect from Others
Aries ♈	Thoughtlessly	Unquestioning
Taurus ♉	Generously	Dependable
Gemini ♊	Wittily	Versatile
Cancer ♋	Intuitively	Sensitive
Leo ♌	Warmly	Heart-centered
Virgo ♍	Self-sacrificingly	Sensible
Libra ♎	Sensually	Harmonious
Scorpio ♏	Passionately	Devoted
Sagittarius ♐	Spontaneously	Exciting
Capricorn ♑	Carefully	Practical
Aquarius ♒	Innovatively	Unusual
Pisces ♓	Sensitively	Compassionate

The astrological house in which each of your asteroids resides will reveal the *style* of how you express your signs. Here are key term reminders for each astrological house.

Astro House	Key Terms
1st	Identity
2nd	Self-worth
3rd	Knowledge
4th	Home and family
5th	Creativity
6th	Work and service
7th	Relationships
8th	Transformation
9th	Beliefs
10th	Ethics and career
11th	Community
12th	Spirituality

Let's look at an example we first explored in Chapter 3, the elemental pairing of Fire and Earth in the Knight of Wands and the 9 of Pentacles. Whether this becomes a long-lasting match may be more apparent in forces below the Elemental surface. Suppose for this particular Fire/Earth couple, Juno ⚵ in Aries ♈ in the 2nd house fires the impulsive Knight of Wands in his quest for an equally fiery response. Meanwhile, Juno ⚵ in Taurus ♉ in the 6th house makes for a committed partner in the 9 of Pentacles who expects security. It looks as if these Juno ⚵ approaches and expectations will make a long-lasting relationship between these two individuals difficult to maintain, unless other factors are present to temper them.

When we place the Knight of Wands and the 9 of Pentacles face to face, the potentials and challenges in such a relationship rise to the surface. He's charging off to battle, while she's perfectly content in her garden. Will they live happily ever after? Take a look at the astrological sign and house for each partner's asteroids to gain important insights.

After you've made a note of the sign and house for both your and your partner's asteroids, select Tarot cards whose images represent each of these concepts, as we've done above. Choose cards that match your elemental signature, too. Set each pair of cards next to each other and consider what the images have to tell you about your love strengths and challenges. Be sure to make some notes about what you discover.

Chiron ⚷ Heals All Wounds

In addition to the asteroids, Chiron ⚷, a planetoid representing the wounded healer of myth, can help you understand an aspect of your needs that you may have not previously considered. That's because astrologers now agree that Chiron's position in your chart reveals your psychic wound, and how you can first heal yourself, and then reach out to heal others.

According to Greek myth, Chiron was the only one of the half-man, half-horse centaurs who was not violent. Chiron became so renowned for his unusual goodness and wisdom that the scions of well-connected families often sent their sons to him for their educations, and in this way, Chiron raised the warrior Achilles, the physician Aesculapius, and the hunter Actaeon, to name but three. Unfortunately, the immortal Chiron was wounded in battle, and ultimately Zeus persuaded Chiron to give up his immortality so that he didn't need to live forever in pain.

To discover your own love relationship Chiron wound—and how you can heal together—begin by finding the position of Chiron ⚷ in each of your astrological birth charts. Note the astrological signs and houses for each of you.

	Name: ______________		**Name:** ______________	
Chiron ⚷ In	**Your Sign**	**Your House**	**Partner's Sign**	**Partner's House**
Ceres ⚳	________	________	________	________
Juno ⚵	________	________	________	________
Pallas Athene ⚴	________	________	________	________
Vesta ⚶	________	________	________	________

Use the following table to learn what your Chiron placement reveals about your psychic wound, and then about how you can heal both yourself and others—as well as what you need from others to heal yourself.

Chiron ⚷ In	**Wound**	**Heals By**	**Chiron House**	**Wound**	**Heals By**
Aries ♈	Impatience	Patience	1st	Self-doubt	Self-love
Taurus ♉	Doubt	Understanding	2nd	Lack of self-faith	Faith
Gemini ♊	Self-distrust	Wisdom	3rd	Feelings of ignorance	Study
Cancer ♋	Indifference	Gentleness	4th	Not belonging	Family
Leo ♌	Overenthusiasm	Tolerance	5th	Boredom	Creativity
Virgo ♍	Servility	Strength	6th	Irresponsibility	Service
Libra ♎	Indecision	Steadfastness	7th	Loneliness	Partnership
Scorpio ♏	Possessiveness	Selfless love	8th	Apathy	Devotion
Sagittarius ♐	Restlessness	Inner peace	9th	Aimlessness	Belief
Capricorn ♑	Fear	Courage	10th	Irreputability	Responsibility
Aquarius ♒	Aloofness	Sharing	11th	Loneliness	Friendship
Pisces ♓	Paranoia	Self-transcendence	12th	Secretiveness	Sharing

Suppose your Chiron ⚷ is in Sagittarius ♐ in your 6th house. Your wound is restlessness, which you express through irresponsibility. This wound can be healed by inner peace achieved through service, and could be represented by the Knight of Swords Tarot card.

Now suppose your partner's Chiron ⚷ is in Taurus ♉ in his or her 11th house. The wound is doubt, expressed through loneliness, and can be healed by understanding achieved through friendship, and could be represented by the 2 of Swords Tarot card.

When you put the psychic wounds of the Knight of Swords and the 2 of Swords next to each other, misunderstanding is inevitable.

Because of the way Chiron ⚷ manifests in the pairing of the Knight of Swords and the 2 of Swords, it's all too likely that the Knight of Swords partner (whether male or female), may interpret the 2's tendency to express doubt as a condemnation of the Knight in the form of restlessness and irresponsibility. The 2 of Swords partner may interpret the Knight's tendency to express restlessness as a condemnation of the 2's doubting nature. This merry-go-round of misunderstanding will go round and round and round—unless each partner recognizes the psychic wounds within both self and beloved, and mutually decide to learn to heal them together.

After you've made a note of the astrological sign and house for both your own and your love partner's Chirons, select Tarot cards whose images represent each of these concepts. Set these two cards next to each other and consider what the images have to tell you about each of your psychic wounds and how you can heal them. Be sure to make some notes about what you discover.

Breaking Up Is Hard to Do

The next thing to consider in terms of deciding whether your relationship can (or should) continue is your astrological aspects—in this case, more specifically, how your two birth charts aspect each other. Remember, aspects are the geometric relationships between any two planets in your own chart, as well as in relation to another chart, whether for another person, a moment in time, or your own progressed chart. Let's review the astrological aspects and their meanings.

Astro Aspect	Symbol	Keyword(s)
Conjunction	☌	Focus, shared energy
Sextile	⚹	Favorable
Square	□	Challenging—pushes for change
Trine	△	Ease, extremely favorable
Opposition	☍	Difficulty, extremely challenging
Quincunx	⚻	No shared energy, nothing in common

Depending on how your charts aspect in a number of key areas, you will either be challenged to move your relationship to a new level, or to walk away from it. To show you how this works, we've again selected Bruce Willis and Demi Moore to represent a couple whose marriage relationship didn't work out. The synastry grid for Bruce and Demi follows.

The challenges for Bruce Willis and Demi Moore begin right away in their personal planets—the Sun ☉, Moon ☽, Mercury ☿, Venus ♀, and Mars ♂, where we find a preponderance of oppositions ☍, squares □, and trines △. Arlene likes to call the combination you can see here "opposition equals," out-of-balance energy that's in constant need of coming back to balance.

In any synastry grid, squares □ represent frustrations and difficulties related to growth. When this aspect is present, growing together won't be easy, as one or the other will often feel as if he or she has to make a "sacrifice." Another possibility is that, due to distractions or interruptions, any growth the relationship had will suddenly stop. In Bruce and Demi's synastry grid, we are immediately struck by the squares these two make to each other's Venuses ♀. There are also ascendant and midheaven squares, compounding the frustration.

Across	Down
Bruce Willis	**Demi Moore**
Natal Chart	Natal Chart
Mar 19 1955	Nov 11 1962
6:33 pm CET -1:00	2:16 pm MST +7:00
Idar-Oberstein GER	Roswell NM
49°N42' 007°E19'	33°N23'39" 104°W31'21"

	☽	☉	☿	♀	♂	♃	♄	♅	♆	♇	⚷	⚶	⚴	⚵	⚳	☊	☋	As	Mc	⊗	⚸
☽				□ 1S13	☌ 3S44	⚹ 1A21	☍ 2A21			□ 6A16				☍ 0S39	△ 2S53			△ 9A20			
☉		△ 9A20		□ 1S41	☍ 4S12	△ 0A53	☌ 1A53	△ 4A40		□ 5A49				☌ 1S06							
☿		⚼ 2A19	△ 8S39	□ 6A17	☍ 3A46	△ 8A52	☌ 9A51						∠ 0S46	☌ 6A52			△ 9S36	∠ 1A50	⚼ 1A16		
♀		△ 7S48		□ 3A13	☍ 5A44	△ 0A39	☌ 0S21	△ 3S08		□ 4S16		⚻ 1S59		☌ 2A39							
♂		⚼ 1S16		☍ 2A43	□ 0A12		□ 6A17							□ 3A17	⚻ 1A03	⚼ 1A49	∠ 1A49	∠ 1S44			
♃	⚺ 0S36		☌ 0S44			⚼ 1A46			△ 5S30		⚺ 0A44					⚹ 1S41	△ 1S41		△ 5S50	⚻ 1S04	□ 2S06
♄	☌ 3S09										☌ 1S48	⚼ 1A51						△ 7S48		☍ 3S37	
♅			☍ 2S31		△ 9A54	∠ 0S01					⚻ 1S02		△ 9S39			△ 3S28					□ 3S52
♆		⚼ 0S06		□ 3A53	☍ 1A22	△ 6A27	☌ 7A27							☌ 4A28	⚹ 2A14	∠ 3A00	⚼ 3A00	∠ 0S34	⚼ 1S09		
♇					△ 2A56				∠ 0A45						△ 3A47						
⚷			☌ 3A46			⚼ 1A16			△ 8A32								△ 4A44		△ 8A52		□ 5A08
⚶					△ 2A17				∠ 0A06						△ 3A08						
⚴		△ 7A36				☌ 0S51	△ 0A09	☌ 2A55	□ 6A53			⚺ 1A47		△ 2S51	☍ 5S05						
⚵					△ 0A54				∠ 1S17					⚹ 3A59	△ 1A45						
⚳			☍ 2S46		△ 9A39	∠ 0S16					⚻ 1S18		△ 9S54			△ 3S43					□ 4S08
☊	☍ 0A08	△ 4A19	⚻ 0A16					☌ 8A59	□ 5A02		☍ 1S12					⚻ 1A13	⚺ 1A13			☌ 0A37	△ 1A38
☋	☌ 0A08		⚺ 0A16					☍ 8A59	□ 5A02		☌ 1S12					⚺ 1A13	⚻ 1A13	△ 4A47		☍ 0A37	⚹ 1A38
As		☌ 5A56				△ 2A30	△ 1A31	△ 1A16		⚻ 2A25		□ 0A08	□ 2A52	△ 4A30				☍ 5A28	□ 4A54	△ 9A39	△ 8A38
Mc		□ 2A55						⚻ 1A45	⚹ 2A12	△ 0A36		☍ 2A53	☌ 0A10			☌ 6A01	☍ 6A01	□ 2A27	☍ 1A52		
⊗		☍ 6A24			△ 7A08	⚹ 2A03	⚹ 1A03	⚹ 1A44				□ 0A35	□ 3A19		△ 6A17			☌ 5A56	□ 5A21		
⚸	△ 9S36			△ 5A12	⚻ 2A41						△ 8S15				□ 3A32						

Synastry grid for Bruce Willis (read across) and Demi Moore (read down).

Trines △ allow for an ease of movement between periods of stress, and with this aspect between both their Suns ☉ and their Mercuries ☿ (as well as between a number of other planets), Bruce and Demi will have rapport regarding both their children and their belief systems. This same trine, however, may also cause them to become complacent about each other and so not force issues until they come to a critical point. Trines often lead to a kind of a live-and-let-live attitude, and, although this may seem desirable, the problem is that squares and oppositions often take over precisely when one partner needs the other. To a pair with aspects set up this way, it will seem as if the other is nowhere to be found when there's a crisis.

For Bruce and Demi, sometimes the problem is a conflict between work and home, emotion and cooperation (Moon ☽ Saturn ♄ opposition ☍); sometimes, when a crisis occurs, one or the other can't maintain a balance to help the other. (Remember their *yin* and *yang* from Chapter 2?) Either way, there's a constant see-sawing of energies. For the pendulum to not swing too far off course, these two lovers would need to really be in tune with each other on a daily basis.

The many squares □ to Bruce's Venus ♀ from all of Demi's personal planets are particularly dramatic in this grid. With such volatile energy contained within, this relationship seems to live for crisis. In addition, oppositions ☍ and squares □ to Bruce's Saturn ♄ mean Demi is a challenge to Bruce as well. All these Saturn aspects suggest that there's a lot of karmic duty at work between these two, connecting them in a powerful, intense way that they may not consciously understand.

At the same time, the Moon ☽ and Saturn ♄ oppositions in these two charts reveal a powerful sense of duty, creating a push … pull between the desires to protect each other and restrict each other. Sometimes Saturn ♄/Moon ☽ aspects such as these can bring about a strongly devoted relationship, but it may become demanding and critical over time. How this aspect evolves depends on how a couple evolves as a couple. If both are career-oriented rather than focused predominantly on their marriage and family, then the relationship may work out.

Still, this marriage could work only if one or the other would submit to Saturn's influence. In other words, one partner would have to allow for the other to shine while the other takes the backseat to that recognition. This is because a Sun ☉ or Moon ☽ opposition to Saturn ♄ is hard to break, and, for Bruce and Demi, the rest of the grid has friction in it as well as harmony. This is truly a roller-coaster relationship. Although it might be all right if it were a business association, this relationship encompasses family *and* marriage *and* business *and* the public besides? It's way too much of a strain on these two charts.

The only hope for these two would be to evolve to where they could handle time away from each other and make sure they allow for quality time when they are together. Still, Arlene believes that despite the strain, stress, and even volatile energy evident in this synastry grid, Bruce and Demi may very well be connected on and off throughout their entire lives. How much harmony would prevail? The answer is that these two charts are in a constant tug of war involving unusually intense personal emotional cycles. Could Bruce and Demi learn to give fairly and unconditionally to each other? If they could, this relationship could succeed.

Challenging Your Aspects

To explore your own charts for favorable and challenging aspects, begin with a synastry grid. If you already created one for the Chapter 5 exercise, retrieve that grid now. You can also ask a professional astrologer to prepare a synastry grid for you. Remember, aspects represent either a flow between you or a lesson to be learned.

When you have your synastry grid in front of you, follow these steps one at a time:

1. Review the luminaries. The Sun ☉ and Moon ☽ need connections to both personal planets and outer planets for a relationship to succeed.
2. Look for all aspects in the grid between all personal planets: Mercury ☿, Venus ♀, and Mars ♂.
3. Review the Sun ☉ and Moon ☽ aspects between the two charts to focus on both the ego and emotions.
4. Conjunctions ☌ are focal points. Pay special attention to what they reveal about the two of you.
5. Look at trines △ and sextiles ⚹, which allow for harmonious flow between the charts. Sextiles allow free-will decisions into the relationship.
6. Check the oppositions ☍ and squares □. These aspects allow for challenges (and maximum growth); squares also set up the need to push the envelope.
7. Don't forget quincunxes ⚻, which can reveal areas where one—or both—of you might need to make an adjustment.
8. See which planets have no aspect between them. Although this can be considered positive because it means there are no issues in this area, there won't be any growth here, either.
9. Look to Saturn ♄ and Nodal ☊ ☋ connections for longevity and endurability. Saturn and the Nodes of the Moon also relate karmic lessons and conditions of duty.

Learning to Love Yourself

If you've decided to end your present relationship and move on to whatever new love may be on the horizon, you already know that when you're first on your own after being in a relationship, the world can be a scary place. Learning to love—and trust—yourself again is the most important step you can make toward learning to love and trust others in order to once again face the world—and love. Fortunately, your own birth chart can help you, well, chart the way.

Just as your birth chart reveals the difficulties you've been having in your relationship, it can also help you explore your own strengths. Returning to the birth charts of Bruce Willis and Demi Moore in Chapter 2, for example, we see both are individually strong people, with personal squares □ to their Marses ♂ and Saturns ♄ pushing them to grow, and personal trines △ helping them to recover. For this reason, each has been able to create a strong and separate identity. This means that when they are each on their own, they are able to function quite well, maintaining public personae, connecting to others, and maintaining enough interest in a variety of things to keep them fulfilled. These two function amazingly well on their own, which is why they've been able to create separate worlds since their breakup, while still remaining committed to their work, their public, and, most important, to their family.

Finding the strengths in your own birth chart that can help you survive a love breakup is easy. Just follow these tips to discover resources of inner energy that you can count on to help you love yourself after the romance is over:

- Your focal points can be found in your conjunctions ☌—gatherings of planets that show where you like to focus your energy.
- You'll find the ways you are strong in the aspects to your luminaries, the Sun ☉ and the Moon ☽. Trines △ and sextiles ⚹ may make it easier, whereas squares □ and oppositions ☍ may make it more difficult; however, those difficulties will in turn make you much stronger in the long run.
- Take your time studying your Mars ♂ and Saturn ♄ aspects. Mars, with its focus on power, and Saturn, with its focus on discipline, can each reveal your particular strengths as you embark on a life after love.
- Venus ♀ and Jupiter ♃ aspects can be very helpful at a time like this. Trines and sextiles, especially to the luminaries and to Mars and Saturn from Venus and Jupiter, can go a long way toward easing you into a life on your own you love.

- Don't forget to look at your Nodes ☊ ☋. Nodes reveal both your karmic challenges and those things that come easily to you. At a time like this, you may want to lean a little more heavily on your South Node ☋ karmic strengths until you're ready to face your North Node ☊ karmic challenges again. If your Nodal positions make trines △ or sextiles ⚹ to Venus ♀, Mars ♂, or the Moon ☽, they will help you deal with challenges such as loss, competition, and separation from a loved one.
- You can also look for strengths in aspects such as the trines △ and sextiles ⚹ between your Sun ☉ and Moon ☽ and Saturn ♄. These aspects are particularly helpful for handling a loss due to conflict.
- Quincunxes ⚻ show the areas where you're willing to adjust when the need arises. This is where to look for potential compromises and areas you're willing to fine-tune.

Is There Life After Love?

Now that you've discovered where your personal strengths lie, you may be comfortable enough to think about loving someone new. If you're wondering what that special someone might be like, Tarot's Mission Spread can help you discover the answer.

Tarot's Mission Spread can help you discover what's next for you in your love life.

A Mission Spread uses 21 cards to discover the past, present, and future mission and purpose regarding a question. You might, for example, ask what kind of love would really make you happy, or how you can best meet that special someone.

The top row of cards in a Mission Spread represents what you've done so far regarding the question, or, to put it another way, this particular mission's past. The middle row concerns your present mission—what you're doing now (or should be doing) to make this mission successful. The bottom row shows this mission's future—both things that may happen and things you can do to make sure they do.

Unlike some of the other Tarot spreads we've shown you, the cards in each row of a Mission Spread should be read together rather than separately. To show you how this works, here's a sample Mission Spread for Michael, who asked what he hoped to find in his next love.

The top row concerns Michael's past mission and purpose regarding this question. Twice-married, twice-divorced Michael has been single for a number of years now, and is good friends with both of his ex-wives. In each marriage, both partners knew when it was time to let go, and settled into their separate existences fairly easily because of their interests outside the marriages.

The middle row addresses where Michael is now regarding this question. Michael is very interested in taking a relationship with someone he already knows to the next level, but because of some lingering health problems for her, he's been careful about pushing her. Recently, however, she's made it clear that she may be ready to move their friendship toward something more, and Michael's become a bit more impatient than usual.

The bottom row shows this question's future mission and purpose. Someone from the past is at the center of this row, and Michael seemed to think it was the woman he's been interested in. Although a number of unexpected difficulties kept them apart in the past, these are now behind them; they can move forward with renewed purpose toward what, knowing Michael as we do, will almost certainly be a third-time charm.

Now that you've seen how Michael's Mission Spread worked, you can try one of your own. We've provided a meditation you can do after you've completed the Tarot portion of the exercise.

Michael's Mission Spread: "What do I hope to find in my next love?"

First decide what question you want to ask of your Mission Spread. Note that question here:

____

Thinking about your question, shuffle your Tarot deck until you feel it is ready to answer the question for you. Cut the deck if you'd like, and then lay out the cards. As you begin to examine the images on the cards, remember to consider each grouping of cards together, looking first at your past mission and purpose regarding the question in the top row, second at your present mission and purpose in the middle row, and finally at your future mission and purpose in the bottom row. You can use the space provided to record your initial impressions, or you may want to record the entire reading and make notes in your journal.

Past: ____

____

Present: ____

____

Future: ____

____

After you've finished studying your Mission Spread, don't put it away—you need the cards (or some of them) for the second part of this exercise. Of the 21 cards that comprised your spread, chances are certain cards had particular resonance for you regarding your question. Select those cards now, being sure to select at least one from each row. Michael, for example, was struck by Temperance in the top row, the 3 of Wands in the middle row, and the 6 of Cups and Hierophant R in the bottom row.

Lay the cards that you selected in front of you, and ask them the same question you asked your spread. Rather than interpreting them as you would a Tarot spread, however, use your Psychic Intuition to discover what more these particular cards have to tell you about your question. Michael felt that his cards were reminding him that patience (both Temperance and the 3 of Wands) would ultimately pay off in the kind of unconventional relationship he hoped for with his longtime friend. You'll likely want to make some notes about what *your* intuition tells *you* as you contemplate the cards. Chances are, you'll discover that there really *is* life after love.

chapter 8

Soulmates: Loving for Eternity

That special someone
A love truly made in Heaven
Where's Saturn?
North meets South (Node, that is)
When the Moon (and other planets) are in the 12th house
Karmic warning signs
A love for all eternity

Even if you aren't sure about reincarnation, you probably do believe that there is a special someone somewhere, just for you, or a "Soulmate." When looking for a Soulmate connection, astrologers look at a number of factors to determine your particular karma of love, including the house placement of Saturn, your North and South Nodes, and what's happening in your 12th house. In this chapter, we explore what these various placements can mean for you and your Soulmate(s), as well as show you how you can use the Intuitive Arts to discover karmic connections—and warning signs. The course of eternal love is sometimes no smoother than the course of love over one lifetime, but you can use your Psychic Intuition both to help you understand why the road is rocky—and to learn which warning signs to watch for. With the Tarot, Astrology, and Psychic Intuition to guide you, eternal love is just a (sixth) sense away.

That Special Someone

If you're at all familiar with the term *Soulmate,* you probably heard it in the context of lovers fated to rediscover each other, life after life.

While it's true that this is one type of Soulmate relationship, it's not the only one—but it probably is the one you're most interested in hearing more about. Before we show you how to discover this version of your Soulmate this time around, though, we want to briefly talk about just what "Soulmate" really means in the literature of reincarnation.

Basically, Soulmates are those with whom we travel through many lifetimes, either because there are lessons we are learning together, because there is unresolved karma from past lives between us, or because we share some other sort of karmic connection. It's because of this karmic connection that, when we first meet a Soulmate in our current life, we feel an immediate attraction—or an immediate strong dislike. If you've ever taken an instant dislike to someone, you probably know exactly what we mean! But you may be equally familiar with that "love at first sight" sensation, and that's a Soulmate connection as well. Whether we fall madly in love with or madly in hate with our Soulmates, however, we *will* meet them—because Soulmates need each other to learn the lessons of this lifetime.

For this reason, Soulmate relationships often present challenges. As you've learned in previous chapters, however, it's just such challenges that are more likely to spur us on to new and exciting experiences and discoveries. Take, for example, a friend who keeps meeting people who challenge his impatience with self-centered people. Sure enough, a closer look at this person's birth chart reveals Saturn in Libra in the 3rd house of learning. Translation? In this lifetime, he needs to learn to accept different people's ways of approaching the world—especially those he finds selfish and self-absorbed! And perhaps, as well, be on the lookout for those same qualities in his very own self!

A Love Truly Made in Heaven

Soulmates of our hearts often present us with challenges, and that's why it's worth exploring what your karmic lessons can teach you about the people with whom you tend to fall in love. A Horseshoe Spread uses five Tarot cards to help you understand how your past lives can affect karmic issues your present life. Questions that you might ask this spread include not only why you keep falling in love with the same kind of person, but also the types of karmic issues you and your Soulmate share.

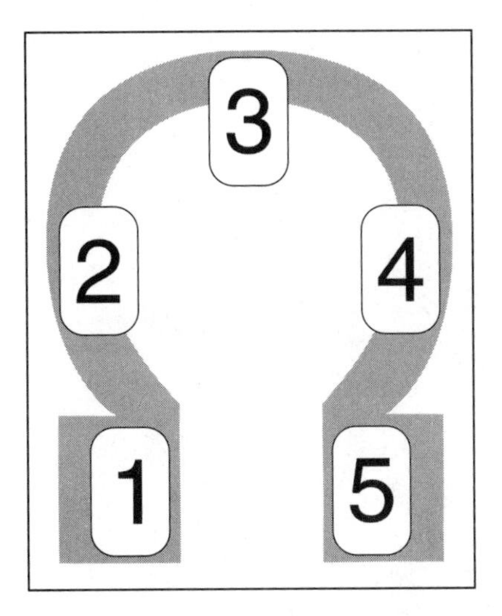

The five Tarot cards of a Horseshoe Spread can help you discover how past-life issues affect your present life.

Here's what the five cards mean:

- The first card in a Horseshoe Spread is the one that concerns how your past lives and ongoing karmic issues affect the question.
- The second card concerns how the question's past life lessons are manifesting in this life.
- The third card, at the top of the horseshoe, represents where you are now regarding the question.
- The fourth card reveals your present lessons concerning this question.
- The fifth card represents the question's future karmic lessons.

Let's try a Horseshoe Spread to see exactly how this works.

Mickey's partner's work keeps the partner, Alex frequently away from home. Mickey's question: "Is there a way for my Soulmate Alex and me to be together?"

The first card that came up for Soulmates Mickey and Alex was the 5 of Pentacles R. This card represents how Mickey and Alex's karmic issues may be affecting this question. The 5 of Pentacles in its upright position describes impoverishment, which is a lingering fear for both Mickey and Alex: Their respective jobs and the money they earn are a big part of why they live in two places. But because the 5 of Pentacles is reversed here, it suggests that Mickey and Alex have now learned this lesson in this lifetime and are ready to move beyond it.

Mickey's Horseshoe Spread: "Is there a way for my Soulmate and me to be together?"

The second card reveals past lessons in the present lifetime, and for Mickey and Alex, managing a two-location life has frequently felt just like the juggler in the 2 of Pentacles. "Look at the boats, sailing back and forth!" Mickey added, studying the card's images. "They might as well say 'Southwest Airlines' on their sails!"

The third card represents where Mickey and Alex are now with regard to this question. The Judgement card, key 20 in the Major Arcana, suggests that this particular journey may well have reached its "great a-ha." Mickey and Alex can now sit up and change the way they live, and their desire to do so is evident in this question. With this Major Arcana card, a new lesson will likely open between them, so now the question might be whether there's a way to continue receiving a good income while spending more quality time together. The answer is a resounding yes: As they work on these seemingly conflicting issues, this couple will come to the conclusion that anything is possible. Judgement tells us that these two will change their direction and come together in one place, especially because the 9 of Cups—the Wish Card—follows Judgement.

The fourth card in this spread is what Tarot readers call the Wish Card—the 9 of Cups. When this card appears in a spread, it means that any wishes you hold regarding the question will come true. Mickey was naturally delighted to see this card—it meant that these two would get their wish of being together. And because this card is in the present position in this reading, it will likely happen very soon!

The last card in this spread shows the question's future karmic lessons, and here we find the Page of Pentacles. Notice that this is the third Pentacle in this reading: Clearly, issues of money have a lot to do with Mickey and Alex's karmic lessons. The Page of Pentacles brings a message of reward for work well done, and in this position suggests that Mickey and Alex will not need to worry about money if they make the choice to live in one place.

Try Your Own Horseshoe Spread

Now that you've seen how a Horseshoe Spread can reveal how past-life lessons can affect your present life Soulmate relationships, you're probably eager to try one of your own. Begin by writing your question here:

____

Next, shuffle the cards, thinking about your question, your Soulmate, and your past-life lessons concerning the question and your Soulmate. When you are ready, lay the cards out.

Before you go on to look at the suggested card meanings provided in Appendix B, study the images on the cards as they tell their "story" in your karma spread. Consider not only the individual cards, but their "relationships" as well. Mickey, for example, noticed how both the 2 of Pentacles to its left and the 9 of Cups to its right seemed to be "supporting" the Judgement card at the top of the reading, as well as how money-centered the reading was. Record your initial impressions here:

____

____

____

____

If you still feel the need to explore the cards' meanings after you've recorded your notes, go ahead and see what we have to say about each of these cards in Appendix B. Just remember that no card's meaning is cast in stone!

If your Horseshoe Spread doesn't seem clear to you, one of the nice things about this particular spread is that you can "double" it, or even "triple" it. If you decide to do this, simply lay another row of cards above (for doubling) and below (for tripling), and then interpret all 10 or 15 cards together. Think of the cards you add as spices, whose flavors can enhance your reading both subtly and dramatically.

Where's Saturn ♄?

The placement of Saturn ♄ in each of your astrological birth charts can reveal not only the lessons you need to learn in this lifetime, but also what you'll look for others to teach you. For this reason, your Saturn placements can be key to your Soulmate relationships—both those that give you joy and those that you find more challenging. Let's begin by charting Saturn through the houses, because it's Saturn's house placement that reveals your most important Saturn lesson in this lifetime.

Saturn ♄ In	Your Lesson	What Others Can Teach You
1st house	Responsibility	Self-discipline
2nd house	Self-esteem	Security
3rd house	Sharing	Cooperation
4th house	Emotional security	The importance of family
5th house	Having fun	How to relax
6th house	Conscientiousness	Understanding
7th house	Dealing with others	Fairness/cooperation
8th house	Prudence	Emotional expression
9th house	Learning	Anything you want to learn!
10th house	Leadership	The value of teamwork
11th house	Security	Friendship/trust
12th house	Fear	Obligations/karmic duty

Now look at Saturn in each astrological sign to discover the way you can learn this planet's lesson. Remember, your Saturn lessons involve others—especially your Soulmates; so as you read these lessons, think about how others might teach your lessons to you.

Saturn ♄ In	How You Can Best Learn Your Saturn ♄ Lesson
Aries ♈	Learn the difference between selfishness and self-interest.
Taurus ♉	Learn the difference between possessions and things of value.
Gemini ♊	Learn the difference between talking and listening.
Cancer ♋	Learn the difference between giving and taking.
Leo ♌	Learn the difference between pride and dignity.
Virgo ♍	Learn the difference between practice and perfection.
Libra ♎	Learn the difference between cooperation and compromise.
Scorpio ♏	Learn the difference between what's revealed and what's hidden.
Sagittarius ♐	Learn the difference between excitement and excess.
Capricorn ♑	Learn the difference between ambition and success.
Aquarius ♒	Learn the difference between detachment and freedom.
Pisces ♓	Learn the difference between kindness and self-sacrifice.

Now let's apply these Saturn lessons to one of our celebrity pairs. We once again picked Joanne Woodward and Paul Newman, because their charts show these connections so clearly.

Joanne's Saturn ♄ is in Capricorn ♑ in her 2nd house. This means that, in this life, she will need to learn the difference between ambition and success through self-esteem, and her Soulmate can help her by teaching her the value of security. In this case, Paul has given Joanne this security via the innovation of his 2nd house ruler, Uranus ♅.

Paul's Saturn ♄ is in Scorpio ♏ in his 10th house. This means that, in this life, he will need to learn the difference between what's revealed and what's hidden through leadership, and his Soulmate can help him by teaching him the value of teamwork. Joanne has given Paul this teamwork via the communication of her 10th house ruler, Mercury ☿.

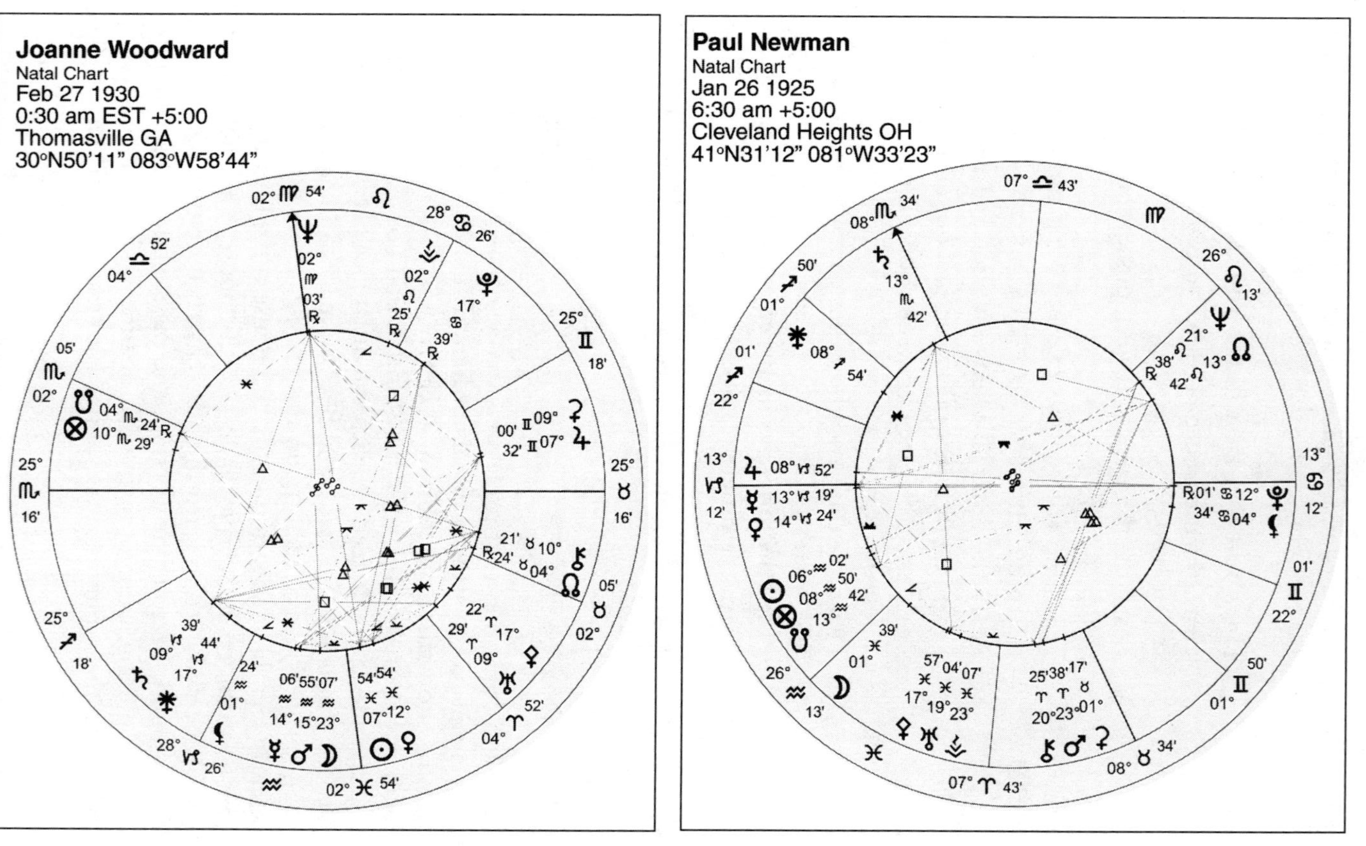

Birth charts for Joanne Woodward and Paul Newman.

Next we look to see where the Saturn of one's chart falls in the other's chart, to discover the lessons that will endure. Paul's Saturn is in Scorpio, which falls in Joanne's 12th house, pointing once again to the value of teamwork. Because this is the 12th house, however, Paul can nurture Joanne from behind the scenes. In other words, Paul won't interfere with Joanne's desire to do her own thing, or her need for privacy from the public.

Joanne's Saturn is in Capricorn, which falls in Paul's 12th house. Can you believe this? What an amazing connection! (And we'll be talking more about 12th house Soulmate connections in a few pages.) This means that Joanne in turn can nurture Paul from behind the scenes. Remember the old saying that there is a "strong woman behind every successful man"? It certainly applies here—but so does the other side, that there is a strong man behind every successful woman!

As we know, these two have long been a team who know how to lean on each other's strengths to cover for each other's weaknesses. Their birth charts merely confirm what they learned about each other a long time ago! All we can say is "Wow! A Saturn Soulmate connection written in the stars!"

Your Saturn ♄ Lessons

For the following exercise, first determine both your and your partner's Saturn lessons. Ideally, perform this exercise together, in the same room at the same time; if that's not possible, be sure to write down your responses so that you compare notes later.

Tarot's Emperor represents traditional Saturn ♄ values as embodied in the father figure. The Empress represents the mother figure who helps you with these lessons.

Begin by removing the Emperor and the Empress from your Tarot deck. Like Saturn is in Astrology, the Emperor is the father figure of the Tarot. All of these aspects of the father are embodied in the imagery of the Emperor card of the Tarot. The Empress card embodies all the aspects of the mother figure in its imagery, and helps you to deal with the karmic Saturn ♄ lessons the Emperor represents. Contemplate the images of the Emperor and the Empress, considering the Saturn ♄ lessons your birth chart has suggested you need to learn in this lifetime. You might want to ask some of these questions of each card:

- What does the Emperor represent to me about my Saturn lessons in this life?
- How do I feel about these lessons? Am I resistant? Do I feel I've already learned them?
- Who are some of the people who have appeared in my life to teach me these lessons? How do I feel about them? Have I learned from them?
- How might the Empress help me learn this lesson? Do I pay attention to her when she speaks to me? Comforts me?

As you contemplate the Emperor and the Empress and consider these questions, you may want to make some notes about your meditation on them. Feel free to return to these cards again whenever your Saturn ♄ lessons come into your life.

North Meets South (Node, That Is)

The Nodes of the Moon, points that relate to the Moon's orbit around the Earth, can be important keys to Soulmate connections as well. That's because they represent your past and your future—both in this life and in future ones. Taken together, they can reveal what will be easy for you in this life, and the challenges you will need to meet in order to grow.

Your South Node ☋ reveals the lessons you learned in your past lives, whether they're skills, talents, or dealing with certain types of people. You'll be drawn to people and situations that reflect your South Node because the South Node represents your comfort zone. Its lessons still apply, but you've incorporated them into your life already.

Your North Node ☊ indicates karmic lessons that you haven't mastered. Going your North Node route isn't easy, as following your South Node path is, but if you choose to accept its challenges, you'll find everything from self-fulfillment to rewards from the world around you.

When we look at the Nodes astrologically, we always look at them together, because they appear in opposition to each other in your birth chart. The reason for this is that once you've mastered one side of the coin, your challenge will lie on the other side. Your Soulmate can either help you or hinder you in your Nodal lessons, so it's important to consider the role they play here as well.

Let's look first at the Nodal pairs' signs. Your Soulmate will often connect to your challenges here. For example, if your challenge is to learn to be independent, your Soulmate may be independent him- or herself, or may conversely challenge your independent urges.

If your **North Node ☊** is **in Aries ♈** and your **South Node ☋** is **in Libra ♎**, then you've learned about cooperation. Your challenge is to learn to be independent.

If your **North Node ☊** is **in Taurus ♉** and your **South Node ☋** is **in Scorpio ♏**, then you've learned about power. Your challenge is to learn about material values.

If your **North Node ☊** is **in Gemini ♊** and your **South Node ☋** is **in Sagittarius ♐**, then you've learned about freedom. Your challenge is to learn new communication skills.

If your **North Node ☊** is **in Cancer ♋** and your **South Node ☋** is **in Capricorn ♑**, then you've learned about responsibility. Your challenge is to learn to share your emotions.

If your **North Node ☊** is **in Leo ♌** and your **South Node ☋** is **in Aquarius ♒**, then you've learned the value of detachment. Your challenge is to learn about generosity.

If your **North Node ☊** is **in Virgo ♍** and your **South Node ☋** is **in Pisces ♓**, then you've learned to be compassionate. Your challenge is to learn to be practical.

If your **North Node ☊** is **in Libra ♎** and your **South Node ☋** is **in Aries ♈**, then you've learned to lead. Your challenge is to learn to cooperate.

If your **North Node ☊** is **in Scorpio ♏** and your **South Node ☋** is **in Taurus ♉**, then you've learned about material values. Your challenge is to learn about power.

If your **North Node ☊** is **in Sagittarius ♐** and your **South Node ☋** is **in Gemini ♊**, then you've learned how to communicate with others. Your challenge is to seek the truth.

If your **North Node ☊** is **in Capricorn ♑** and your **South Node ☋** is **in Cancer ♋**, then you've learned about nurturing. Your challenge is to learn to be responsible.

If your **North Node ☊** is **in Aquarius ♒** and your **South Node ☋** is **in Leo ♌**, then you've learned how to be generous to those you care about. Your challenge is to learn to be generous to all.

If your **North Node ☊** is **in Pisces ♓** and your **South Node ☋** is **in Virgo ♍**, then you've learned to be practical. Your challenge is to learn to be understanding.

Next we look at what the Nodal pairs mean in each of the astrological houses. Here is where you can find where your Soulmates can help you achieve your karmic challenges, by presenting you with opportunities for developing your karmic challenges in the houses. So, for example, if your karmic challenge is a 1st house North Node ☊ need to develop leadership, your Soulmate will provide an environment that allows you to do so.

If your **North Node ☊** is **in the 1st house** and your **South Node ☋** is **in the 7th house,** then you need to develop your leadership skills. Chances are, you're happiest fading into the background, but if you wish to grow, your Soulmate can help you step out of the shadows and take the reins.

If your **North Node ☊** is **in the 2nd house** and your **South Node ☋** is **in the 8th house,** then you need to establish values of your own. Chances are, you've learned how to go with the flow and assume others' values as your own, but if you wish to grow, your Soulmate can help you decide where your own beliefs lie.

If your **North Node ☊** is **in the 3rd house** and your **South Node ☋** is **in the 9th house,** then you need to learn more about communication skills. Chances are, you've mastered the "learn it and go" approach, but to grow, your Soulmate can help you learn to stick around for the long haul.

If your **North Node ☊** is **in the 4th house** and your **South Node ☋** is **in the 10th house,** then you need to learn to build a solid foundation. Chances are, you know how to make leaps of faith, but to grow, your Soulmate can help you learn how to establish a safety net.

If your **North Node ☊** is **in the 5th house** and your **South Node ☋** is **in the 11th house,** then you need to learn how to establish goals and follow through on them. Chances are, you know all about having your head in the clouds, but for you to grow, your Soulmate can help you learn how to follow through on your dreams.

If your **North Node ☊** is **in the 6th house** and your **South Node ☋** is **in the 12th house,** then you need to learn to trust other people. Chances are, you're most comfortable in your own world, but if you wish to grow, your Soulmate can help you learn the pleasures of being with others as well.

If your **North Node ☊** is **in the 7th house** and your **South Node ☋** is **in the 1st house,** then you need to learn to cooperate. Chances are, you know about individuality and self-expression, but to grow, your Soulmate can help you understand the value of sharing and caring as well.

If your **North Node ☊** is **in the 8th house** and your **South Node ☋** is **in the 2nd house,** then you need to learn about global values. Chances are, you know all about your own value system, but to grow, your Soulmate can help you learn how to share what you know with humankind.

If your **North Node ☊** is **in the 9th house** and your **South Node ☋** is **in the 3rd house,** then you need to learn to move beyond details to the big picture. Chances are, you know lots of people's stories—as well as the petty details of their day-to-day lives—but if you wish to grow, your Soulmate can help you look beyond your own insular world to expand your horizons.

If your **North Node ☊** is **in the 10th house** and your **South Node ☋** is **in the 4th house,** then you need to establish a career. Chances are, your family provides an easy diversion from this outside role, but for you to grow, your Soulmate can help you move away from personal responsibilities toward a rewarding life outside the home.

If your **North Node ☊** is **in the 11th house** and your **South Node ☋** is **in the 5th house,** then you need to learn objectivity and acceptance of others. Chances are, you're proud of your own creativity, but to grow, your Soulmate can help you see that others have a lot to offer as well.

If your **North Node ☊** is **in the 12th house** and your **South Node ☋** is **in the 6th house,** then you need to learn to get in touch with your higher self. Chances are, you know all about self-sacrifice, but if you wish to grow, your Soulmate can help you move beyond codependence and toward transformational understanding.

Now, when we look at Joanne Woodward's and Paul Newman's Nodal positions, we get the essence of what they are learning from each other. We note that Joanne's North Node ☊ is in Taurus ♉ and that her South Node ☋ is in Scorpio ♏. This suggests that Joanne already knows about power and self-empowerment. What she needs to learn about is the material world—finding her self-worth and how to be valued. Her Soulmate can help her move beyond any of her self-doubts by supporting the houses they fall in. Her Nodes come from the 12th house of higher self/private self to her 6th house of work and service, so Paul can support her work and the service she would like to do for the public or her career.

Paul's North Node ☊ is in Leo ♌ and his South Node ☋ is in Aquarius ♒, which reveals that Paul already knows about independence and detachment. What he needs to learn about is leadership within a partnership: North Node ☊ in the 7th house. Because the 7th house rules both types of partners (business and marriage), Joanne's support through their mutual business ventures also can support Paul's development in that arena. Both of these Nodal relationships show clear Soulmate connections. We're not even surprised anymore!

Now let's try the same thing for Jennifer Aniston and Brad Pitt. Note that Jennifer and Brad's charts are noon birth charts. We won't go into the in-depth analysis we did for Joanne Woodward and Paul Newman, however. Instead, use these charts to see what *you* can discover about this pair.

To get you started, we'll locate Jennifer and Brad's North ☊ and South ☋ Nodes.

Jennifer Aniston

North Node ☊		**South Node ☋**	
Astro Sign	*Astro House*	*Astro Sign*	*Astro House*
Aries ♈	11th	Libra ♎	5th

Brad Pitt

North Node ☊		**South Node ☋**	
Astro Sign	*Astro House*	*Astro Sign*	*Astro House*
Cancer ♋	4th	Capricorn ♑	10th

Now, using this Nodal information, discover what Jennifer's and Brad's Nodal pairings suggest they already know and need to learn. How can these two help each other? Can you see their Soulmate connections?

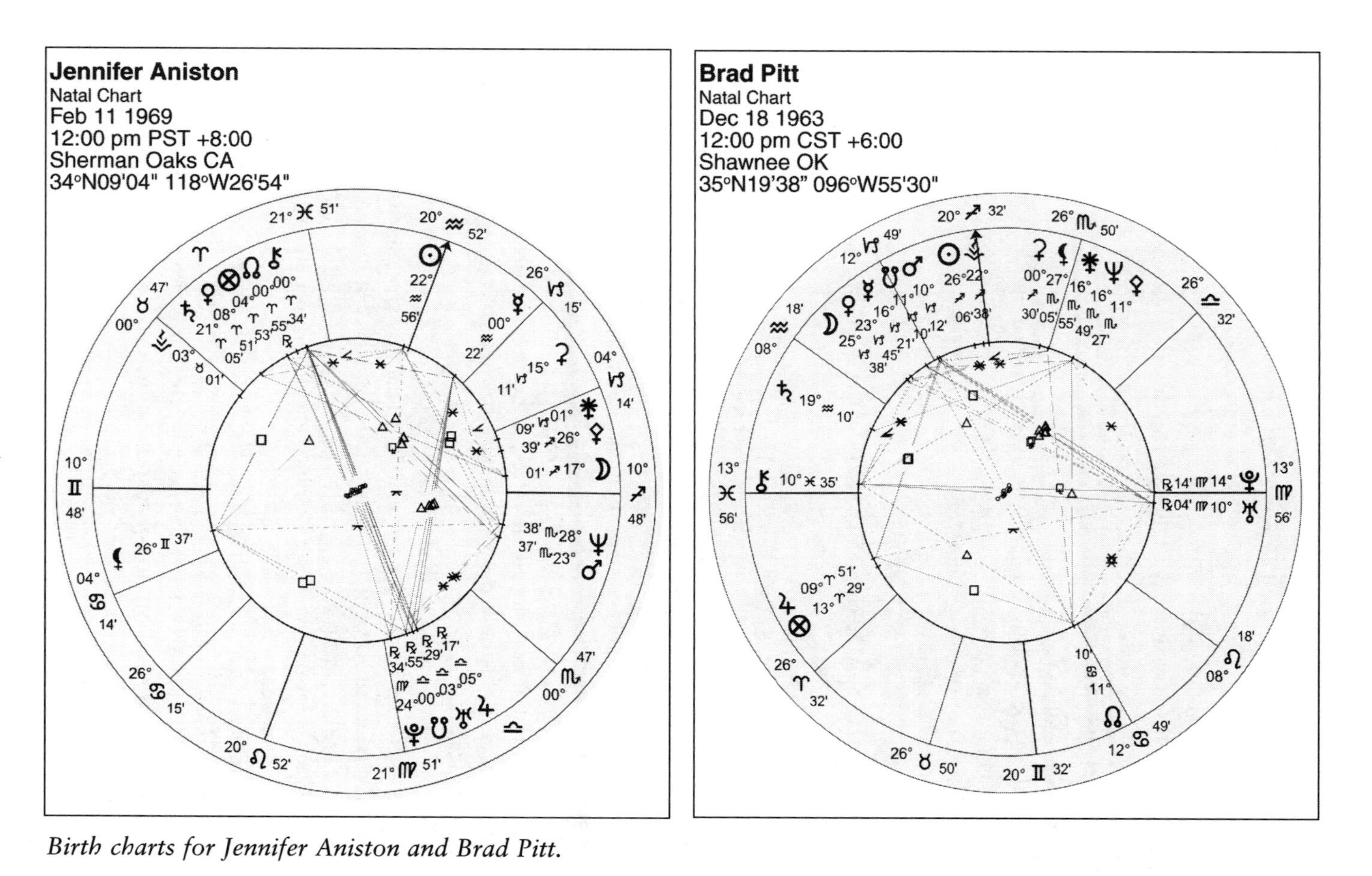

Birth charts for Jennifer Aniston and Brad Pitt.

You can discover your own Nodal couple karma lessons by following these simple steps. Follow these steps slowly, for one partner at a time, to make certain that you get it right:

1. Find your Nodal signs.
2. Note the lesson and challenge for this pairing.
3. Note how your Soulmate(s) can help you meet your Nodal astrological sign challenge.
4. Find your Nodal houses.
5. Note the lesson and challenge for this pairing.
6. Note how your Soulmate(s) can help you meet your Nodal astrological house challenge.

When the Moon (and Other Planets) Are in the 12th House

The 12th house is the most misunderstood of the astrological houses, and a lot of this has to do with old-fashioned male/female dichotomies. You know—the ones that go "men are logical, women are emotional." As we discussed in Chapter 2 when we looked at *yin* and *yang*, this foolish male/female stereotype no longer has a place of value in our world. So rather than say your 12th house is where you'll find your "irrational" or "chaotic" side, we like to say your 12th house is where you'll find your unconscious, your connection to your higher self—and your past-life connections. This latter, of course, means that your 12th house can also help you discover where to find your Soulmate, if you haven't already.

The first thing to consider when looking at your 12th house for past-life information is its ruler. Every house has a planet (or planets) that is considered to be its natural ruler—the 12th house's rulers, for example, are Neptune ♆ and Jupiter ♃. Depending on where the planets were when you were born, it's likely a different planet will rule your 12th house.

The ruler of your 12th house is the planet associated with the sign on the 12th house cusp in your birth chart. If you look at Paul Newman's birth chart earlier in this chapter, for example, you will see that the sign on his 12th house cusp is Sagittarius ♐. The planetary ruler of Sagittarius ♐ is Jupiter ♃, so this is the planet that rules Paul Newman's 12th house.

What does this mean about Paul? First of all, he will seek to fulfill his unconscious desires with optimism and confidence (Jupiter ♃). At the same time, to learn his karmic lessons, he will seek out others who can help him learn optimism and confidence. He will unconsciously connect to others who have an "affinity with his past," meaning people with like souls or like energies.

Our Soulmates will be people who will be particularly good at fulfilling our 12th house needs, and the planetary ruler represents the types of people or conditions; so, because it's Jupiter here, Paul will seek out positive and affirming people—those who are pretty darn supportive of him. He is lucky in this life to have the optimistic and positive sign ruling his 12th house. It means that he will naturally attract luck in this life, and luck is part of his lesson on earth this time around.

To discover how a partner fits your unconscious (12th house) Soulmate desire, look for the archetype of the planet that rules your 12th house. Paul, for example, will attract Soulmates who are of Jupiter's archetype: beneficial.

Let's try this in reverse, looking at Joanne's 12th house ruler. The sign on her 12th house cusp is Scorpio ♏, which is ruled by Pluto ♇ and Mars ♂. This means that Joanne will seek to fulfill her unconscious desires through transformation (Pluto ♇) and decisive action (Mars ♂). At the same time, to learn her karmic lessons, she will seek out others who can help her learn how to transform and be decisive.

In Joanne's chart, we find both Pluto ♇ and Mars ♂ rulership. Joanne will unconsciously attract others who will transform her and "push" her into growing. The types of people or conditions that Pluto and Mars rule are aggressive, motivational, and deeply intense creative types. So in this life, Joanne will attract people to "push her envelope," so to speak: Dramatic growth and personal transformation will be what she needs to learn.

In addition to the 12th house ruler, we look to see whether there are any planets within the 12th house. Paul Newman's Jupiter ♃ is here—reinforcing his karmic lesson of optimism and confidence. And so is Joanne Woodward's South Node ☋—reinforcing her karmic lesson of learning to trust others. The 12th house is one of mystery for any astrologer, beginner or professional! One thing is certain, however: This is the house of deep bonds and obligations. All of us have a 12th house to consider, and yours is likely asking questions like these: What are my obligations in this life? And how can a Soulmate support or connect me to those lessons? Pay attention to your 12th house and you can learn your karmic lessons well.

Tracking Soulmate connections through your own 12th house should be done slowly and carefully, one step at a time. The following steps are the ones we took to discover the Soulmate connections for Joanne Woodward and Paul Newman. To chart your own Soulmate connections, follow these same steps:

1. Find the planet(s) that rules your 12th house.
2. Note that planetary ruler's archetype.
3. Note how your Soulmate can help you achieve that archetype.
4. Look for planets within the 12th house.
5. Note how your Soulmate reinforces these 12th house karmic lessons.

Karmic Warning Signs

Sometimes Soulmate relationships present karmic challenges that produce the wrong kind of sparks. If you've ever been in a relationship where your partner sometimes did things that frightened you, you may well know the kind of push/pull codependency we're talking about. In addition to day-to-day warning signs, you can use the Intuitive Arts to guide you toward determining whether this is a karmic issue, and if so, what you can do about it.

If you are in a dangerous situation, however, *the most important thing you can do is get appropriate help now.* Every locality has agencies to help you, from your local police force to social service agencies and shelters for victims of domestic violence or rehab clinics for substance abusers. *No one should remain in an abusive relationship.*

Perhaps the sparks in your relationship are not putting you or your partner in danger, per se, but you realize that you are never joyous together, or to quote a cliché, you and your partner find yourselves "holding on to the sunny hours to forget the rainy days." If your experience of the love relationship diminishes or impoverishes you as a couple rather than nurtures you and your partner with a synergy that makes you both together a unique and positive pair, the reasons may have karmic import.

Pay attention to your Psychic Intuition. Has your charming and generous partner ever suddenly transformed, leaving you to wonder if you're in love with Dr. Jekyll and Mr. or Ms. Hyde? What was your gut reaction when this happened? Do you get the same feeling every time it happens? Do you find that you don't like yourself when you are with your partner, that you find yourself behaving in uncharacteristic ways? Your intuition can be one of your best barometers for your own truth. Both women and men need to pay attention to what their sixth sense is trying to tell them.

If your answer to any of these questions is yes, your Psychic Intuition is screaming for you to pay attention. If you can, try to recall the exact way you felt during intense episodes with your partner. Here are some questions that may help you:

- How did I feel physically during the episode? Did my heart beat faster and my pulse race?
- What was I thinking? Did I think I'd done something, or did I wonder what had made my partner act the way he or she did?
- Did I like or respect myself and my actions? Did I like or respect my partner?
- How did I respond? Did I choose to be quiet or did I respond with strong emotions or actions of my own?
- After the episode was over, what were my feelings? Did I want to leave? Did I feel overwhelming love for my partner, despite whatever happened?
- Did I act on my feelings?
- If I didn't act on them, why didn't I?

The last question in particular is a definite karmic warning sign. If you and your partner seem to have such collisions again and again, and you do nothing to act on your feelings, you need to consider whether you're headed for karmic disaster. Ask your intuition for guidance. Pay attention. And then follow through, by contacting a professional counselor who can help you and your partner sort out your karmic challenges and make positive changes for yourselves and your love relationship.

If you're feeling that "intuitive nudge," but don't feel it's necessary to contact a professional counselor, you can ask the Tarot for guidance. If you're having trouble figuring out how you might end this relationship, for example, you could use a Mission Spread to ask how best to do so. Or you could try a Celtic Cross to tell a story of the relationship, asking for its potential outcome. You could also ask the Tarot, "What do I need to know about my relationship as it stands?"

Finally, you can look at your astrological birth charts to see whether there are karmic warning signs. Some potential areas of conflict include:

- ☯ One's Mars conjunct the other's Moon ♂☌☽
- ☯ One or the other's Mars ♂ and Pluto ♇ are conjunct ☌ in the 8th house, or make challenging aspects such as squares □ or oppositions ☍ to the other's Mars or Pluto
- ☯ One's South Node conjunct the other's Pluto ☋☌♇ or Mars ☋☌♂
- ☯ One's Saturn square the other's Venus, Sun, or Moon ♄□♀☉☽
- ☯ Either one's Aries ♈ or Scorpio ♏ in the 4th, 8th, or 12th houses
- ☯ Either one's Uranus ♅ in the 1st, 4th, 7th, or 10th houses

Astrologers have long noted that these aspects between the planets of two people's charts can be very difficult when it comes to love. Mars ♂, Saturn ♄, Pluto ♇, and the South Node ☋ are considered by astrologers to be the most difficult karmic points. When these particular planets or points are aspected by squares □ or oppositions ☍ between the two charts, there is always some kind of loss attached. This means that karmic meaning is destined to come into the relationship—even if it is not apparent at the relationship's beginning.

When we look at Jennifer Aniston's and Brad Pitt's synastry grid, we note two major aspects that may prove difficult for the relationship over time. First, Jennifer's Aries ♈ Saturn ♄ is square □ Brad's Capricorn ♑ Venus ♀. Aries Saturn may fear that Capricorn Venus will not fulfill his responsibilities to the relationship. Over time, her suspicion and doubt may lead to mistrust, which may in turn make him want to escape or otherwise compromise their relationship.

In addition, Brad's Aquarius ♒ Saturn ♄ squares □ Jennifer's Scorpio ♏ Mars ♂. Aquarius Saturn can irritate, unsettle, and create strong insecurities in Scorpio Mars, leading to problems similar to those just outlined. How these aspects turn out for this pair—as jealousy between careers or abuse and mistrust in the home—could make for overwhelming challenges if they don't adjust. Being aware that these conflict points exist, however, can help them understand and overcome them. Karmic challenges can offer potential relationship problems, but they can also offer couples powerful opportunities to grow themselves and the relationship.

Across
Jennifer Aniston
Natal Chart
Feb 11 1969
12:00 pm PST +8:00
Sherman Oaks CA
34°N09'04" 118°W26'54"

Down
Brad Pitt
Natal Chart
Dec 18 1963
12:00 pm CST +6:00
Shawnee OK
35°N19'38" 096°W55'30"

	☽	☉	☿	♀	♂	♃	♄	♅	♆	♇	⚷	⚶	⚴	⚵	⚳	☊	☋	As	Mc	⊗	⚸
☽			☌ 4A44		⚹ 2S01	△ 9A38	□ 4S33	△ 7A50	⚹ 2A59	△ 1S05	⚹ 4A56					⚹ 5A17	△ 5A17	⚼ 0A10			⚻ 0A59
☉		⚹ 3S10					△ 5S00			□ 1S32	□ 4A29	△ 6A55	☌ 0A33	☌ 5A03		□ 4A50	□ 4A50		⚹ 5S14		☍ 0A32
☿							□ 4A45								☌ 1S09						
♀			☌ 6A37		⚹ 0S08		□ 2S40		⚹ 4A52	△ 0A49							△ 7A10	⚼ 2A03			
♂				□ 1S21		□ 4S56						△ 7S11			☌ 4A59			⚻ 0A36			
♃	△ 7A10	∠ 1S55		☌ 1S00	⚼ 1S13	☍ 4S34									□ 5A20			⚹ 0A57		☌ 4S57	
♄	⚹ 2S09	☌ 3A46			□ 4A28	⚼ 1A07	⚹ 1A55	⚼ 0S41											☌ 1A42	∠ 0A43	△ 7A28
♅				⚻ 1A13								△ 7A03			△ 5S07			□ 0S44			
♆		□ 6A07			☌ 6A49			∠ 1A40			⚼ 1S14			∠ 0S40	⚹ 1S37	⚼ 0S53	∠ 0S53		□ 4A03		
♇	□ 2S47		⚼ 1S08												△ 0S57			□ 3A26			
⚷	□ 6A26														⚹ 4A36			□ 0A13			
⚶	☌ 5S37	⚹ 0A18					△ 1S33			□ 1A56			☌ 4A01	☌ 8A31					⚹ 1S46		☍ 3A59
⚴													∠ 0A12		⚹ 3A44			⚻ 0S39			⚼ 0A10
⚵		□ 6A01			☌ 6A42			∠ 1A34			⚼ 1S21			∠ 0S46	⚹ 1S44	⚼ 1S00	∠ 1S00		□ 3A57		
⚳			⚹ 0S08		☌ 6S53	⚹ 4A46		⚹ 2A59	☌ 1S52		△ 0A04				∠ 0S19	△ 0A25	⚹ 0A25			△ 4A23	
☊				□ 2S19					⚼ 2A28						☍ 4A01						
☋				□ 2S19					∠ 2A28						☌ 4A01			⚻ 0S22			
As	□ 3A05		∠ 1A26												⚹ 1A15			□ 3A08			
Mc	☌ 3A31	⚹ 2A24					△ 0A33			□ 4A01			☌ 6A06						⚹ 0A19		☍ 6A05
⊗	△ 3A32			☌ 4A38			☌ 7A36		⚼ 0A09						□ 1A42			⚹ 2A41		☌ 8A36	
⚸		□ 4S09	⚹ 3A17		☌ 3S28				☌ 1A33	⚹ 2S31	△ 3A29					△ 3A50	⚹ 3A50			△ 7A48	⚻ 0S28

Synastry grid for Jennifer Aniston and Brad Pitt. Jennifer: Across. Brad: Down.

A Love for All Eternity

By now you know that the course of eternal love is sometimes no smoother than the course of love over one lifetime. Still, you can use the Intuitive Arts to help you understand why the road is rocky—and how you can learn to handle the bumps.

For this exercise, go through your Tarot deck, one card at a time, thinking about your relationship with your Soulmate. Every time a card seems to speak to your love relationship in some way, set it aside. Do this until you have gone through all 78 Tarot cards.

You may have 2 cards set aside; you may have 20. You may even have 78—although that's rather unlikely. If you have more than 10 cards, go through them again, thinking about a more specific issue you and your Soulmate have.

After you've found the cards that speak to your relationship, lay them out in front of you. Move them around until you feel they're arranged in a way that feels "right" to you.

Then "read" the cards as if they have a story to tell you. They *do* have a story to tell you, and it's a story you already know on a "gut" Psychic Intuition level. Write down the story the cards tell you about your Soulmate relationship, and reread what you've written. Consider what this story has to tell you about both your and your Soulmate's approach to eternal love, and what each of you can do to make the road smoother.

There is no road without those bumps, and even Soulmate relationships offer challenges along with the joys. But learning to negotiate the rough parts makes the ride more than worthwhile—life after life after life!

chapter 9

Create Your Love Portrait

An Intuitive Arts love portrait of *you*
A love-ly day
Transits: Knowing your challenges
Progressions mean progress
Make an astrological event chart—and check it twice
Your personal love profile
The best of your love

It's time to put together everything you've learned throughout this book to create a portrait of your own Intuitive Arts style of love. From visualizing a love-ly day to knowing your challenges, understanding yourself is the first step toward that intuitive love relationship with a special someone. In this chapter, we explore how astrological transits and progressions can reveal how the ways you change through the years can be opportunities for further growth together, as well as on your own. We introduce you to event charts and show you how you can pick a moment in time for that special celebration you want to remember forever. And finally, we show you how to put it all together, creating a personal love profile that will help you understand both yourself and your honey—and the kind of love you can make together. Whether you're already in a committed partnership or still dreaming about the person you'll spend your life with, using the Intuitive Arts of Astrology, the Tarot, and Psychic Intuition will help you discover how to get—and give—the best of your love.

An Intuitive Arts Love Portrait of You

As you've learned, love is everywhere in your astrological birth chart, beginning with your Sun sign, which reveals the uniqueness of *you.*

We begin this chapter with an exercise that combines Astrology, the Tarot, and your Psychic Intuition to create a visual portrait of your unique love style.

Begin with your astrological birth chart. List the sign for each of your planets, asteroids, and rising sign in the following table.

Planet	Astro Sign
Sun ☉	______________
Moon ☽	______________
Mercury ☿	______________
Venus ♀	______________
Mars ♂	______________
Jupiter ♃	______________
Saturn ♄	______________
Uranus ♅	______________
Neptune ♆	______________
Pluto ♇	______________
North Node ☊	______________
South Node ☋	______________
Ascendant	______________
Ceres ⚳	______________
Juno ⚵	______________
Pallas Athene ⚴	______________
Vesta ⚶	______________
Chiron ⚷	______________

After you've completed this list, the fun begins! Get out your Tarot deck and place it face up, so you can see the Tarot card images. Beginning with your Sun ☉ sign, say aloud the words, "My Sun sign card." As you repeat these words, go through your Tarot deck. You will be seeking a card that represents the Sun sign part of you. As you look at the pictures on the cards, don't think about which card you might select; rather, use the words as a sort of mantra, so that your Psychic Intuition will pick the card. When you've selected a card, write it down in the following table and then lay it face up on a flat surface.

One at a time, do the same for each of your other planets' signs. Take your time, but don't "think" about your choices. Just go through your Tarot deck saying the words "my Moon sign card," or "my Vesta card" as you work your way through the cards. If two cards seem to resonate for you when it comes to a particular planet, go ahead and lay them out together.

After you've selected a card for each of your planets, list each of these cards here (so that if you decide you want to revisit this portrait at a later time, you'll have a record of the cards you selected).

Heavenly Body	Tarot Card
Sun ☉ sign card	______________
Moon ☽ sign card	______________
Mercury ☿ sign card	______________
Venus ♀ sign card	______________
Mars ♂ sign card	______________
Jupiter ♃ sign card	______________
Saturn ♄ sign card	______________
Uranus ♅ sign card	______________
Neptune ♆ sign card	______________
Pluto ♇ sign card	______________
North Node ☊ sign card	______________
South Node ☋ sign card	______________
Ascendant sign card	______________
Ceres ⚳ sign card	______________
Juno ⚵ sign card	______________
Pallas Athene ⚴ sign card	______________
Vesta ⚶ sign card	______________
Chiron ⚷ sign card	______________

Now comes more fun! Using your birth chart as a guide, lay out your cards to represent where each of the planets lies in your birth chart. If you've got a "full house," as Lisa does, you'll want to come up with a way of overlapping the cards. You can even go to your local copy shop and have your birth chart photocopied to poster size, so you can literally lay the Tarot cards on the symbol for each planet. Once you've created your visual love portrait, laying the Tarot cards in the places where their corresponding planets appear on your birth chart, take some time to study it, making whatever notes you'd like in your journal. Chances are, you'll want to return to this intuitive portrait often—we know we will! We thought you might be interested in our "portraits," so here are the ones we created for ourselves:

Arlene's Intuitive Arts Love Portrait

Heavenly Body	Tarot Card
Sun ☉ sign card	6 of Cups
Moon ☽ sign card	4 of Cups
Mercury ☿ sign card	The Star
Venus ♀ sign card	Ace of Swords
Mars ♂ sign card	7 of Cups R
Jupiter ♃ sign card	Strength
Saturn ♄ sign card	3 of Swords R
Uranus ♅ sign card	3 of Cups
Neptune ♆ sign card	The World
Pluto ♇ sign card	Temperance
North Node ☊ sign card	10 of Cups
South Node ☋ sign card	2 of Wands
Ascendant sign card	Queen of Pentacles
Ceres ⚳ sign card	Queen of Wands
Juno ⚵ sign card	6 of Wands
Pallas Athene ⚴ sign card	The Magician
Vesta ⚶ sign card	2 of Swords R
Chiron ⚷ sign card	Page of Pentacles

When Arlene pulled out her cards and put them in their corresponding places on her birth chart, she knew she had picked not only herself, but how she sees love! She immediately looked toward the houses where her Sun ☉ and Moon ☽ are. The 6 of Cups, which she selected to represent her 12th house Sun ☉ sign, describes the nature of her love: She wants to share and be a friend to her loved ones. Arlene selected the 4 of Cups to represent her 3rd house Moon ☽. This card describes exactly how she "feels" about romance: sometimes detached and sometimes withdrawn. What she really prefers is a partner who loves to speak his feelings.

For her Mercury ☿ card, Arlene selected the Star to show how she communicates her love: She is always hopeful and optimistic (or at least she communicates that way!). Mercury falls in Arlene's 11th House, so a friend can become the love interest. Her Moon in the 3rd House and the mental planet Mercury in the 11th draw Arlene's romantic signature to the heart and mind. She always tries to think positively about love and understanding human nature.

Arlene's need for love, the Venus ♀ card, is the strong Ace of Swords, because Arlene needs a strong partner who can match her both mentally and intellectually. In her chart, Venus falls in her 10th house of Career, so might she find her mate through her work, too. Her Mars ♂ card, the 7 of Cups in its reversed position, says that Arlene is focused on the type of energy she needs from herself and others. Mars is in Arlene's 8th house of intuition. This suggests that she has her "knowing" about what chemistry is important in a relationship.

All these cards truly describe who Arlene is and what she needs in a love relationship! Arlene's reaction to trying this exercise: "*Wow,* it is pretty revealing!" The most interesting part of this exercise is that when you do it, you really start going within and contemplating your own needs.

Lisa's Intuitive Arts Love Portrait

Heavenly Body	Tarot Card
Sun ☉ sign card	Queen of Cups
Moon ☽ sign card	The Moon
Mercury ☿ sign card	The Hermit
Venus ♀ sign card	The Empress
Mars ♂ sign card	The High Priestess
Jupiter ♃ sign card	9 of Pentacles
Saturn ♄ sign card	7 of Cups
Uranus ♅ sign card	The Fool
Neptune ♆ sign card	Temperance

Lisa's Intuitive Arts Love Portrait (continued)

Heavenly Body	Tarot Card
Pluto ♇ sign card	The Chariot
North Node ☊ sign card	The Magician
South Node ☋ sign card	Queen of Wands
Ascendant sign card	Strength
Ceres ⚳ sign card	Queen of Pentacles
Juno ⚵ sign card	Hierophant R
Pallas Athene ⚴ sign card	Justice
Vesta ⚶ sign card	Queen of Swords
Chiron ⚷ sign card	2 of Swords

The love portrait that emerged when Lisa laid her cards out to represent her horoscope wheel was no surprise to her: While her many 12th house planets in Cancer ♋ make her an empathetic lover—these planets are represented by the Queen of Cups, the Moon, the Hermit, the Empress, and the Fool in her "portrait"—they are all opposed by her 6th house Chiron ⚷ in Capricorn ♑, the 2 of Swords, which makes her fearful as well. Still, her Leo ♌ ascendant, Strength, gives her fortitude and optimism, both of which are helpful considering her unconventional North Node ☊, the Magician, and Juno ⚵, the Hierophant R, which reflect her rather unconventional marriage. Lisa felt her love portrait was very revealing, and she made far more notes than she has room to share with you here!

If you enjoy doing this exercise for yourself, you will likely want to try it for your partner as well. Or you may want to ask your partner to do it with you, and then lay out your love portraits side by side. If you lay the Tarot cards on a poster-size photocopy of your birth charts, you can tape the cards to the chart and hang your portraits on the wall for further meditation. Or take a photo of each portrait, so you can return to it any time you'd like.

The cards you select to paint your portrait may change over time, even though the planets' signs remain the same. This is because all of us grow throughout our lives, so it's only natural that our perceptions about what our signs mean will change as we do. You may, for example, view your Capricorn ♑ Sun ☉ as the Devil when you are young, especially if you're obsessive about planning things out. As you age, however, you may find that same Sun more Temperance-like, offering a much-needed balance between your emotional and practical sides.

How you view your planet's signs will likely change over the years.

A Love-ly Day

Now that you've got an Intuitive Arts portrait of your love, it's time to consider your love goals. For this exercise, once again get out your Tarot deck, although you won't need it right away. For the first part of this exercise, you need nothing more than a quiet place to spend some time in meditation.

1. Get yourself comfortable, and then either close your eyes or look at something that relaxes you, such as a nice view out a window or something pleasing in the room you are in. Once you're relaxed, picture your perfect day with someone you love.
2. Begin picturing your perfect day at the point when you wake up. Where are you? In your own bed? Somewhere exotic? Another city, not your own? What time is it? How did you awaken?
3. Is there someone there with you? If so, is it someone you already know? Is he or she awake? If not, do you plan to wake your lover up? If so, how?
4. Picture yourself getting up. What can you see out your window? What's the weather like? Do you have plans for this perfect day? If so, what are they? Or do you, delightfully, have no plans whatsoever?
5. What happens once you're out of bed? Where do you go? What do you do? With whom do you do it? If there wasn't someone else in the bed with you last night, when and how do you two connect today?
6. Proceed step by step in this way, all the way through your perfect love day. The last thing you'll do at the end of the day is go

back to bed, whether it's nighttime or early morning that ends your perfect day. Be sure to note if your lover goes to bed with you, or if you choose to end your perfect day alone.

7. After you've finished creating this day step by step, go back over some of the details in your mind, refining them or changing them until you just know they're perfect. Only then should you get your journal and make some notes to record your perfect love day. You need your written notes to continue this exercise, so be sure to keep them!

For the next step of this exercise, find a Tarot card to represent each moment of your perfect day. Begin by retrieving the journal notes you created from your perfect love day meditation. Revisualize each moment as you read through your notes once, and then, reading through them again, on a new page, write down a few words that represent that moment.

When you've finished making notes for each moment, you're ready to begin the Tarot card part of this exercise. Begin with the first moment of your perfect day. Visualizing that moment, go through your Tarot deck looking at the card images until you come to a card that perfectly represents it. You may find more than one card on your first pass through the deck; if that's the case, consider the cards you've selected until you find the *one* card that most perfectly describes that moment.

Go through your Tarot deck for each moment in your perfect day until you have one card to represent each moment. Now line these cards up however you'd like to represent that day. You may decide on a simple linear left-to-right alignment, or you may decide one of the Tarot spreads we've presented in this book is more apt. You may even choose a circular layout so that your perfect day will never end!

Once you've laid out the images of your perfect love day, consider their progression as if they were a story, which, of course, they are: They're *your* story! Be sure to make a note of the cards you select for each moment. We've provided some space for you to do just that.

The Story of Your Perfect Love Day

____

____

____

____

Transits: Knowing Your Challenges

As you've learned throughout this book, challenges come to us in many forms. There are the personal challenges of our own squares □ and oppositions ☍, and Nodal ☊☋, Saturn ♄, and 12th house lessons; and the challenges we face with others, including our *yin/yang* complementarity, our Romantic Signature, how we aspect each other in our relationship analysis, and our asteroid signatures. In addition, challenges come to us from outside our love life. Being aware of our personal astrological transits can prepare us for when these challenges are likely to occur in our lives, so we can be better equipped to meet them.

Every day planets move through their Zodiacal sky. Transits are where the planets are now, in the present tense, today and every day. Showing planetary transits for a specific day helps an astrologer compare how the planets' positions are for that day. Astrologers like to think of transits as trigger points, because they often take the form of events, external circumstances, or other outside influences.

The transits that most intrigue astrologers are the outer planet cycles, which take longer to develop and so have far more powerful impacts than the quick returns of the luminaries and inner planets. We explored Pluto square Pluto ♇□♇ in Chapter 6. Here we focus on how particular planetary challenges can affect your love life.

When a Pluto ♇ transit aspects one of your planets, your challenge will be to transform the area of your life that planet affects.

Pluto ♇ = Transformation. Like the Tower card of the Tarot, Pluto transits bring enormous change. Whether you resist the demands of a Pluto transit or choose to accept that some of your old behaviors must go will make a big difference in how you negotiate these periods in your life. Many relationships that seemed to have been going along just fine come to a sudden crisis point during one or the other partner's Pluto transit, so knowing when yours occur can help you prepare for such a crisis in advance.

When a Neptune ♆ transit aspects one of your planets, your challenge will be to find a more spiritual approach to problems you haven't been able to resolve in the past.

Neptune ♆ = Questioning. Like the Hanged Man card of the Tarot, Neptune transits cause you to stop and question everything you've believed up until now. Because Neptune is the planet of dreams, however, it's not always clear to your conscious mind exactly *how* you're questioning everything, let alone *why*. In relationships, partners who've always seemed sure of themselves may suddenly turn needy and dependent when a Neptune transit occurs, and depending on the other partner's own transits at the time, the relationship may or may not survive.

When a Uranus ♅ transit aspects one of your planets, your challenge will be to see old things in new ways.

Uranus ♅ = Reinvention. Like the Judgement card of the Tarot, Uranus transits call for reinvention. Because a Uranus transit sometimes feels like a "last chance" to get things right, this transit is the one that heralds career change, a move, or, in the case of relationships, the discarding of an old love for a new one. If you know this one's coming, you might be able to settle for a trip to Paris instead of a new partner!

When a Saturn ♄ transit aspects one of your planets, your challenge will be to move on to still greater challenges.

Saturn ♄ = Challenge. Like the Knight of Swords card of the Tarot, Saturn transits spur you on to fight greater battles against still-more-challenging opponents. If the previous battle wasn't successfully fought, however, you may face this same challenge all over again when this transit occurs. When it comes to relationships, Saturn transits can mean a dredging up of the same old baggage all over again—or tossing it all out so that you can buy a new set!

When a Jupiter ♃ transit aspects one of your planets, your challenge will be to expand your horizon in an exciting new direction.

Jupiter ♃ = Expansion. Like the Knight of Wands card of the Tarot, Jupiter transits encourage you to try riding a new horse—or to ride the same horse to a new location. Either way, when Jupiter transits occur, you'll be hot to trot somewhere you've never been, and whether it's taking a gourmet cooking class or trekking Mount Everest will depend on where Jupiter falls in your own birth chart. In terms of your relationship, it will just be a question of whether your partner wants to join you. But *you're* going anyway, even if that means going solo.

Astrologers like Arlene have noted that relationship breakups often occur when either Saturn ♄, Uranus ♅, or Pluto ♇ form aspects to the 1st, 4th, 7th, or 10th house angles of a couple's natal charts. Of these transits, the most challenging is when one of these planets—Saturn, Uranus, or Pluto—passes over the ascendant or descendant of a natal chart. An equally challenging trigger point occurs when Saturn, Uranus, or Pluto moves over the natal Moon ☽ or Venus ♀. At the very least, these transits will bring the relationship under the microscope, but relationship blowups are an all-too-frequent result as well.

If you become aware of these potential trouble spots in advance, however, the difficulties can be understood rather than magnified during these transits. Here are some more Tarot planetary transit guideposts to help you negotiate the curves—and curveballs!

Saturn ♄, the Emperor, is the planet of lessons; Uranus ♅, the Hierophant R, is the planet of freedom; and Pluto ♇, Death, is the planet that transforms the "old" of the relationship into the "new."

Remember, challenging transits don't necessarily mean your relationship will end. Rather, they can serve to awaken both of you to necessary work on your personal love relationship issues.

Progressions Mean Progress

Progressions are the way you and your astrological birth chart change throughout your life. To "progress" a chart, the astrologer plots the planets a day forward in time for every year you have been alive. So if you are 24 years old this year, your astrologer would progress your chart by 24 days to see how time has brought evolution to your life path. Just as we do for transits, we can make a number of general statements about how planets will progress through the signs during your lifetime based on planetary cycles. Here are some of the things that will happen as you age:

- Your Sun ☉ will move into a new sign every 30 years, with the first Sun sign change dependent on the degree of the Sun in your birth chart.
- Your ascendant will also move into a new sign over time, depending on where you were born and whether your ascendant is one of long or short ascension. Astrological signs of long ascension are Cancer ♋, Leo ♌, Virgo ♍, Libra ♎, Scorpio ♏, and Sagittarius ♐. Signs of short ascension are Capricorn ♑, Aquarius ♒, Pisces ♓, Aries ♈, Taurus ♉, and Gemini ♊. For example, people born in New York at 41° latitude will have an Aries ♈ ascendant for 16 years and a Libra ♎ ascendant for 36 years.
- The Moon ☽ moves 1° per month of time. Your progressed Moon represents how you have evolved emotionally since birth.
- Planets that have gone retrograde ℞ since birth can signal rethinking in these areas.
- Planets that have gone direct since birth can indicate a change in direction in your life, perhaps even a complete reversal of consciousness that results in a new path to follow.

When we decided to look at progressions for Paul Newman and Joanne Woodward, our love longevity couple, we made a startling discovery: Their 45th wedding anniversary was to take place three days after Paul's 78th birthday! For this reason, we decided to show progressions for that birthday to show you where this couple was at this particular moment in time.

When we look at a progressed chart, we study the aspects at the center of the wheel, which show the relationship between the birth chart and the progressed chart. In this case, we noted immediately that

Paul Newman's progressed Moon ☽ is in Capricorn ♑ in his 12th house of past lives and karmic duty. In addition, his natal 7th house of marriage is ruled by the Moon: Cancer ♋ is on the 7th house cusp in Paul's birth chart! Any time a progressed Moon goes through the 12th house, the person is completing another cycle of karmic duty, and future plans are being incubated. It often marks inner changes and correlates with important outer events, including meetings with new people who will be important for some time to come.

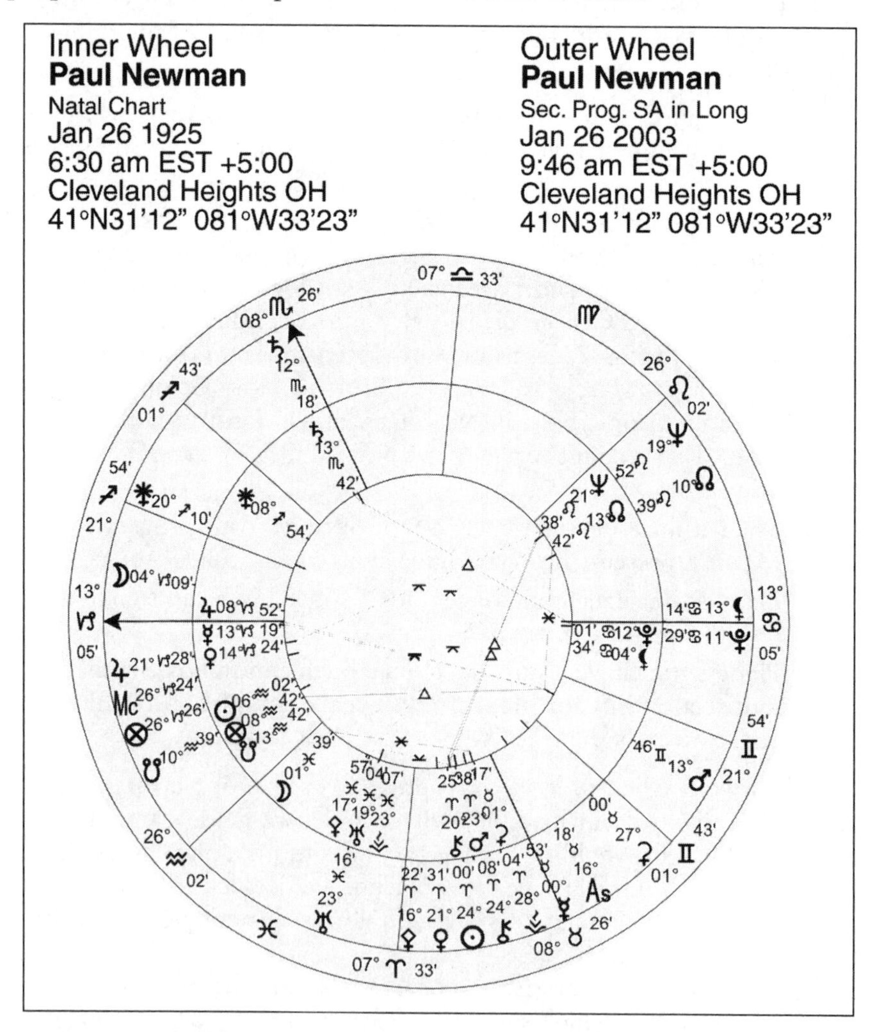

Paul Newman progressed to his 78th birthday (and his 45th wedding anniversary with Joanne Woodward).

In 2003, their marriage only grew stronger. They continue to collaborate on both creative projects and service-oriented activities. It's likely their businesses will grow even further, and that there will be public recognition for their marriage, their service, and their careers. This is reinforced because Paul's progressed Moon ☽ will conjunct his natal Jupiter ♃ in Capricorn ♑ in the 12th house of karmic duty and karmic reward, which equals public recognition.

Arlene does sound a note of caution here: Paul needs to take care of a health issue so it does not get out of control. Despite his busy schedule, he should not ignore health matters. So get thee to a doctor, Paul—and may you and Joanne enjoy many more years of happiness together.

Make an Event Chart—and Check It Twice

One of the nifty things an astrologer can do because of planetary cycles is help you choose the perfect time for a big event like a wedding, marriage proposal, or romantic getaway.

1. First the astrologer will ask exactly what type of event you are planning. Is it a marriage proposal? Your wedding date? For either of these events, the Moon ☽, Venus ♀, and Jupiter ♃ should make good aspects to the personal planets of both charts or connect to the 1st house and 7th house of both charts.
2. The New Moon phase is in general a good time to start anew, and three days after the exact New Moon is a good time to "grow" or "birth" a plan.
3. It is best to have a good transit to the natal charts of both partners. For example, transiting Venus ♀ conjunct ☌ either person's Sun ☉, Moon ☽, ascendant, or descendant will bode well for the future.
4. The progressed Venus ♀ conjuncting ☌ either person's Sun ☉, Moon ☽, ascendant, or descendant is another good marker. Conjuncting both can mean heaven on earth! This phenomenon is more rare than the previous three we've listed; you might not see this for years, or never for some people.

Planning your wedding date is more than just that day—it's the rest of your life. So go ahead and chart your event time. Chances are, your astrologer's fee will be the smallest check you write—but will have the greatest return on investment—of all.

Your wedding day is the beginning of your "happily ever after." You can choose the date and time with care by consulting an astrologer to create an event chart.

Your Personal Love Profile

Now that you've learned how the Intuitive Arts can help you not only make more of your love life, but also the *best* of your love life, it's time to put it all together to create a Personal Love Profile. We'll help you compile information from throughout the book into one convenient worksheet that you can use to see how you and your partner fit together when it comes to love.

To start, retrieve your *yin/yang* complementarity from Chapter 2, as well as your partner's. We've provided spaces throughout for both you and your partner, but you can leave the partner space blank if you prefer. Are your planets mostly *yin* or mostly *yang?*

	You	**Your Partner**
Yin or *yang?*	________	________

In Chapter 3, you discovered your Elemental Romantic Signature. Add that to your personal love profile here:

	You	**Your Partner**
Fire, Earth, Air, or Water?	________	________

Now note the astrological signs and houses for your personal planets and your rising sign, which you first charted in Chapter 4.

	You		Your Partner	
	Astro Sign	**House**	**Astro Sign**	**House**
Sun ☉	________	________	________	________
Moon ☽	________	________	________	________
Mercury ☿	________	________	________	________
Venus ♀	________	________	________	________
Mars ♂	________	________	________	________
Ascendant	________	________	________	________

Next note the placements for your outer planets and asteroids.

	You		Your Partner	
	Astro Sign	**House**	**Astro Sign**	**House**
Jupiter ♃	________	________	________	________
Saturn ♄	________	________	________	________
Uranus ♅	________	________	________	________
Neptune ♆	________	________	________	________
Pluto ♇	________	________	________	________
Ceres ⚳	________	________	________	________
Juno ⚵	________	________	________	________
Pallas Athene ⚴	________	________	________	________
Vesta ⚶	________	________	________	________
Chiron ⚷	________	________	________	________

Finally, retrieve the list of chart strengths you prepared in Chapter 7. As you may recall, there are a number of places to look when you're assessing your own positive traits:

- **Sun ☉ and Moon ☽ aspects.** Trines △ and sextiles ⚹ make things easier, while squares □ and oppositions ☍ may make them more difficult—but it's the difficulties that will make you much stronger in the long run.

- **Mars ♂ and Saturn ♄ aspects.** Mars, with its focus on power, and Saturn, with its focus on discipline, reveal your own unique strengths in these areas.
- **Venus ♀ and Jupiter ♃ aspects.** Trines △ and sextiles ⚹ here, especially to the luminaries and to Mars and Saturn, show your sensual nature and native optimism.
- **Nodal ☊☋ aspects.** Your North Node ☊ reveals your challenges, while your South Node ☋ shows the things that come easily to you.
- **Aspects between Sun ☉ and Saturn ♄, Moon ☽ and Saturn ♄.** When Saturn aspects the Sun or the Moon, it can be particularly challenging, but, like all challenges, these conflicts can spur you toward success.

It's important to remember that although trines △ and sextiles ⚹ mean an easier time of it, these aren't always your strengths. The places we are strongest are usually those we've striven the hardest to achieve. They were worth the effort, and we're not going to give them up.

Where are *your* birth chart's strengths? Maybe your Sun ☉ and Moon ☽, or your Sun ☉ and ascendant, share a sign, creating a focal point. Any time two or more planets appear in one sign, you should consider it a focal point, where a lot is happening in your chart. Or perhaps your Saturn ♄ or Mars ♂ squares □ your Venus ♀, creating the potential for conflict, but also the impetus for learning more about love. Does cheerful Jupiter ♃ or sensual Venus ♀ support you in matters of the heart with a sextile ⚹ or trine △? And how does your Saturn ♄ square up □ against your Sun ☉ and Moon ☽—does it push them with a challenging aspect, or just let them be, with an easier one?

When considering the strengths in your birth chart, try not to think in terms of good and bad. Yes, we've provided keywords throughout to help you codify all these new astrological concepts, but you will do best if you consider those keywords starting points rather than absolutes. So, using your Chapter 7 analysis as a guide rather than copying it verbatim, list your particular strengths when it comes to love.

My strengths:

____

____

____

____

____

____

The Best of Your Love

Like everything that really matters, your Personal Love Profile won't be a simple matter of black and white. Rather, you'll find strengths that help you succeed and challenges that either can keep you from finding your heart's desire or push you to work harder to achieve it, depending on how you choose to work with them.

Comparing your Personal Love Profile to your partner's can help both of you visualize your problem areas intuitively, while at the same time help you take advantage of each other's strengths and the strengths you share together as a couple. Like all such exercises, however, you should consider your Personal Love Profile only the beginning of a beautiful lifetime of ever-evolving and deepening love, in yourself and with your partner.

We hope you'll see this book as a beginning, too. With the Intuitive Arts of Astrology, the Tarot, and Psychic Intuition now firmly in your grasp, there's not much you won't be able to face, whether it comes to love or life itself. We wish you much luck, much happiness, and, most of all, much love!

appendix A

Love Stars

The wheel of the Zodiac
Planets in houses
Signs in houses
Planet personalities and rulers
House keywords
Elements, energies, and qualities
Aspects
Looking for love in all the right places
Ordering birth charts and synastry grids online

We've put together this quick-reference appendix as a guide to understanding Astrology's signs, planets, and houses. Use this information to aid you in interpreting love in your own birth chart—and your loved one's chart, too!

The Wheel of the Zodiac

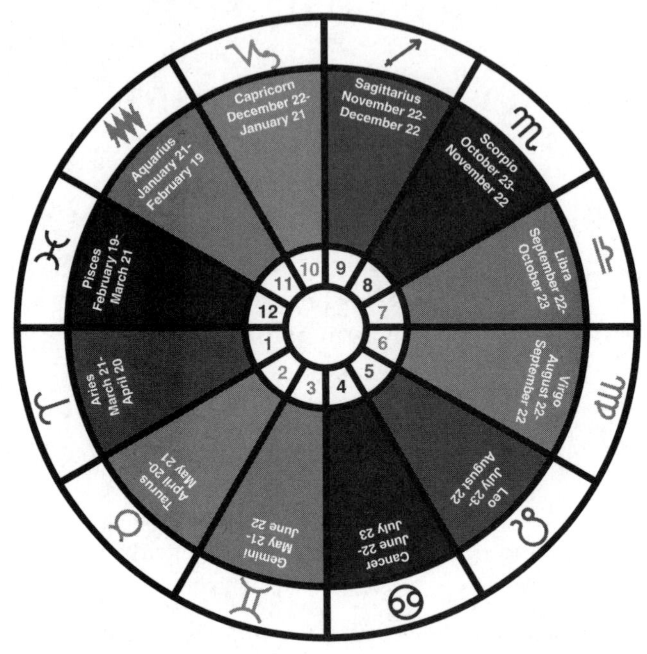

By the Signs

Here's a quick, handy reference to the astrological signs.

Aries, the Ram ♈	**March 21 to April 20**
Element:	Fire
Quality:	Cardinal
Energy:	*Yang*
Rulers:	Mars and Pluto
Anatomy:	Brain, eyes, face
Keywords:	Pioneering, initiating, beginnings

Taurus, the Bull ♉	**April 20 to May 21**
Element:	Earth
Quality:	Fixed
Energy:	*Yin*
Ruler:	Venus
Anatomy:	Neck, throat, thyroid
Keywords:	Ownership, dependability, sensuality

Gemini, the Twins ♊	**May 21 to June 22**
Element:	Air
Quality:	Mutable
Energy:	*Yang*
Ruler:	Mercury
Anatomy:	Hands, arms, shoulders, lungs
Keywords:	Mentality, communication, versatility

Cancer, the Crab ♋	**June 22 to July 23**
Element:	Water
Quality:	Cardinal
Energy:	*Yin*
Ruler:	Moon
Anatomy:	Stomach, breasts
Keywords:	Feeling, sensitivity, nurturing

Leo, the Lion ♌	**July 23 to August 22**
Element:	Fire
Quality:	Fixed
Energy:	*Yang*
Ruler:	Sun
Anatomy:	Back, spine, heart
Keywords:	Willpower, creativity, expressing the heart

Virgo, the Virgin ♍	**August 22 to September 22**
Element:	Earth
Quality:	Mutable
Energy:	*Yin*
Ruler:	Mercury
Anatomy:	Intestines and colon
Keywords:	Service, self-improvement, sacred patterns

Libra, the Scales ♎	**September 22 to October 23**
Element:	Air
Quality:	Cardinal
Energy:	*Yang*
Ruler:	Venus
Anatomy:	Kidneys, lower back, adrenal glands
Keywords:	Balance, harmony, justice

Scorpio, the Scorpion ♏	**October 23 to November 22**
Element:	Water
Quality:	Fixed
Energy:	*Yin*
Rulers:	Pluto and Mars
Anatomy:	Genitals, urinary and reproductive systems
Keywords:	Desire, transformation, power

Sagittarius, the Archer ♐	**November 22 to December 22**
Element:	Fire
Quality:	Mutable
Energy:	*Yang*
Ruler:	Jupiter
Anatomy:	Liver, hips, thighs
Keywords:	Understanding, enthusiasm, exploration

Capricorn, the Goat ♑	**December 22 to January 21**
Element:	Earth
Quality:	Cardinal
Energy:	*Yin*
Ruler:	Saturn
Anatomy:	Bones, joints, knees, teeth
Keywords:	Achievement, structure, organization

Aquarius, the Water Bearer ♒	**January 21 to February 19**
Element:	Air
Quality:	Fixed
Energy:	*Yang*
Rulers:	Uranus and Saturn
Anatomy:	Ankles, circulation
Keywords:	Humanitarian, unique, innovative

Pisces, the Fishes ♓	**February 19 to March 21**
Element:	Water
Quality:	Mutable
Energy:	*Yin*

Pisces, the Fishes ♓	**February 19 to March 21**
Rulers:	Neptune and Jupiter
Anatomy:	Feet, immune system, hormonal system
Keywords:	Compassion, universality, inclusiveness

By the Planets

Here's a quick, handy reference to the energy of each planet.

Planet	**Symbol**	**Energies**	**Action Keyword**
Sun	☉	Self, essence, life spirit, creativity, willpower	Explores
Moon	☽	Emotions, instincts, unconscious, past memories	Senses
Mercury	☿	Mental activities, communication, intelligence	Communicates
Venus	♀	Love, art, beauty, social graces, harmony, money, resources, possessions	Enjoys
Mars	♂	Physical energy, boldness, warrior ways, action, desires anger, courage, ego	Acts
Jupiter	♃	Luck, abundance, wisdom, higher education, philosophy or beliefs, exploration, growth	Benefits
Saturn	♄	Responsibilities, self-discipline, perseverance, limitations, structures	Works
Uranus	♅	Sudden or unexpected change, originality, liberation, radical thinking, authenticity	Innovates
Neptune	♆	Idealism, subconscious, spirituality, intuition, clairvoyance	Dreams
Pluto	♇	Power, regeneration, destruction, rebirth, transformation	Transforms

Signs in Houses

House	Astro Sign
1st	Aries ♈
2nd	Taurus ♉
3rd	Gemini ♊
4th	Cancer ♋
5th	Leo ♌
6th	Virgo ♍
7th	Libra ♎
8th	Scorpio ♏
9th	Sagittarius ♐
10th	Capricorn ♑
11th	Aquarius ♒
12th	Pisces ♓

Planetary Rulers

Planet	Signs Ruled
Sun ☉	Leo ♌
Moon ☽	Cancer ♋
Mercury ☿	Gemini ♊, Virgo ♍
Venus ♀	Taurus ♉, Libra ♎
Mars ♂	Aries ♈, co-ruler of Scorpio ♏
Jupiter ♃	Sagittarius ♐, co-ruler of Pisces ♓
Saturn ♄	Capricorn ♑, co-ruler of Aquarius ♒
Uranus ♅	Aquarius ♒
Neptune ♆	Pisces ♓
Pluto ♇	Scorpio ♏, co-ruler of Aries ♈

House Key Terms

House	Key Term
1st	Identity
2nd	Self-worth
3rd	Knowledge
4th	Home and family
5th	Creativity
6th	Work and service

House	Key Term
7th	Relationships
8th	Transformation
9th	Beliefs
10th	Ethics and career
11th	Community
12th	Spirituality

Natural Planets and Natural Signs in Their Houses

Here are the natural planets and natural signs in their astrological houses.

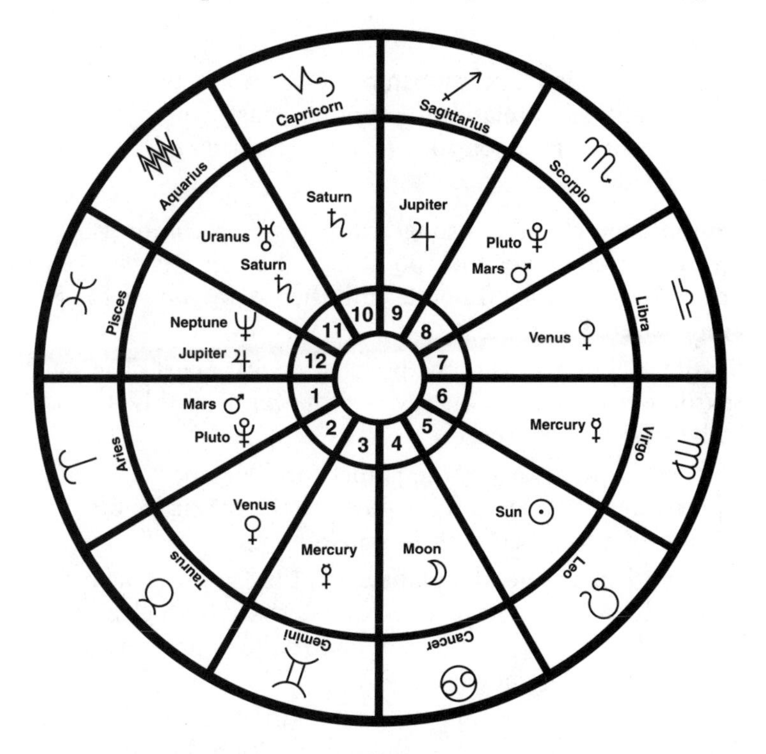

Asteroids and Planetoids

More than just the planets move through your birth chart! Here are the asteroids and the planetoid Chiron, and their areas of influence.

Asteroid	Realm	Areas of Influence
Ceres ⚳	Motherhood	Natural cycles, fertility, crops, relationships between parents and children
Juno ⚵	Marriage	Partnerships, contracts and agreements, social obligations
Pallas Athene ⚴	Wisdom	Intelligence, knowledge, understanding, equality
Vesta ⚶	Power	Sexuality, devotion, health, service to others
Planetoid		
Chiron ⚷	Healing	Transformation, personal growth

Aspects

Aspects are the geometric relationships between any two planets in your own chart, as well as in relation to another chart, whether for another person, a moment in time, or your own progressed chart. The main aspects to consider are:

- **Conjunction** ☌ The strongest aspects. In a conjunction, the planets are placed at the same point in a chart or charts. Conjunctions are considered a focal point, with the interaction of the two planets emphasized.
- **Sextile** ⚹ In a sextile, the planets are 60° apart. The signs in a sextile share the same energy (*yin* or *yang*), so this is considered to be a favorable aspect.
- **Square** □ In a square, the planets are 90° apart. Although squares are considered to be chart challenges, they often provide the impetus for change and improvement.
- **Trine** △ In a trine, the planets are 120° apart. This most favorable of the aspects means the planets share both element and energy. Trines indicate positive connections, often made so easily you may not even notice.
- **Opposition** ☍ In an opposition, the planets are 180° apart. There's little in common with an opposition, but, like squares, their difficult energy can spur us on to meet challenges.
- **Quincunx** ⚻ In a quincunx, the planets are 150° apart. Quincunxes are interesting—nothing is shared between the two signs, so some adjustment is usually required in order for them to interact.

Astrological Extras

The astrological charts and grids you see as examples throughout this book contain two symbols we don't include in our discussions but that might interest you in your further explorations of Astrology. These are the Part of Fortune ⊗ and the minor asteroid Lilith ⚸. The Part of Fortune, sometimes called the Lot of Fortune, derives from ancient Astrology and represents the intersection in the Zodiac where your Sun ☉, Moon ☽, and ascendant converge. The Part of Fortune in its basic symbolism is a "point of karmic reward" in your birth chart. The ancients believed the Part of Fortune is what you would receive as a cosmic gift as you grew in this lifetime. Lilith, also called the Dark Moon, represents primal and emotional connections to your shadow side, and "liberation from conformity" in present-day interpretations.

Looking for Love in All the Right Places

Love is everywhere on your birth chart, but a few special places will give you a quick love assessment. We've used Julia Roberts's birth chart and numbered the areas to pay special attention to when you're looking for love. We've also cross-referenced the chapter that covers this area in detail.

1. In Chapter 1, we showed you where to look for your Sun ☉, your approach to exploration, and your Moon ☽, your sensual approach.
2. Also in Chapter 1, we introduced you to Mercury ☿, your way of communicating, Venus ♀, how you approach enjoyment, Mars ♂, how you engage, and your ascendant, the mask you wear for the world.
3. In Chapter 2, you learned about your *yin/yang* equation: which planets have a *yin* quality and which have a *yang* quality.
4. In Chapter 3, we introduced you to your Elemental Romance Signature, how many personal planets you have in Fire, Earth, Air, and Water signs.
5. In Chapter 4, you learned how to look at your personal planets and their houses to determine your approach to romance, as well as how to identify your aspects.
6. In Chapter 5, we introduced you to synastry, and showed you how to use an aspect grid to find your compatibility ratio with the birth chart of another person.

7. Also in Chapter 5, we explained how aspects between planets and the North ☊ and South ☋ Node, aspects between Saturn ♄ and the ascendant, and retrogrades that made connections to the Nodes, Saturn ♄, and ascendant, can help you determine whether your relationship will last, and showed you how to use sign, planet, and house keywords to make your own relationship analysis.
8. In Chapter 6, we walked the Moon ☽ through the signs. We also looked at lunar cycles, Saturn ♄ returns, and Pluto ♇ transits, so that you could find times when your birth chart might be generating personal change.
9. In Chapter 7, we introduced you to the asteroids, Ceres ⚳, Juno ⚵, Pallas Athene ⚴, and Vesta ⚶, and showed you how these planetary wildcards can reveal how you mother, partner, find strength, and give, as well as your expectations in these areas. We also introduced you to Chiron ⚷, the wounded healer, whose sign in your birth chart shows your own particular psychic wound and potential for healing.
10. Also in Chapter 7, we showed you how to explore aspects in more depth, including the conjunction ☌, sextile ⚹, square □, trine △, opposition ☍, and quincunx ⚻. We also revealed how certain, more difficult, aspects can create an atmosphere more conducive to breakup than longevity.
11. In Chapter 8, we explored Saturn ♄, the Nodes ☋ ☊, and the 12th house in more detail to help you uncover your Soulmate.
12. Finally, we showed you how to chart your transits and progressions, as well as the best way to create an event chart to schedule that perfect moment.

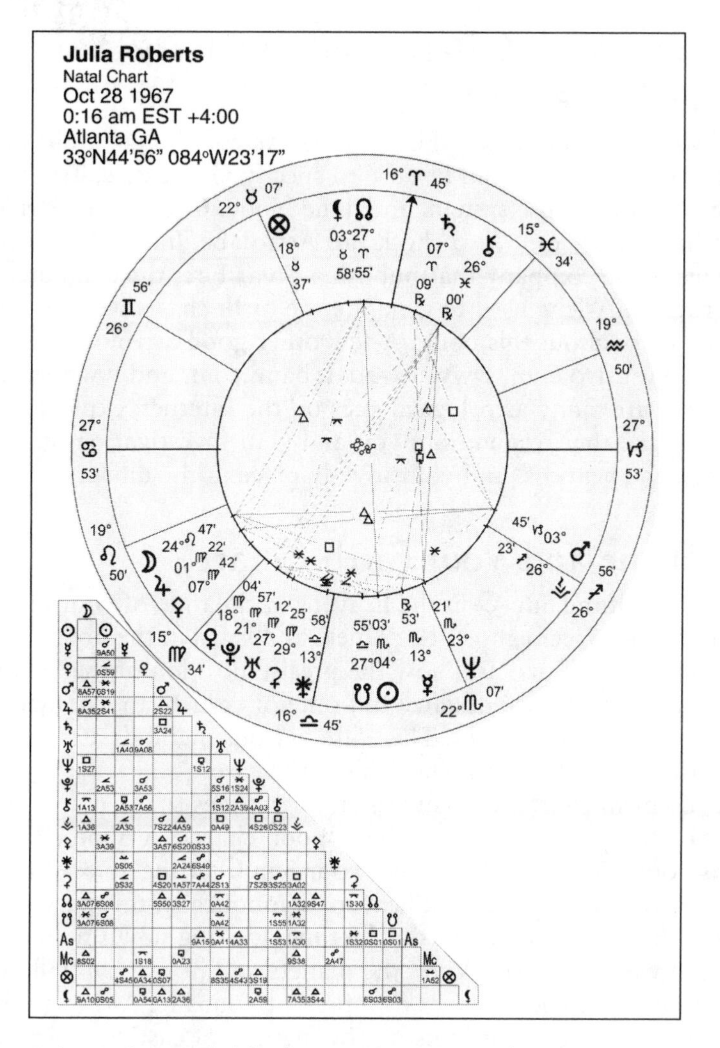

Julia Roberts's birth chart and aspect grid.

Ordering Birth Charts and Synastry Grids Online

Several websites will prepare birth charts for you. To get a birth chart you can use with this book, be sure to specify Geocentric, Tropical Zodiac, Placidus house system, and True Node. Check out Arlene's site at www.mellinetti.com. Also check out Astrolabe, Inc., at www.alabe.com. This is the company that publishes Solar Fire, the computer software program Arlene used to generate the birth charts we used as examples throughout this book. A few other good astrology websites include www.astro.com, www.astrodatabank.com, and www.stariq.com. There are many astrological sites on the Internet; explore and choose the site that resonates to you and your investigation of Astrology, the heavens, and your love-ly place in the universe.

Birth Time and Your Birth Chart

The position of the Sun ☉ in the heavens at the time of your birth determines the placement of the planets and signs in the houses of your astrological birth chart. To know the precise position of the Sun, you need to know the location, date, and time of your birth. Many people don't know their birth times. There are various methods astrologers can use to cast birth charts when this is the case.

For the birth charts with unknown birth times that we used in this book, Arlene used the method called "noon chart." A noon chart uses noon as your time of birth, placing your Sun ☉ at the apex of the horoscope wheel—on your midheaven. Symbolically, this puts your soul at its highest potential in this lifetime, looking down with an eagle's-eye view, so to speak, on the planets and how they "fall" into place in the astrological houses to represent your life. Although there are some imprecisions with this or any method of casting a birth chart without a precise time of birth (for example, the ascendant sign changes every two hours), Arlene finds the noon chart allows the most accurate interpretations for the broadest range of people.

appendix B

Love Cards

No Tarot card's meaning is absolute, and for that reason, we encourage you to make personal interpretations of the cards, both by studying their individual images and examining the stories told by the cards' interrelationships. These images you see here are from the Universal Waite Tarot Deck published by U.S. Games Systems, Inc.

At the same time, knowing the traditional meanings of the cards can often give you an additional spin you might not have considered in your initial interpretation. That's why we've taken a fresh look at the cards' meanings as they apply specifically to love.

Tarot's Major Arcana

The Fool
A brand-new love
Endless possibilities
Naivete and innocence

The Fool R
Uncertainty
A wrong direction
Look before you leap

The Magician
The power to manifest desire
Ask and ye shall receive
A creative or inventive person

The Magician R
Possibility of manipulation
Lack of follow-through
A user or abuser

The High Priestess
Intuition and inner knowing
Yin *and* yang—
emotions + logic
Going with your gut

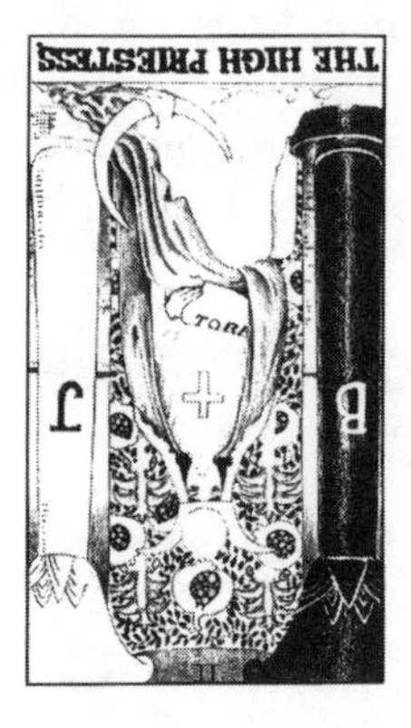

The High Priestess R
Dream or illusion
A hidden agenda
Lack of insight

The Empress
A happy home
Harmony in love
An environment for growth and prosperity

The Empress R
Disagreements at home
Too much focus on physical appearance
Domination rather than dominion

The Emperor
Father figure
Past experience can guide the present
Self-discipline

The Emperor R
Insecurity
Stubbornness
Self-centeredness

The Hierophant
A traditional marriage
Staying between the lines
A solid spiritual foundation

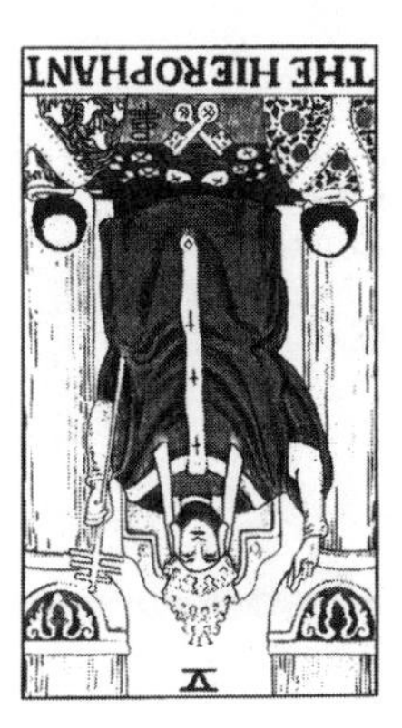

The Hierophant R
An unconventional approach to love
A risk-taker
A relationship with freedom

The Lovers
A new romance
Good start for a relationship
Peaceful coexistence

The Lovers R
Separation or division
Obstacles to desires
A need for better emotional communication

The Chariot
Ability to meet challenges
Focus and determination to achieve goal
Positive outcome after difficult time

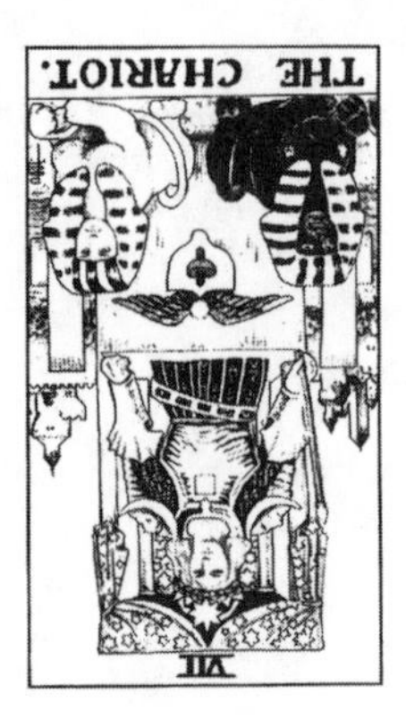

The Chariot R
Confusion
Someone else in control
A battle not worth fighting?

Strength
The inner strength of unconditional love
Love without fear
The power of gentle persuasion

Strength R
A power struggle
Intense emotions that can lead to upset
Uncontrolled passions

The Hermit
Introspection and solitude
A desire for truth
Trust own inner voice for guidance

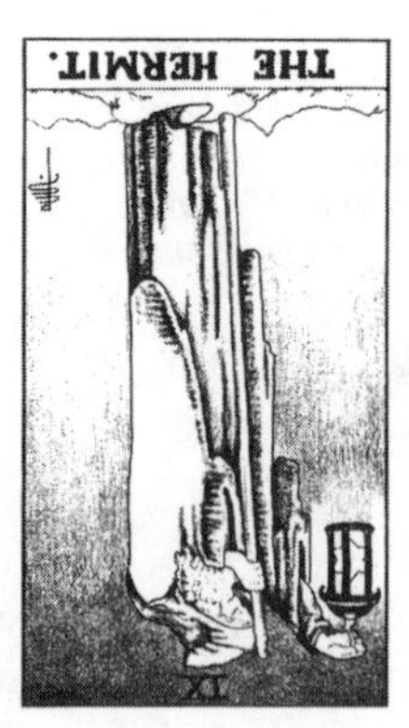

The Hermit R
Inability to see clearly
Wishing instead of acting
A reminder to pay attention to past lessons

Wheel of Fortune
Destiny comes calling!
Lucky in love
True love comes around

Wheel of Fortune R
What goes up must come down
Love slips away
A grinding halt

Justice
Fairness and a desire for balance
A legal agreement or marriage
Universal laws will prevail

Justice R
Unwise counsel
Conditions that are out of balance
Too much subjectivity

The Hanged Man
Desire for a different lifestyle
Need to reflect on the past
A lack of motion—feeling "stuck"

The Hanged Man R
Inability to give up old lifestyle
Inability to give up old love
Fear of change

Death
The end of an old love makes way for new
A catalyst for change
A new dawn

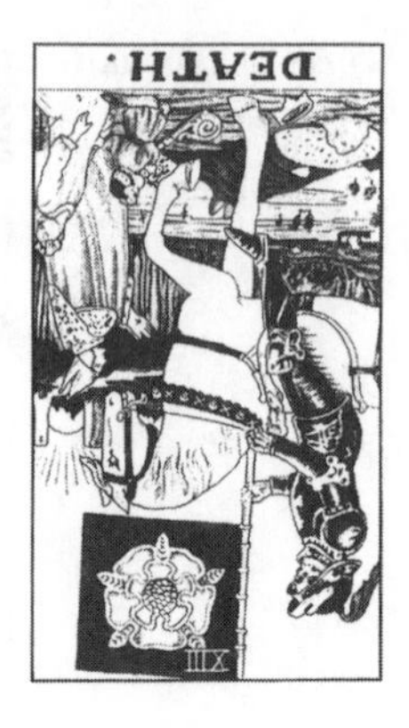

Death R
Past blockages impede progress
Stagnation and stalemate
Arguments; too tired to care

Temperance
A balance between emotion and desire
Giving and taking in equal measure
The importance of moderation

Temperance R
Impatience
Inability to listen to partner
Pushiness instead of patience

The Devil
Sexual obsession
Addictive behaviors
Wrong application of force, aggression

The Devil R
Freedom from fear
Ability to unlock own chains
A burden lifted

The Tower
Surprise!
Collapse of a faulty foundation
Don't depend too much on man-made things

The Tower R
A surprising nuance to a situation
Pay attention to intuitive nudges
Renewed faith after difficult life change

The Star
A faith in love
Giving and taking of love in balance
Return of hope

The Star R
Insecurity
Not receiving as much as you give
A feeling of loss—not always warranted

The Moon
Emotions at full force
A reminder to trust your intuition
Is someone trying to hide something?

The Moon R
Understanding after initial confusion
Clarity of light after darkness
Relief after worry

The Sun
Personal contentment
Sunny outlook for relationships
A good marriage; possible pregnancy

The Sun R
Partnership problems
Marital insecurity
Cloudy forecast

Judgement
A new understanding of past lessons
"I can see clearly now!"
An awakening to cosmic awareness

Judgement R
At a crossroads
Fears holding you back
Frustrating delays

The World
Successful culmination
Your new lifestyle is ready!
Freedom to do as you desire

The World R
A bit more work is needed to achieve goal
Life—and love—is what you make it
You're almost there!

Tarot's Minor Arcana

In romance, the Minor Arcana Tarot suit of Cups is the love suit, Pentacles represent sensuality, Swords show heartache and actions toward resolving love issues, and Wands reveal creative partnering.

Ace of Cups
Beginning of new love
Desire to experience love and joy
New direction of the heart

Ace of Cups R
Insecurity
Inability to connect with others
Too much focus on self

2 of Cups
Mutual emotional understanding
Desire to begin relationship
Developing friendship

2 of Cups R
Need for cooperation
Negative emotions
Jealousy or possessiveness

3 of Cups
The honeymoon phase
Happiness all around
Cause for celebration

3 of Cups R
Unhappiness not being communicated
Pettiness, overindulgence
Need to check emotions

4 of Cups
The thrill is gone
Fantasy more interesting than reality
Don't take your love for granted

4 of Cups R
Emotionally ready to love again
Ready to reconnect with others
Ability to visualize and create Love

5 of Cups
Love's sorrow
It's okay to cry
Need to recognize loss

5 of Cups R
Return of positive energy and hope
Letting go of negativity
Knowledge gained through heartbreak

6 of Cups
Nostalgia for old love
A past love returns
Sharing good memories

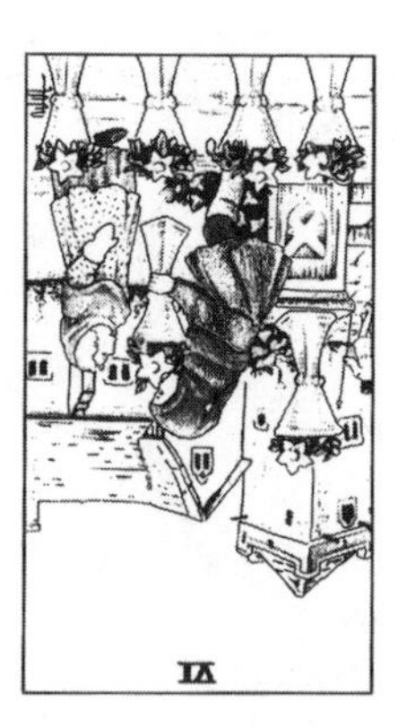

6 of Cups R
Hurtful past situation has current echoes
Emotional need to seek out past
Wishing for the past instead of the present

7 of Cups
Too many choices!
Pay attention to what's beneath
Indecisiveness

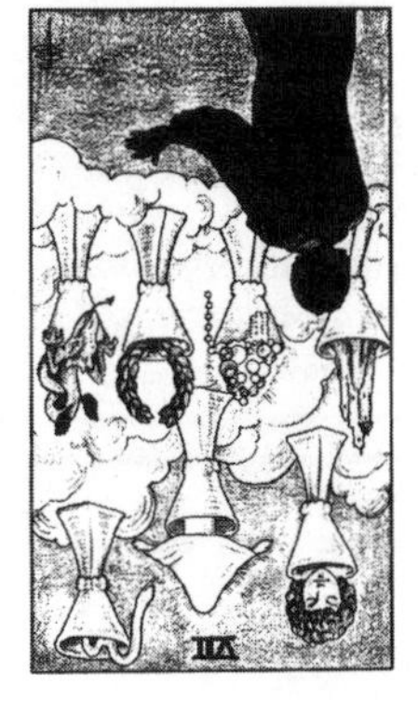

7 of Cups R
The fog has lifted
A plan has been made
You finally took action!

8 of Cups
Emotional surrender to a higher calling
Leaving the past behind
Dissatisfaction with current love
New relationships now possible

8 of Cups R
Time to follow your bliss
Taking pleasure in life's good things

9 of Cups
Happy days are here!
Your wish will come true
A new relationship

9 of Cups R
Expecting too much
Wishes postponed
A need to develop patience

10 of Cups
The best emotional relationship
Happily ever after!
Joy and happiness in abundance

10 of Cups R
Things you haven't told each other?
Fear of ultimate commitment
Troubled family life

Page of Cups
Kindness and compassion
Someone who cares
An offer of happiness

Page of Cups R
Someone feeling sorry for themselves
An immature view; a drama queen/king
Someone who's oversensitive

Knight of Cups
Movement toward emotional goal
A new relationship coming
Action toward developing relationship

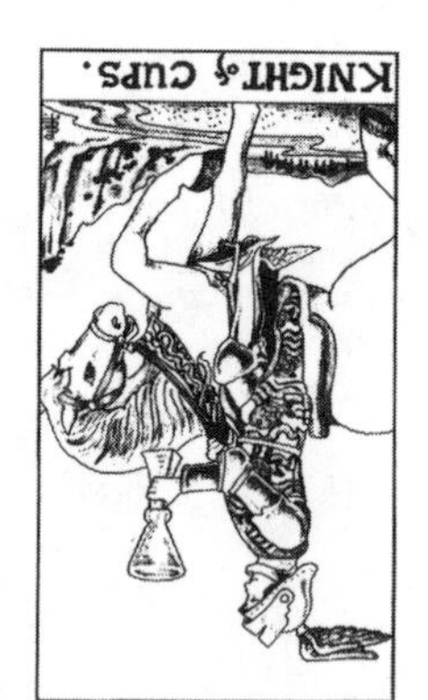

Knight of Cups R
Vacillating emotions
Emotionally unable to give
Living in the past

Queen of Cups
A nurturing, caring person
A focus on feelings and sensitivity
Someone concerned for others

Queen of Cups R
Someone who exaggerates feelings
Tendency toward secrecy or self-deception
A worrier; an overactive imagination

King of Cups
A giving, caring person
Someone who understands others
A desire to help others

King of Cups R
A recent emotional loss
Hidden emotions
Potential for manipulation of feelings

Ace of Pentacles
Focus on good home environment
Good common sense
Happiness of solid foundation

Ace of Pentacles R
Frustration and delays
Need to hold tight to what you have
Need to reassess priorities

2 of Pentacles
Juggling more than one thing
Confidence despite stress
Balance is essential

2 of Pentacles R
A hard time deciding something
Need to simplify; let something go
Need for caution

3 of Pentacles
A time to learn new things
Approval for work and talent
An award or honor

3 of Pentacles R
The reality doesn't look like the plan
Lack of passion
Sloppy workmanship

4 of Pentacles
Holding tight to what you have
Conservative about money
A miserly person

4 of Pentacles R
Spending more than you have
Use caution when spending
Generosity; overgenerosity

5 of Pentacles
A deep sense of personal loss
Feelings of separation
Lovers without a trysting place

5 of Pentacles R
Renewed hope and optimism after loss
Negative cycle ends
Can now reap what was sown

6 of Pentacles
Extra help is offered
Sharing with others
Financial reward; a new job

6 of Pentacles R
Be cautious of what others offer
More giving than taking
Bribery and chicanery

7 of Pentacles
Self-confidence
Payment for your skill
Financial independence

7 of Pentacles R
Poor speculation
Problems with land or real estate
A need for caution when speculating

8 of Pentacles
Social approval
Development of greater skill
Recognition for job well done

8 of Pentacles R
Delayed production
Lack of balance in personal life
Someone's burning out

9 of Pentacles
The comforts of home
Self-sufficiency and independence
Prosperity to share

9 of Pentacles R
Financial insecurity
Shaken foundations
Uncertainty about future

10 of Pentacles
The height of familial security
Assured future security
A stable and secure maturity

10 of Pentacles R
Family feud!
Family wealth at risk
Be cautious with investments

Page of Pentacles
An eager learner
A message of happiness
Good news—good results

Page of Pentacles R
A selfish or demanding child or person
Differing values
Prejudice or rebellion

Knight of Pentacles
Slow and steady wins the race
Development of prosperous future
Wise counsel and good stewardship

Knight of Pentacles R
Discontent with present work
Absent father figure
Trying to keep up with the Joneses

Queen of Pentacles
A kind, gentle person
The Earth Mother personified
Always something cooking on the stove

Queen of Pentacles R
A needy or dependent person
A lack of confidence
Losses in the home

King of Pentacles
A good parent figure
Assured prosperity
Someone who will share the wealth

King of Pentacles R
Laziness or lack of motivation
Ill-equipped for financial success
Disorganization, discontent about money

Ace of Swords
A new situation
A new way of communicating
A sword can cut two ways

Ace of Swords R
The need to be cautious and vigilant
Beware of aggression or force
Listen before acting

2 of Swords
Disconnected from emotions
Indecision or stalemate
Need to concentrate and focus

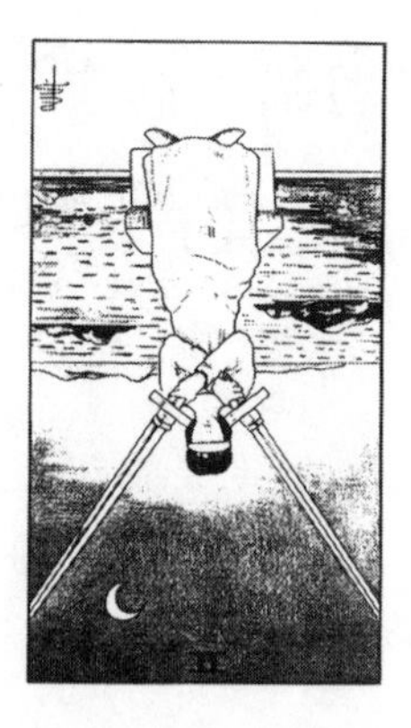

2 of Swords R
Remember to connect to intuition
Use caution to maintain balance
Freedom to make own decisions

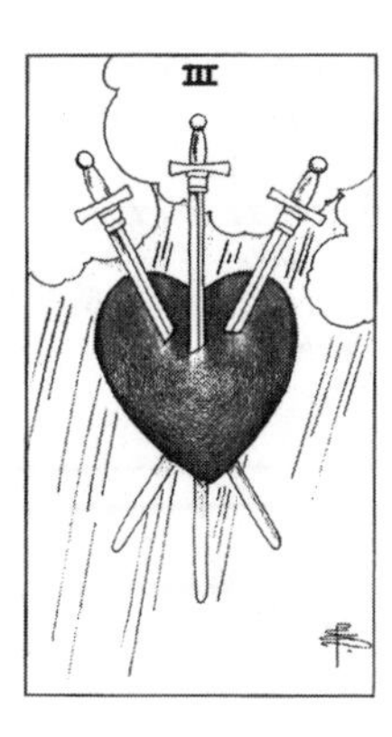

3 of Swords
Heartbreak and sorrow
Pain, loss, and grief
Learning about loss and sadness

3 of Swords R
Passing sadness
Dissatisfaction, but all is not lost
A different result than what was expected

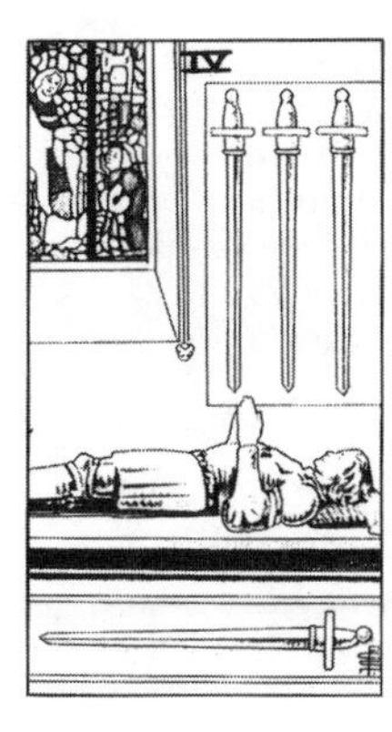

4 of Swords
R & R required!
Need for retreat and meditation
Inner work being done

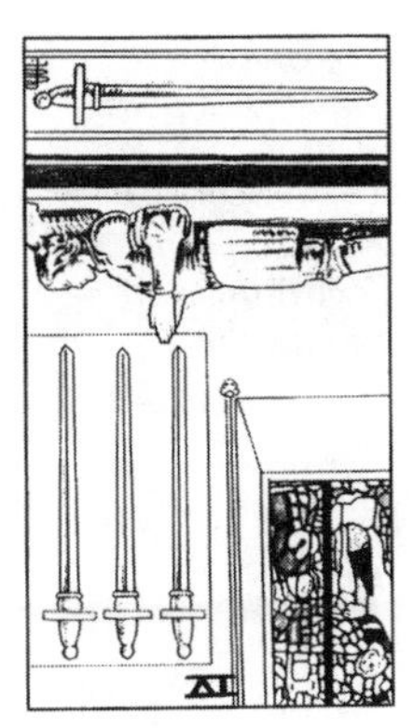

4 of Swords R
Ready for renewed action
Ready to fight for own rights
Opportunity to change existing condition

5 of Swords
Stormy weather
Someone taking unfair advantage
Loss, possible slander

5 of Swords R
Feeling too weak to fight
Someone being sneaky
The truth, however difficult, will come out

6 of Swords
Moving away from sorrow
Acceptance of better things to come
Leaving regrets behind

6 of Swords R
Stuck in a difficult situation
Better to wait and see
Learn to be patient

7 of Swords
Someone's being sneaky
A need for the truth to come out
Contradictions and duality

7 of Swords R
Wise counsel will return
What was hidden will be revealed
Freedom to move on

8 of Swords
Self-bound to fears
Abuse of mental power
Are you hurting yourself the most?

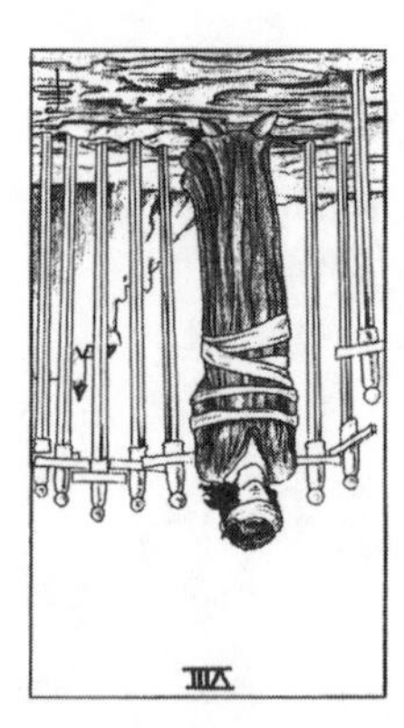

8 of Swords R
Letting go of fear
Facing one's own restrictions
Ability to move about freely once more

9 of Swords
Grief, sadness, and sleeplessness
Learning to deal with loss and regret
Emotional depression

9 of Swords R
The nightmare is over now
Negative energy is dissipating
The light at the end of the tunnel

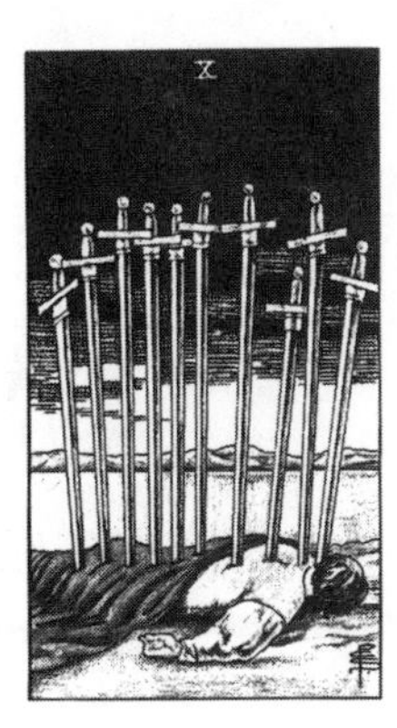

10 of Swords
End of a karmic pattern
End of a difficult relationship
Deep sense of loss or separation

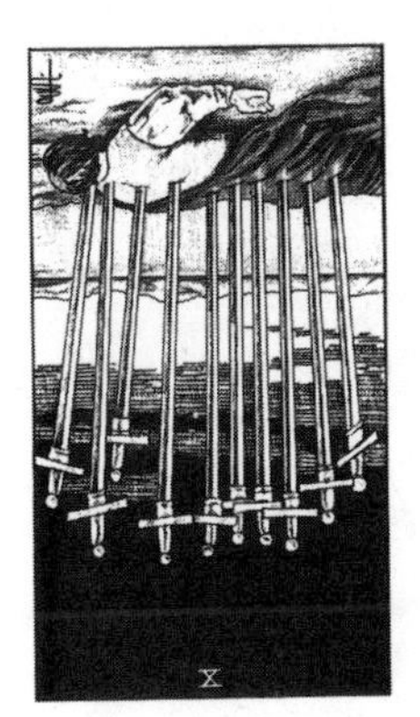

10 of Swords R
Releasing of a karmic debt
Prepared to move ahead
End of long, stressful cycle

Page of Swords
Courage when needed most
Using common-sense approach
Pay attention to details

Page of Swords R
Overly emotional communication
Need to speak mind
Importance of truth

Knight of Swords
Sudden change of direction
Direct honesty—sometimes too direct
Awakening to truth

Knight of Swords R
Out of control!
Arguments and disruptive behavior
Lack of emotional insight

Queen of Swords
Ability to get to heart of matter
Joy of debate
Honesty and forthrightness

Queen of Swords R
Overly critical person
Anxiety and miscommunication
Judgmental or contentious behavior

King of Swords
Logical analysis
Ability to probe beneath surface
Rational counsel

King of Swords R
Preconceptions without basis
Stubbornness and unfair judgment
Selfishness or aloofness

Ace of Wands
A fresh start
The first step toward creating passion
A new love or a new baby!

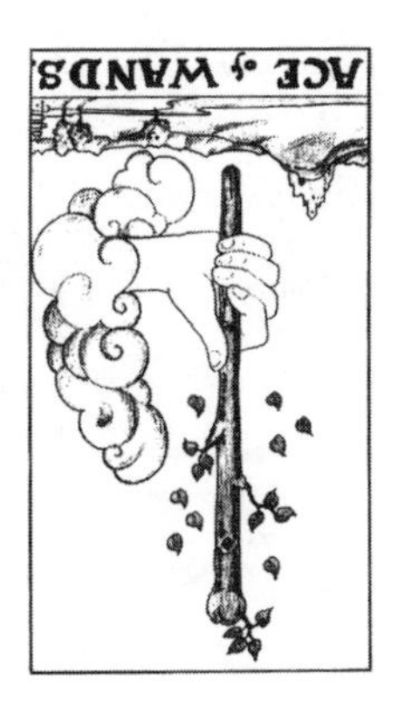

Ace of Wands R
Overenthusiasm gets in your way
Delays or frustration
Pushiness or aggression

2 of Wands
Waiting for results
A good perspective
A positive attitude

2 of Wands R
Lack of follow-through
Delays because of others
A hidden agenda

3 of Wands
Cooperation and partnership
Good results forthcoming
Competition

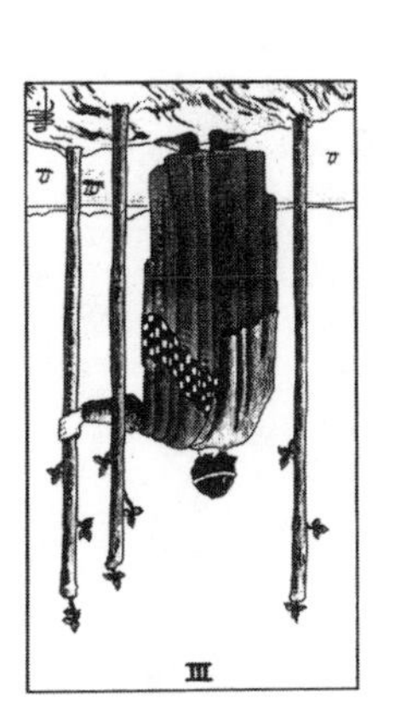

3 of Wands R
Wasted energy
Inadequate resources
No one in the lead

4 of Wands
A ceremony
(a wedding?!)
Happiness and success
A dream come true

4 of Wands R
Life's little joys
A gathering of family
Enjoyment of small pleasure

5 of Wands
Getting up on the wrong side of bed
Disagreement and crossed purposes
Aggression and misplaced energies

5 of Wands R
A win-win situation
Compromise and conciliation
Negotiation and constructive talks

6 of Wands
Good news comes home
A happy journey with loved ones
Company coming

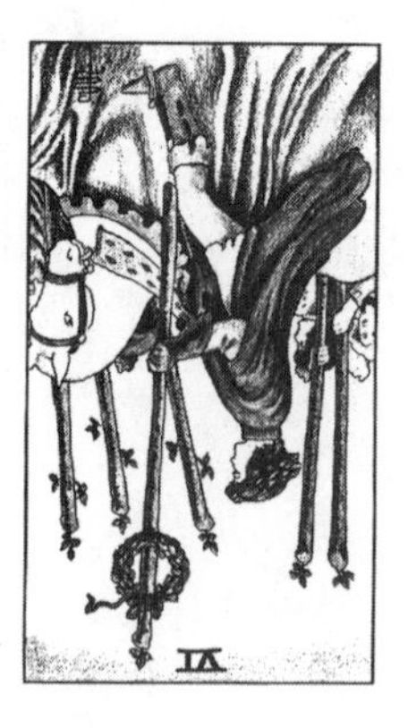

6 of Wands R
Stressful conditions
Need to ride out the storm
Just not your day

7 of Wands
Anxiety and cautiousness needed
A good offense is the best defense
Need to face fears and turn them around

7 of Wands R
The storm is passing
A sense of personal empowerment
Difficulties are over

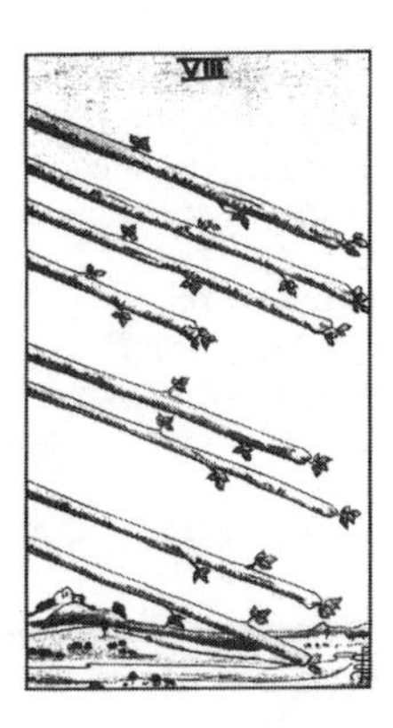

8 of Wands
The arrows of love are arriving!
Shared passions
Common goals and ideals

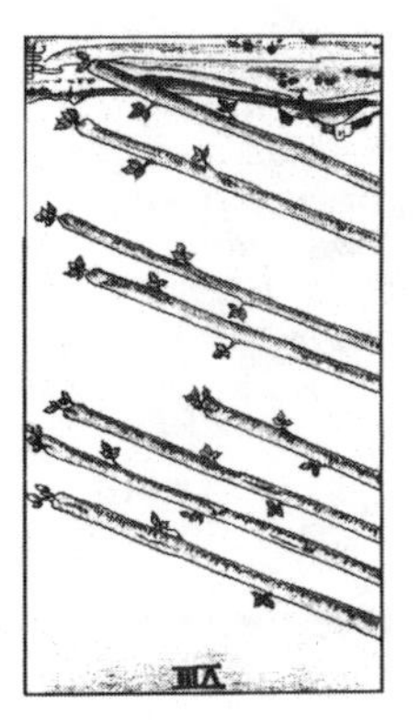

8 of Wands R
Disagreement and discontent
Jealousy or envy
Domestic disputes

9 of Wands
Safeguarding the family
Forewarned is forearmed
Well prepared to handle crisis

9 of Wands R
Vulnerable and tired
Desire to be left alone
Anxiety and poor health

10 of Wands
Helping too many others at once
Stressful conditions at home
Overwhelming obligations

10 of Wands R
Shifting the burden
Learning to delegate
Taking the right approach to responsibility

Page of Wands
An exciting message
An encouraging companion
Good tidings arrive

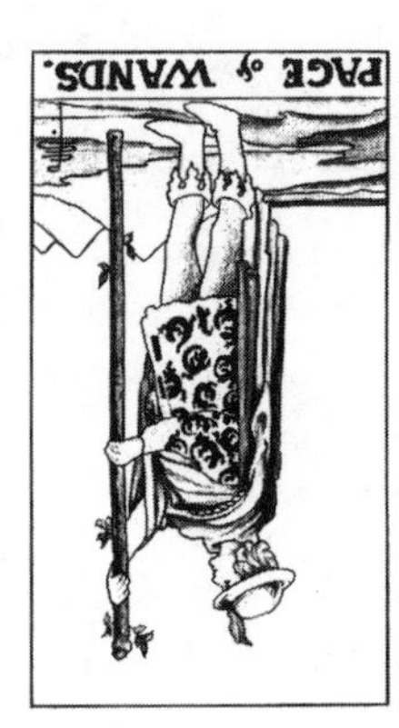

Page of Wands R
Disappointing news
Delay in receiving expected information
A preoccupied young person

Knight of Wands
Enthusiasm and renewed energy
A new adventure
A generous loved one

Knight of Wands R
Postponed journey
Jealousy, arrogance, or self-doubt
An unstable person

Queen of Wands
In command of domestic life
Someone who encourages others' self-sufficiency
Feminine ambition

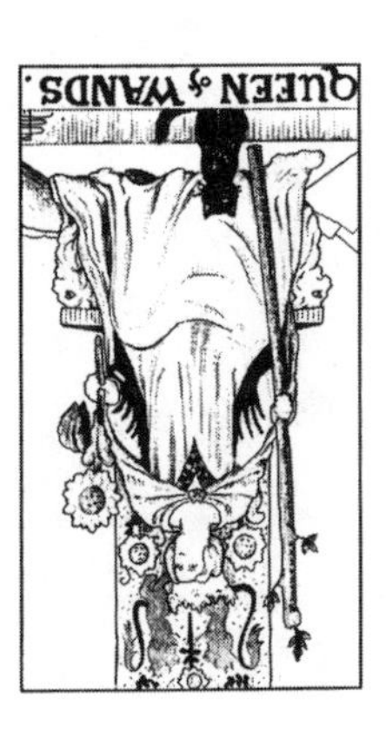

Queen of Wands R
Discomfort on the home front
Possessive and domineering behavior
Confusion and obstinacy

King of Wands
Someone willing to lend a helping hand
A good man to have around in a crisis
A passionate mentor

King of Wands R
Lack of confidence
Feeling grumpy and detached
Pessimism or doubt

About the Authors

Arlene Tognetti grew up in a home where religion and spiritual ideas came together. Her mother, a traditional Catholic, and her father, a more Edgar Cayce–type individual, helped her to understand that there's more to this world than what's obvious. Arlene began studying the Tarot and Astrology in the 1970s and started her own practice in 1980. She began teaching the Tarot at the University of Washington in the Experimental College in 1982, and currently teaches the Tarot at Pierce College in Tacoma. Arlene's focus is on enlightening her students and clients: "I want everyone to learn what Tarot, Astrology, and Psychic Intuition are all about and how these Intuitive Arts can help them grow and look at the choices and alternatives in their lives." Arlene is expert author, with Lisa Lenard, of *The Complete Idiot's Guide to Tarot, Second Edition.* Arlene lives in the Seattle area. Her website is www.mellinetti.com.

Lisa Lenard's most recent book is the *KISS Guide to Dreams.* She is also co-author of *The Complete Idiot's Guide to Astrology, Third Edition* (with Madeline Gerwick-Brodeur), *The Complete Idiot's Guide to Numerology* (with Kay Lagerquist), and *The Complete Idiot's Guide to Palmistry* (with Robin Gile). Lisa lives in Corrales, New Mexico.

Amaranth Illuminare is a leading book producer, developing New Age and holistic wellness books for mainstream readers. Amaranth's goal: Touch readers' lives. In addition to the *Intuitive Arts* series, Amaranth has developed many books, including *The Thyroid Balance* by Glenn Rothfeld, M.D., and Deborah S. Romaine, *Releasing the Goddess Within* by Gail Feldman, Ph.D., and Katherine A. Gleason, and *Menu for Life: African Americans Get Healthy, Eat Well, Lose Weight, and Live Beautifully* by Otelio S. Randall, M.D., and Donna Randall. Amaranth's founder and creative director, Lee Ann Chearney, is the author of *Visits: Caring for an Aging Parent* and editor of *The Quotable Angel.*